Conversations with Russell Banks

Literary Conversations Series
Peggy Whitman Prenshaw
General Editor

Conversations
with Russell Banks

Edited by David Roche

University Press of Mississippi   Jackson

www.upress.state.ms.us

The University Press of Mississippi is a member
of the Association of American University Presses.

First printing 2010

∞

Library of Congress Cataloging-in-Publication Data

Banks, Russell, 1940–
  Conversations with Russell Banks / edited by David Roche.
    p. cm. — (Literary conversations series)
  Includes index.
  ISBN 978-1-60473-745-5 (cloth : alk. paper) — ISBN 978-1-60473-746-2 (pbk. : alk. paper) 1.
Banks, Russell, 1940-—Interviews. 2. Novelists, American—20th century—Interviews. 3. Au-
thors, American—20th century—Interviews. 4. Fiction—Authorship. I. Roche, David, 1976– II.
Title.
  PS3552.A49.Z46 2010
  813'.54—dc22   2010007047

British Library Cataloging-in-Publication Data available

Books by Russell Banks

Fifteen Poems. With William Matthews and Newton Smith. Chapel Hill, NC: Lillabulero Press, 1967.

Waiting to Freeze: Poems. Northwood Narrow, NH: Lillabulero Press, 1967.

30/6. New York: Quest, 1969.

Snow: Meditations of a Cautious Man in Winter. Hanover, NH: Granite, 1974.

Searching for Survivors. New York: Fiction Collective, 1975.

Family Life. New York: Avon, 1975.

The New World: Tales. Urbana: University of Illinois Press, 1978.

Hamilton Stark. Boston: Houghton Mifflin, 1978.

The Book of Jamaica. Boston: Houghton Mifflin, 1980.

Trailerpark. Boston: Houghton Mifflin, 1981.

The Relation of My Imprisonment. Washington D.C. and Philadelphia: Sun & Moon Press, 1983.

Continental Drift. New York: Harper & Row, 1985.

Success Stories. New York: Harper & Row, 1987.

Affliction. New York: HarperCollins, 1989.

The Sweet Hereafter. New York: HarperCollins, 1991.

Rule of the Bone. New York: HarperCollins, 1995.

Cloudsplitter. New York: HarperFlamingo, 1998.

The Invisible Stranger: The Patten, Maine, Photographs of Arturo Patten. Photos by Arturo Patten. New York: HarperCollins, 1999.

The Angel on the Roof: The Stories of Russell Banks. New York: HarperCollins, 2000.

The Darling. New York: HarperCollins, 2004.

The Reserve. New York: HarperCollins, 2008.

Dreaming Up America. New York: Seven Stories Press, 2008.

Contents

Introduction

The interviews included here span a period of over thirty years, from 1976 with the publication of Banks's first novel *Family Life* and his first collection of short stories, *Searching for Survivors*, to 2008 with *The Reserve*. If his breakthrough novel, *Continental Drift*, drew wide acclaim in 1985 and remains to this day one of his best-selling books as well as the book which has received the most scholarly attention, it is undoubtedly the publication of Pulitzer-finalist *Cloudsplitter* in conjunction with the back-to-back release of film adaptations *The Sweet Hereafter* and *Affliction* in the late 1990s that suddenly put Banks in the spotlight as "Hollywood's Hottest New Property."[1]

The contents of this book testify to this accession to celebrity status, with only five conversations over the first twenty years of Banks's career. Since 1998, Banks has been very generous in giving interviews, and very articulate when doing so, not only to newspapers and academic journals, but also to readers who keep up non-profit internet blogs, ex-students, or Ph.D. candidates. If Banks says he doesn't "think about [his] reader at all when [he's] writing" (Trucks), he clearly enjoys talking with his actual readers about his life and work, *their* life and work, literature, history, politics, and cinema. He also delights in the diversity of his audience and in the "greater democratization of commentary"[2] provided by alternative media—most recent interviews are available on-line either as transcriptions or podcasts. Clearly, Banks applies his democratic ideals of allowing various voices to express themselves not only to his narrative strategies, but also to his career.

Although Banks says that literary criticism is not particularly "useful" to him as a writer (Checkoway), he respects it as a field and is familiar with many critical concepts; Banks admits that reading Bakhtin on polyphony in Dostoevsky was "reassuring" to him and that Freud's analysis of Oedipal tensions "corresponds to [his] perceptions of human affairs and human relationships," but insists that this realization is "after the fact" and that he doesn't "see [himself] in any way as operating from a theoretical or psychoanalytical theory or political theory."[3] Banks himself takes pleasure in returning to his work as an intelligent reader and is very open to readings and analyses made by his readers. When we first met in 2003, I asked him, rather awkwardly, if his male characters' anxiety of being "inherently evil" and their perception of female characters as somewhat "saintly" was rooted in his own life experience. He replied a bit teasingly: "You think they're evil?"[4] Two years later, however, he would tell me that my remark was certainly valid for most of his work up to *The Darling*. Banks has always considered writing as a "search for clarity" (Reeves), a process which makes him more intelligent, each work building on previous works and leading to another. Clearly, Banks sees exchanging with his readers as part of a collaborative search for clarity.

This book reveals that Banks's vision of the purpose of fiction has not changed, while his approach to form has. For him, the writer plays "the role of the storyteller, in a very primitive sense of what a storyteller is in the tribe" (Davidson and Arroyo). Like the bard (Reeves), the storyteller fulfills very basic and universal human needs, "which is to tell us who we are, and where we came from, and what are the limits of our power [...] to talk about the human condition, to tell us something about ourselves" (Davidson and Arroyo). This must be linked to Banks's "longing [...] for there to be such a thing as wisdom" (Reeves). Because literary fiction relies on the telling mode, voice is, perhaps, the main vehicle for wisdom. The diversity of voices implies that, if the desire for wisdom may be universal, there is no universal truth, just as there is ultimately no explanation for the tragic school bus accident in *The Sweet Hereafter*. This paradox, it seems to me, is at the heart of Banks's postmodern realism.

Such a volume, of course, highlights the writer's evolution. The most significant change, obviously, is Banks's clear adhesion to postmodernist fiction in the 1970s and his embracing realism in the 1980s. Banks partly attributes this change to his stay in Jamaica, which gave him perspective on his personal life and American history and culture, and enabled him to articulate the two through what remain to this day his main obsessions: "the mystery of race, sex and class"[5] and death (Benedict). He also thinks his early use of in-your-face artifice reveals his insecurity as a writer from a lower-class background who needed to prove to himself he was "smart enough" and was afraid that "the stories [he] could tap into" weren't "sufficiently meaningful material for fiction" (Roche). One need only compare *Hamilton Stark* to *Affliction* to perceive this evolution, but other details, such as Banks's depreciation of E. L. Doctorow in 1976 (Rooke) and his later acclaim of this same writer (Reeves, Faggen and Munger), testify to this change. This is not to say that Banks now rejects artifice: on the contrary, he sees it as a "useful" and "not necessarily *undesirable*" part of writing fiction (Roche).

This book has been several years in the making. Selection has been a painful process, what with the number of interviews and their length, and was determined by three criteria: quality, availability, and the overall coherence of the book. The interviews have not been edited for redundancies to underline Banks's main concerns and preserve the spontaneity of the conversations. My transcription attempts to reproduce, within the limitations of written text, the oral quality of our conversation in order to give an idea of the way Banks speaks, picks his words, sometimes thinks out loud.

This book could not have been made without Russell Banks who backed up the project from the start and has always made himself readily available, nor without his assistant, Nancy Wilson, who helped out in so many generous ways. I want to thank all the contributors to this volume, as well as those who helped me collect the material over the past five years: Jill Anderson at the Harry Ransom Center, Supriya Bhatnagar at *AWP Chronicle*, Robert Birnbaum, Phil Brown at the *Adirondack Explorer*, Jean Adamoski and Philip Gourevitch for the *Paris Review*, Tessa Joseph at the *Carolina Quarterly*, Vicki Lawrence at the *Michigan Quarterly*, Fran Maas and William Smith at Western Washington University, Nell McClister at *Bomb*, Sylvain Nicolo at *La Femelle du Requin*, Laurence Patri at Biblioblog.fr, Beth E. Robertson at Purdue University Press, Philippe Romanski at Cercles.com, Minh Tran Huy at the *Magazine Littéraire* and Joel Wendland at PoliticalAffairs.net. Finally, I am grateful to Walter Biggins and Leila W. Salisbury at the University Press of Mississippi for making this volume possible, and to the Centre Interlangues TIL of the Université de Bourgogne for financial assistance.

DR

1. Joyce, Cynthia. "Antihero: The Salon Interview: Russell Banks." Salon.com (Jan. 5 1998).
2. Birnbaum, Robert I. "Russell Banks: Author of *The Darling* Converses with Robert Birnbaum." IdentityTheory.com (Jan. 18, 2005).
3. From an unpublished interview included in the annex of my dissertation, *L'Imagination malsaine et ses ambiguïtés*, but not in the book version.
4. Ibid.
5. Ibid.

Chronology

2000   Purchases house in Saratoga Springs, New York, where he spends winters.

2001   Visits West Africa to research for *The Darling*. Russell receives an honorary degree from Skidmore College.

2002   Russell becomes the third president of the IPW; tours the Palestinian and Israeli territories at the request of Palestinian poet Mahmoud Darwish.

2003   Founds Cities of Refuge North America after the dissolution of the IPW. Purchases an apartment in Miami where he spends more and more time year after year during the winter months. Russell receives an honorary degree from Paul Smith's College of Arts and Sciences.

2004   Is New York State writer till 2008.

2005   Russell receives an honorary degree from Clarkson University.

2006   *The Darling* wins the Laure-Bataillon Prize for best work of fiction translated into French.

2007   Russell receives the eighth annual Jean Kennedy Smith NYU Creative Writing Award of Distinction.

2008   Wins Thornton Wilder Award for his career.

Conversations with Russell Banks

Russell Banks: An Interview

Constance Rooke/1976

From *Fiction International* 6/7 (1976): 37–45. Reprinted by permission of Leon Rooke.

CR: I'll start with something impossible, if that's all right with you. Can you define the new fiction, and perhaps locate your own work in those terms?
RB: I'm glad you asked me that. Actually, I'm not. It's a topic a wise man would avoid. Attempts to define in critical terms what appear to be tendencies in contemporary writing, or clottings among writers (social or otherwise), are obviously better left to people who make a profession out of making those definitions—critics, teachers, social and cultural historians, etc. Clearly a writer is no more likely to be skilled at making those definitions than he is at political commentary. Writers are at heart the last true amateurs at everything in the universe, so one's attempts to dance around questions like "Can you define the new fiction?" ought to be seen as instinctive attempts to protect one's amateur standing. I'd hate to have them take all my medals away. Still . . . well, still, I'm not an idiot, and I do read a lot of contemporary fiction, and I love it, and I have a few ideas about why I love it. So, what the hell, maybe just this once won't taint me with professionalism, he said, slipping off his New Fiction tee shirt and pulling on the star-studded New Critic leathers . . . .

What's called the "new fiction"—what Barth calls "irrealism," Sukenick calls "bossa nova," Federman calls "surfiction," Klinkowitz and Bellamy call "superfiction," and Gore Vidal calls "boring"—is, in most cases, writing that has little or no concern with psychological or social realism. It's image-making of a different order, with a different intent. All serious writing seems to function essentially to create an image that lets us recognize what it is to be human. I think it's W. S. Merwin who said that man is the only creature who has to learn what it is to be itself. That's why man is the only image-making creature. As far as we know, gods and beasts don't bother. They don't have the need. Anyhow, only a fool would believe that the psychological image of man, say, or the sociological image (the beehive, for example) sufficiently describes him. But for the last hundred years or so, these two senses of man have been at the center of our bewilderment. What are we psychologically? What are we socially? (Maybe prior to that it was, what are we physically?) Darwin, Marx, and Freud. But it would seem that the center of our puzzlement has shifted lately (not that we've necessarily answered the earlier questions once and for all; we've perhaps just become distracted by more pressing questions), and now we want to know what we are in an anthropological sense, and what we are in a purely spiritual sense. Enormous generalizations, I know. Our center of puzzlement has shifted, but we still seek the thing that art provides: wonderment, the cessation of need that occurs when we meet an image that lets us recognize in a crucial way what it is to be a human creature. And writers correspondingly and as usual have let themselves pursue their own puzzlement. This pursuit is what is producing what we're calling the "new fiction." As a result, we're now getting images made from language conscious of itself and its own process. We're getting images arbitrarily organized by systems like logic, alphabets, spatial organization, I Ching. We're getting images from Jung rather than Freud, from sufis rather than Hegelians, from linguists rather than naturalists. Please understand that by "image" I mean the whole thing, not just a part of it. The tapestry itself, not just the greyhound in the corner—the entire novel as a coherent image of what it is to be a human creature . . .

Okay, then, the shift in our puzzlement has necessitated a corresponding shift in what will suffice for an image adequate to produce wonderment. There has to be a corresponding shift in the image-making tools. The old tools of, say, observation and memory, great for social or psychological realism, won't work for us. So we start scratching around for new tools, rocks of different consistency and texture, sticks of different length, and pigments of a different color. That's how a tradition gets created. Writers start to look around the tool chest of the past, and they rediscover Sterne, Rabelais, and Hawthorne; they look around their immediate environment, and they discover Borges, Beckett, Nabokov, Flann O'Brien, Calvino, Marquez, and poets like Wallace Stevens, Pound, and Olson. They go after fables, folk tales, parables, anything that'll help make an image on the cave wall that'll fill us with wonderment, that'll produce the cessation, however momentary and fleeting, of bewilderment.

I'm afraid this is turning into an essay, so I'll move on. The second part of your question calls for me to "locate" my own work in those terms, presumably the above terms. Naturally I can only do that in terms of intent, and my intent has increasingly become conscious of itself as working out of the above sense of image-making. It's been a gradual coming to consciousness, and I hope naturally that it's a continuing process. It'll make it easier for me to get my hands on the proper tools. I don't rely on memory or observation. I rely on hallucination, what John Hawkes calls "vision," dream, fable, fantasy, and system (i.e., logic and symmetry). I don't think these tools are peculiarly my own, God knows, and I don't feel particularly lonely or cut off from the essential needs of the community. That old sense of the storyteller in the community, providing not information but images, is very sustaining to me, and I don't feel deprived of that function.

CR: Your fiction, and at least to some extent the image of the human creature which it supplies, seems to me consistently ironic. Do you think that your work is *necessarily* ironic as well, that it will always be so?

RB: I think my work is consistently ironic, but not necessarily so. I don't want to spend my life without at least once being straightforwardly sincere. It's just that certain apparently sincere relations to the reader can't be trusted any longer. We've spent so much time deliberately "getting in touch with our feelings" in the last few decades that we've probably lost the ability to do it. We're so informed now about what those feelings in any given situation are supposed to be that we're probably only capable of feeling guilt or self-satisfaction, guilt if we come up without the appropriate feeling and self-satisfaction if we can come up appropriately hurt, angry, hostile, content, whatever. Irony is a way to avoid that dichotomy between guilt and self-satisfaction. But the naif in me longs for it to be merely a stopgap measure. I mean, there *must* be a point where you become clear enough about your feelings to be as sincere as a tractor, say, or a tree. I have a fear, though, that if once I were wholly straightforwardly sincere, I would black out. Language would become impossible. The signal would cease and all I'd be able to give off would be some kind of verbal test pattern.

CR: To what extent is the self-conscious voice a necessary ingredient in the fiction which is of interest to you now?

RB: I'm not yet able to imagine a voice that isn't self-conscious. Perhaps it's because I don't really believe in the existence of the nuclear ego. [*Laughs nervously.*]

CR: Do you really believe that straight realistic fiction has ground to a halt, that it has all become repetitive or invalid?

RB: I think I touched on this question earlier, all that business about psychological and social realism. The reason for its uselessness (maybe a better word would be its "inappropriateness") is that it's not able to produce wonderment in us right now. It produces instead boredom; and if there's puzzlement, it's only as to why anyone would care to take the immense time and effort to describe yet another middle-class living room in "telling detail."

CR: Can a nineteenth-century sort of novel be written successfully today?

RB: Not without the author's awareness of the fact that his readers will already bear in their own imaginations a very clear idea of what a nineteenth-century novel is, and thus his novel will necessarily have to be a commentary on that already existent image. A realistic painting today, to function meaningfully as an image, must take into consideration the fact that the viewer automatically organizes form and space into the conventions of realistic painting, or else the artist will be doing nothing more interesting than showing over once again what the viewer was practically born seeing on his own. To write a nineteenth-century novel today would be either a meaningless act or an act of disrespect—disrespect for the reader's own already existent set of images. Such an author would be presuming that the reader didn't already order his experience into the conventions of nineteenth-century fiction and that he didn't find that unsatisfactory.

CR: Does much or all of your fiction have a moral impetus? Do you intend it to have a moral effect?

RB: I *hope* that much or all of my fiction has a moral impetus, because I *hope* that anything one bends all his conscious attention to has a moral impetus. To have a moral impetus, however, is not necessarily to have a moral effect. So whether or not my work has a moral effect, I simply couldn't say.

CR: What pressures do you feel to be peculiarly contemporary?

RB: Economic pressures, mainly. Because of the economic structure of the publishing business, it's extremely difficult to write and expect to publish fiction that cannot be produced, packaged, advertised, and sold the way soap and electric toothbrushes are produced, packaged, advertised, and sold. Thus the serious writer is more than ever forced to rely, first, on his skills as an entrepreneur to get his work published and, second, on his skills as a parasite to house and feed himself and his family. The first set of skills, and the problem to which they're applied, explains why we're seeing so many alternative non-commercial modes of publishing today. Little magazines, small presses, co-ops, universities are coerced into publishing poetry and fiction (unheard of in previous centuries: can you imagine a Heidleberg University Press Poetry Series that would correspond to Yale's or LSU's?). The second set of skills, not all that different, and the problem to which they're applied, i.e., attaching the writer to the side of a large corporate and corpulent host so that he can house and feed himself and his family, explains why today there are so many writers working as teachers in universities. There's no necessary relation between writing and universities—except the obvious and doubtless temporary one of parasite and host—any more than there was a necessary relation in the seventeenth century between the Church and the poets. Writers, in times when the community has been unable to house and feed them for the tales and poems they tell, have traditionally been parasitic, attaching themselves to the Church, to nobility, to government bureaucracies, to whatever corporate host was willing to sustain them. Of course, it's a dangerous way to live. The host will every now and then get irritated by the parasite's presence and will try to rub him off against a rock or the side of a tree. So I'm interested in keeping myself aware of alternative corporate hosts to attach myself to. The university seems to be tiring of us. They're starting to breed their own, less irritating barnacles, with the MFA programs and so on; so we're probably going to have to jump pretty soon, and we ought to have some idea of where we're going to go. I've been looking into the possibilities of attaching myself to the military-industrial complex by becoming a manufacturer of some tiny, absolutely essential electronic component—a fuse, say, or a CB radio antenna, or maybe chrome lug nuts.

CR: That sounds contemporary enough. I was wondering, though, about the ways in which your own work is responsive to other contemporary fiction.

RB: I don't believe that my work is *consciously* all that responsive to the work of contemporaries, though of course their books are in my life, and presumably my work is responsive to whatever is in my life. But in a strictly literary sense, no. I think that most writers use their contemporaries to justify what they were going to do or were doing in the first place. I remember how reassuring it was for me, say, to see how Ishmael Reed was using visual material in *Mumbo Jumbo*, or Paul Metcalf was collaging historical material. It meant that I wasn't schizophrenically lost in my own fantasies. I felt the same way about Coover's use of fairy tales and Gass's theoretical claims for the primacy of language and artifice and Barthelme's use of *dreck*. Those writers didn't so much influence my own writing as they made me feel less crazy and lonely. We don't inherit our traditions; we discover and create them. And Harold Bloom's theories to the contrary, I don't think we discover and create them in order to work out sibling or oedipal rivalries, so much as we do merely to feel less crazy and lonely.

CR: Can you identify any literary influences upon your work?

RB: Nathaniel Hawthorne, Lawrence Sterne, Borges. I know how silly it sounds to invoke names like that, but if you're going to spend your life trying to transcend the limits your genes and environment have placed on you, you might as well set your standards as high as you can imagine.

CR: What about *social* influences?

RB: The same names as above. I refer all personal quandaries to Hawthorne, Sterne, and Borges, and they have agreed to advise me. William Faulkner sometimes helps out. Flann O'Brien too. The work of any apprentice is to keep his masters as fully imagined as possible. It's also important to note that true masters never select their apprentices, and true apprentices never get to choose their masters. The process of writing well creates both of them simultaneously. That's why I don't feel completely silly in answering your last two questions the way I have.

CR: For what audience do you write?

RB: Several, I suppose. An outer circle of strangers who share with me a puzzlement about what kind of creatures we are—that is, people who are puzzled in ways similar to mine. Then an inner circle of friends, people I could name, mostly poets as it turns out—Charlie Simic, Paul Hannigan, Bill Matthews—but not because they are poets so much as because they are friends who have access to my private sense of my own enterprise and thus can tell early if I've lived up to myself or not. My wife is included in this circle, naturally, and a few more friends who are not writers at all. At the exact center of my audience, though, sits myself as reader. So, finally, I'm writing what I myself want most to read. I have no conscious sense of writing for posterity or for or against the past. I can't imagine what that would be like. Too lonely, I think. Too lonely to bear.

CR: Do you have a preference for the short story or the novel? Do you perhaps feel more comfortable in one form than in the other?

RB: Right now I feel more *confident* working with shorter forms, mainly because I've done more work on stories just in terms of word count than on novels. But as the limits on digression, voice, textual shifts, and so on are more immediately present in shorter works, I've become less comfortable there and more comfortable with the novel. As my own needs in writing have changed, I've had to change forms: from writing personal, more or less lyrical verse, to long, meditative verse, to short narrative fiction, to novel-length fictions. Maybe I've just become more gabby, less reticent, less attracted by silence. Novels are a great lot of noise, you know.

CR: Can you describe any writing habits which might be of interest?

RB: No, because I don't seem to have any writing habits as such. The ways in which I organize my writing activity change, not daily, but certainly monthly and seasonally, depending on hundreds of secret, often unconscious mental obstacles and just as many domestic and social obstacles.

CR: Do you engage in very much advance planning?

RB: It varies to a slight degree, but ordinarily I avoid advance planning as much as I can. That's an operating principle. I do try to play to my strengths, though—or what at any given moment I'm able to perceive as my strengths.

CR: What about rewriting?

RB: Yes. A great deal of rewriting, at all stages, even after publication in book form. The only reason I stop revising anything is because I have given up on it, botched it. So far everything I have written in my life is either still under revision or has been botched.

CR: Is it true that you wrote *Family Life* on three-by-five index cards?

RB: Yes. On some cards I had to write tiny letters and risked hand-cramps; on others I was able to use large, round letters. I prohibited myself from making any of the 144 chapters in the book longer than what I could get onto a three-by-five card. It was a mnemonic device. Helped me remember what I didn't know I'd forgotten.

CR: Would you agree with Wright Morris's assertion that any serious writer will be found on close inspection to have been hammering away at a single theme throughout his career?

RB: Yes, sure, because it's kind of a truism. There can't be more than three or four really large themes that have ever occurred to human beings. Our lifetimes are so short we just don't have time to think of more than one of those three or four before it's time to go.

CR: Is there such a theme in your own work, one that you would be able or willing to define?

RB: Not yet. I haven't written enough for me to tell, not in that "large theme" sense, I mean. Over my desk at home I have a plaster cast taken from a seventeenth century gravestone of an angel's head and in a scroll over her, or maybe his, head is the inscription, "Remember Death." I found the cast in a New Hampshire barn about thirteen years ago and have carried it around with me since. Maybe that angel's my "large theme." I don't know. I like to switch the emphasis, though, from "remember" to "death" and back again, and so on.

CR: Perhaps *guilt* will prove to be a part of your "large theme," right up there with the angel where it belongs. Obviously it has had an important place in your fiction so far. Since I'm not angling here for a full confession, I'll merely ask what two of your characters feel so guilty about. What is the guilt experienced by the protagonist of "The Blizzard" (one of your finest stories, I think) or by the King in *Family Life*?

RB: Guilt seems to be one of the ways we avoid accepting our secret ambivalences. Negative capability may be the antidote, the best means at our disposal for simultaneously relating to the world with feeling and also accepting the world for what it is. Anyhow, the protagonist in "The Blizzard" is ambivalent—towards his wife, mainly—and he can't accept that. No, I mean he can't *believe* that about himself, so he alternately assumes that he's guilty of some offense or else slips into adolescent fantasies about some kind of woman he doesn't feel ambivalent towards. The King in *Family Life*, though, is in a somewhat different position. His guilt is a kind of standard male guilt for possessing power. In "The Blizzard" guilt is the psychological consequence of avoiding a metaphysical truth, that two things can be true at the same time, that one can both love and loathe a woman at the same time. But in *Family Life* guilt is the consequence of an anthropological fact, that males in our culture possess by virtue of gender more power than females. Of course, there is a single sensibility driving both "The Blizzard" and *Family Life*. I mean, after all, I was raised Presbyterian Congregationalist in a culture that subscribed in all ways to your basic Calvinist principles if not doctrines, which probably means that I'm likely to be conscious of guilt as a way of being in the world. And since it would be worse not to be in the world at all, I probably tend to cling to guilt a bit more desperately than, say, a Cajun would. Guilt as indirect proof of existence. I'm guilty; therefore I am. It's something to hold onto. [*Shrugs helplessly.*]

CR: How does political consciousness function in your work? Does your fiction propose certain political actions as just, others as irresponsible?

RB: Well, reluctantly I'll admit that *Family Life* is informed to some degree by a feminist view of the family. That is, I don't think I'd have been able to see power in quite the terms that I've tried to describe power within *Family Life* if it weren't for having tried to apply a feminist critique to my own life over the last decade or so. Stories written prior to *Family Life* probably wouldn't be as informed by that critique, naturally. But please, this is an after-the-fact set of observations about the work. I did not consciously set out at any point to scrutinize the family unit from a feminist point of view. And also, please note that I can't propose any solutions. I do have politics, obviously. That is, I do think that people as individuals relate to each other in groups along certain identifiable lines of power, and that injustice is almost always the result. But I don't know of any solutions. Which means that I don't have any ideology to promote. If I did, though, I would. If I thought I knew how to fix something as essential to human life as the family, I would definitely try to fix it. But I don't.

CR: In two of the stories in *Searching for Survivors*, "The Investiture" and

"The Masquerade," as well as in *Family Life*, you are writing (superficially, at least) about royal families. Is there any other relationship between these stories and the novel? And why royalty?

RB: "The Investiture" and "The Masquerade" were written just prior to *Family Life*, so there's certainly a relation in time. Writing about royalty allowed me to write about mother-father-son-brother-daughter-sister figures without having to call them "my father" or "my sister" or "my son" and so on, and thus it gave me access to language that in turn gave me access to basic kinds of *relations* between figures. The language of realism—"*my* father," "*my* sister," etc.—inhibited me, forced me to keep on seeing relations in the same old ways. Folk tales can provide language similarly, can let one take the necessary step outside the social and literary conventions he was born with so that he can see anew what he'd grown blind to.

CR: The King in *Family Life* delivers a short speech that he seems rather proud of, the kind of statement that he might expect to have taken up. I'd like you to discuss it, if you will. I'm wondering how far the King is your persona, rather than (or in addition to) the artist figure whom you call the Green Man. Here's what the King says: "I think that guilt, once perceived, i.e., experienced, is a passion, to be spent, like other passions. The meanings of most things, of passions, certainly, lie wholly in their enactments or in analytical description, i.e., reenactment of those things. The point of human life, when it comes right down to it, is simply to provide content for the otherwise empty forms of reality. The basic difficulty of human life is in knowing when a particular form has been sufficiently filled, or perceived, experienced—knowing when an experience has become redundant. Thus, most of the 'good' life is an exercise in good taste, and I do mean ethically."

RB: I suppose I could back off this one by saying *I* don't know what it means, I didn't say it, *the King* did. And in a sense I do believe that's true. To react to the statement I have to stand strictly in the position of the sympathetic reader of the book, because I discovered that statement as I wrote it, the way we discover most statements. Some days I believe the King is all right, and sometimes I think he's a lying, self-serving bastard. Today, tonight, this minute, I think he's a lying, self-serving bastard, and thus I'm inclined to claim that was my intention in giving him those words. To portray such a man in action, talking. In many important ways the King more closely resembles me than the Green Man does, even though the Green Man at one point confessed to having the name Russell Banks.

CR: What is supposed to happen for the reader when he perceives that young Prince Egress is "melancholy," that he receives a message from some ghost on a parapet, that he visits his mother's bedroom, and so on? Or that Prince Dread comes out of Hemingway? Or that the Queen's interpolated novel employs the style of *True Romance* stories?

RB: One effect I can hope for is that the reader will recognize the obvious literariness of the description and from there can come to an awareness of the entire novel as artifice. One of the virtues of parody is that its presence asserts the artificiality of language, its existence as invention, not as nature. Its humanness, if you will. Hamlet, Nick Adams, and even the heroines of *True Romance* tales all have that essential property—they are images, made up, language acts. And insofar as they share that property, I love them and honor them equally (remember, parody, no matter how cruel, is an affectionate gesture; when there is no affection, parody sinks to sarcasm).

CR: Many of the principal male characters in *Family Life* have homosexual liaisons. Is there any special reason for this emphasis?

RB: It doesn't seem to me to be especially emphasized. You might have asked why the emphasis on sexuality, period. Because I do think that there is such an emphasis in the book, and my answer would concede that I, like most people in our society, am fascinated by the subject, especially its expression in power terms. Given that particular interest in sexuality, not to give equal time to homosexual sexual power would be to over-particularize my interest in sex, would be to misrepresent it. I wasn't so much interested in genital penetration or modes of penetration as I was in dominance and control. Also fear, an important mode of dominance and control. And homosexuality versus heterosexuality, as an issue, taps vast reservoirs of fear.

CR: For my last question, I'd like to return to the difficulties of getting published. Will you describe the context in which the Fiction Collective has arisen? What are the advantages of the Fiction Collective for a book like *Searching for Survivors*?

RB: All right. Let's go back to the business of audience, that outer circle of strangers who share a particular puzzlement about what kind of creatures we are. I believe that the size of the outer circle, its circumference, is the variable between what we think of as "popular" authors and the rest of us, the authors who, in the process of writing, have to discover or invent what kind of creatures we are. That first group has no such puzzlement, or admits to none, and naturally their audience is the same. They *already* know, or want badly to believe they know, how it is to be a human being, and so they clasp to their collective breast anything that confirms that knowledge or the legitimacy of that desire. The rest of us readers, as audience, and writers too, are a much smaller group, numerically. Now, the reason this creates a publishing problem goes back to what I was saying earlier about the machinery of production, distribution, and sales that is used today by the large commercial publishers. They are like dinosaurs who can only eat enormous quantities of one kind of vegetable, leeks, say, and as long as there are plenty of leeks, they function pretty efficiently for their size. But they can only do one thing well—eat leeks. That is, they can make and sell books for mass audiences—books about disasters before the disasters have been properly cleaned up, books about sex scandals before the appropriate wives and husbands have been notified, or novels that tell us we're okay, we're just like we thought we were all along. Books that reassure us that we're not going to have to change our lives. The problem arises mainly for the author who has no interest, desire, or even ability to write books of that sort. For him there's no way that dinosaur can function efficiently, predictably, controllably. I don't think the publishers themselves have quite figured this out yet. Their accountants have, but many of the editors still nurture the fantasy, in themselves as well as in the writers, that a truly inventive, original novel *can* be sold to a wide audience in an efficient manner. And they always point to Pynchon or Gaddis or Doctorow (though I get serious reservations whenever that one's trotted out as an example of serious, inventive work). But they won't admit that these writers (and always, only *one* of their books) are like falling stars, meteors, random events that can only be observed statistically after the fact and cannot ever be predicted the way comets can. Which means simply that they can't publish such books efficiently. They have to take huge risks—inappropriate, unrealistic risks—and they have to count heavily, too heavily, on shameful publicizing, movie tie-ins, paperback sales, tee shirts, national holidays and so on.

What's the solution? Easy. Simply create a mechanism that can function efficiently in manufacture, distribution, and sales of an item for which there probably aren't more than 5,000 willing buyers. And the Fiction Collective, stripped of its rhetoric and aesthetic claims, is essentially an attempt to create such a mechanism. It has succeeded to the degree that it has—and for me it *has* succeeded: it got me an audience for a book that no commercial publisher could have obtained, and while it has not made me rich or famous, no commercial publisher could have done that either, so I can't complain—because of an unusual mixture of large quantities of luck, pluck, hard work, and good books. Out of twelve titles so far, I think that at least five are purely and simply excellent works of fiction. That's an incredibly high percentage, at least to me it is. There are lots of things wrong with the Collective. One of the things wrong with it is that there aren't half a dozen other collectives to publish fiction, so that we would then tend to evolve in a direction that would be more aesthetically coherent, less catholic. Other collectives would help take up the burden and free us from an unspoken, probably unconscious for most of us, but nevertheless active desire to consider all so-called serious, non-commercial fiction equally. But most of the problems seem to me to be mechanical and administrative and could be resolved with increased capitalization. More cash. As it is, every author-member volunteers his time, energy, and talents as manuscript reader, copy editor, publicist, accountant, whatever, and naturally volunteer labor is never as reliable and efficient as labor you can pay for. Not that anyone *other* than the author-members ought to be doing these things. I just think they'd be done more effectively if they could be paid for. Ideally, the decision to have a manuscript considered for publication by the Collective would be a decision by the author about the nature and site of his appropriate audience. The existence of the Collective ought to function to make an author more conscious of the nature of his audience, and it ought therefore to help make him less vulnerable to having his fantasies manipulated by forces outside his own private life.

The Search for Clarity:
An Interview with Russell Banks

Trish Reeves/1987

From *New Letters* 53.3 (Spring 1987): 45–59. Reprinted by permission.

TR: Why do you write?

RB: Not to demean the question, but it's a very hard question to answer the same way twice, probably because one doesn't write for the same reasons twice. So, whenever you answer it you're thinking, why did I write the last time? I think that I began to write for reasons that had to do with the simple desire to be a writer; I had fallen in love with literature. I think Flannery O'Connor said, "Literature attracts literature." I wanted to be one of those people who thrilled me so. I want to thrill others the same way, which is in some important way, perhaps, the wrong reason to write. If that's all you want and that's the only reason you want to write you don't do it for very long. But we always seem to start things for the wrong reasons and then later on we'll straighten out what our reasons are for doing it.

As time went by, I continued to write simply because it seemed I had to write in order to maintain my own clarity, such as it was, in the world. Whatever degree of clarity I could have, whatever knowledge I could have about the world of fact and value, I could only seem to get through writing, through the discipline and rigors of writing fiction particularly. So it goes on for, I suppose, those reasons, because it's how I have learned to know anything of importance to me about the world. One writes a particular story or novel or whatever for different kinds of reasons on the surface of the work—as presented to you in a dream or a newspaper clipping or an anecdote or a memory. You start to unravel it and pull at it the way you pull a thread out and pretty soon you've got a sweater in your lap. But that kind of thing is a different level of reason for writing. The deeper causes, the deeper compulsions come from, finally, the trust in the process as an access route to knowledge; it's epistemological in the end for me. I certainly don't write for money or fame. I'm forty-six now and I've been at it almost twenty-five years, and it's only in the last year where I could say that I am making more money from this than I am making from anything else I am doing. I'm making now about what a cop makes.

The same thing with fame; you're known to a very small number of people who happen to take contemporary American fiction very seriously. You'd be better off designing shoes if fame is what you're after.

TR: Your first two published books were poetry. Do you still write poetry?

RB: No. Well, I doodle at it and noodle at it. I'm not really able to write poetry that seems very good or interesting to me. So I keep going back to it hoping some door will open, and I'll fall through into this room where all the poets stand or sit and work. I'm like most fiction writers in that we secretly feel that poetry is the queen of the arts in some way and that if we could only be a poet we wouldn't be a failed poet. Faulkner said all fiction writers are failed poets, and he was speaking of himself. But I think he was also speaking of many of us as well. I suppose it's an easy analogy, but I think that poets feel like pitchers. They know they can't hit but they feel it's not an important part of the game. And most novelists feel like hitters. We know we can hit, and we secretly think we can pitch if they'd just give us a chance to get in the game.

TR: After reading your work, I think of you as someone who focuses his writing on lives and situations that cause a reader to wish for social change. How much of an activist are you?

RB: I'm not a political activist beyond my writing. And I don't think of my writing as political activism. There was a period in my life, in my twenties and early thirties, when I was a political activist and was involved in the civil rights movement and the protest against the Viet Nam war. But they were very specific events and it wasn't anything I could follow along as a way of life. So my relation to that kind of activity is really marginal. I naturally support specific and particular causes and occasionally even send money for them, sign letters and do the rest of it. But not as a writer, just as John Citizen. As a writer I'm not so much interested in change, as you said, really, as in pointing at and revealing pain. I'm horrified by pain. I'm sensitized, I suppose, to people who are in pain because of political or social reasons, oppression of one form or another, power; they're at the bottom, the weak side of a power relationship. And so I write about that, I try to portray that. All I can do is point at it.

TR: Do you think this pointing will perhaps bring about change?

RB: Well, yes, I hope so. I'm not a nihilist; I have faith in humanity that if we only open our eyes and see, then we will alter how we treat people. If we can only imagine what it's like to be somebody else, then we will treat others better. I really believe that.

TR: I was going to ask you what possible hope we could have, at the end of *Continental Drift*, for alleviating pain after that bleak portrayal. Awareness?

RB: Yeah. If we're aware that a man like Bob Dubois or a woman like Vanise the Haitian woman, if we can somehow know through a book like that—that that kind of person has as complex an inner life as we have—we who subscribe to *The New Yorker*, we who have Quality Paperback Book Club subscriptions and so forth, we who live in this upper-middle-class world—then we can respect them and respect their inner life in a way that we might not otherwise. And yeah, we'll treat them better. I suppose in that sense if the book works, it works that way. I don't expect to affect immigration legislation or the Reagan budget or anything like that. I'm much more interested in humanity on a larger scale and humanity on the one-to-one scale; nothing in-between seems to be able to engage my imagination. And so I have to deal with it that way. Also, I don't think it's that bleak really, *Continental Drift* itself. Certainly Bob Dubois dies, but there's a dramatic necessity for that. Bob is a man whose life is determined so many ways by a failure of imagination. He doesn't imagine his own relation to the larger economy. Bob's substitute for a sense of community is a sense of himself as a consumer; he's victimized, but he participates in his own victimization. And the opportunities that he has to escape, when they present themselves, he declines to really imagine his life and take hold of it and change it. He doesn't have very *many* options. But his wife has more imagination than he has. She knows where she stands in relation to the rest of the world. She doesn't have this kind of macho hang-up on success and on getting ahead and on being somebody. So she's not as easily manipulated as he is. She knows she's somebody already, so she can't be as easily manipulated.

TR: But then there's the other half of the story; the Haitian culture where death was beside the point, almost.

RB: For Vanise. Yeah. They survive as they do because they have a connection to the spiritual world that Bob doesn't have, which allows them to endure things that Bob, under his circumstances, couldn't begin to endure. But their world is much harsher and crueler than his.

TR: That's partly what I was thinking of when I referred to the "bleakness."

RB: Oh yes. The other culture is in the classic position of the working-class immigrant: One generation literally sacrifices itself for the benefit of the next. There is a real act of sacrifice there, an engagement on a biological, historical level. That's what they're going through. Bob is two generations after that, and so his relation to the economy and to the institutionalized world, the United States, is quite different. He's more involved and engaged in his own victimization.

TR: You talked of Bob's wife being ahead of him in this. Do you see his maleness as being part of the problem in the culture?

RB: Sure. He's manipulated by his own macho self-image; I mean who benefits from that kind of a man, that kind of a man's delusions? Only his employers, only the people who sell things benefit from those delusions.

TR: You once said that sometimes your stories have a way of choosing you. Could you expand on that?

RB: I think that most of us sort of start out writing about one thing and as you get into it the story starts to appear on the page in front of your eyes, almost despite you. You thought you were writing about a mother and son but in fact you're writing about a father and his sister or something like that. It unfolds before you the way a painting unfolds; you think you're making a picture of a mountain and it turns out you're making a picture of a tunnel or a hole in the ground. The field reverses itself. And this happens more often than not, I think, for most writers: We discover in the process of writing what it is that wants to be written about.

TR: So, could you say what poets often say, that they really don't have a poem until they've surprised themselves?

RB: Yeah, I don't know how my stories are going to end until the end, until I get there; and then when I know, I stop writing. You discover it in the process. And so in that sense a story's choosing you, you're not choosing it. You just make yourself open, you clear your mind in the act of writing. Some of us do it differently. Some of us take drugs and some of us drink and some of us do this or that to get there; meditation, yoga, sharpen pencils, write letters. But the point is to get there, to where the story can take place through you. I like and try to cultivate, as much as possible, that sense of myself as a vehicle for expression since I'm not truly finally, in the end, interested in *self*-expression or memoirs or any kind of self-portraiture or anything of the sort. Therefore I have to try to make myself as available as possible to be a vehicle for stories to get told through me rather than for me to make them up or tell them.

TR: Do you think writers should be more vocal in support of various causes, in today's world, especially North American writers who are so often accused of being drawn to the insignificant?

RB: There's no reason for writers to be more or less drawn to identify with or support particular causes or issues. What I think depresses me sometimes about American writers is our mistrust of history and our unwillingness to discover and apply to our own work and to the world around us any sense of history. Most of us abandon all hope, in a way, of having an historical perspective, so we tend to write about the domestic most deliberately and pointedly. Only a few writers, like Ed Doctorow, Robert Stone, or one or two others stick right out because they do have a sense of history; a particular view of American history, particularly. They are free and in fact they are obliged to write about different things, not *just* the family, not *just* divorce. Sure, divorce is present in their work, but the scope is much larger, and they end up writing what some of us in our shortsightedness tend to call political fiction; but it's much more than political fiction, it's fiction with a sense of history—and a willingness to fight their way through this maze of histories. I mean, America is a country that is always trying to invent itself over again and pretend it has no history, and so our writers tend to go along with that myth.

I guess there's a big difference between us and most European and Latin American writers who are very conscious of their history and feel strongly that a writer has an obligation to understand the history of his or her society and not just the history of his or her family, which is what we're more inclined to do. A vision of the history of our country is crucial to our understanding of ourselves. This kind of obligation is Homeric. That's what writers have always done: told us who we were, where we came from, where the ends of our lands were, that sort of thing. That's why you brought the bards in from the cold and let them sit around the fires. We've given that function off to the academic specialists, but fiction writers and poets have historically always played that role. And it's only in this country; where we're so terrified of our history, that we seem to have abdicated that in recent times. Our tradition is very much historically preoccupied: Whitman and Melville and Hawthorne and Crane and Twain and so on. And I couldn't say for sure why we seem to have abandoned that. I think it's a temporary aberration.

An awful lot of writers of my generation, those who are now entering maturity as writers, were in adolescence and young adulthood in the sixties. Most of them that I know were very involved in political events of that time. So *their* idea of a meaningful event is one that takes place in a public way, that has to do with society in a larger way than simply the immediate present. Writers such as Stone, Don DeLillo, John Edgar Wideman, or Rosellen Brown or a whole range of American writers in their early forties, middle forties, are really writing some wonderful books that we mistakenly call, because they seem unusual, political fiction. But in fact it's just writers returning to the old obligations.

TR: When you were talking about that, I thought about your *The Relation of My Imprisonment*, which is almost a global history rather than one country's history.

RB: Yeah. I don't know what I think about that book; it kind of came as a gift. I wrote it in a very short time. The voice appeared in my ears and almost dictated it, that strange kind of seventeenth-century English voice or New English voice or whatever it is. Every day I would just go out and sort of tune in a radio station and get it right, and then I would start to transcribe. It was a marvelous event, and one longs for those sort of automatic writing events. They're rare.

TR: Do you think any good came from the much-publicized 1986 International PEN Conference?

RB: I'm not sure. I think it was probably disillusioning for many European and Latin American writers because I think they saw American writers at their worst, at their most parochial and most self-absorbed and most distracted by local quarrels. I think that the bad consequences are that in some way we're not taken as seriously as we probably should be by foreign writers; it helps them not take us seriously. And I would rather that didn't happen. Many good things, I think, did come out of it; it depends upon the individual writer of course. But for me, and I think that my response was typical of many others, it was wonderful and enlightening and very reassuring to meet and hear, talk with writers such as Nadine Gordimer, Gunter Grass, or dozens of others whose sense of the task and of the pleasure of writing was very much close to mine. I felt much closer to them than I feel, say, to writers of the ilk of John Updike or Saul Bellow or most of the American writers who were there. I felt reaffirmed in my own work and commitment. Which is not to compare my work to theirs, but just the way I think about the act seemed much closer to the way they describe their work. So I didn't feel quite as lonely and crazy.

Sometimes you can feel really isolated and a little awed and you say, I just don't understand why what I'm doing doesn't make sense to other people. Then you realize, well, I'm looking at the world from a very small vantage point, I'm looking at it from inside New York, say from 14th Street to 57th Street, between three avenues. I love that wonderful story of Donald Barthelme's called "Balloon," that area is sort of covered by the balloon in his story—from 14th to 57th, I think, and from Lexington to 6th Avenue—right over the publishing center. So the conference was very reaffirming in that sense, I think for a lot of writers it was terrific in that sense. And it's good to see writers have bodies. I like finding out how big they are, how little they are, that Gunter Grass smells like pipe smoke. Just to get that sense of the physical back onto a name is great, it takes them out of this bloodless world and makes them human beings.

TR: Much of your more recent work uses a narrator who speaks directly to the reader. There aren't so many quotation marks, in more than the literal sense. I think this is at odds with most short stories today, which are mostly dialogue; your style seems both old fashioned and quite new. I was shocked by this technique because it seemed a tremendous risk that worked and was moving in the way that it worked. What about the evolution of your fiction, in technique as well as subject matter, and your thinking on this intrusive narrator approach?

RB: OK, I'll try to talk about that particular aspect of my work, because that's a consciously worked-out program, in that I set out some years ago to do what for me was an important thing. I wanted to invent a narrator. I wanted to have a narrator who could tell stories, who played no part in the story itself but who took responsibility for what was being described. I did not want the story to be about the narrator in any way. To do that, I had to go back over the head of realism, naturalism, and Flaubert, back over to the eighteenth-century kind of narrator almost, where there was a different sense of the relationship between the author and the reader so you could in a sense address the reader, Dear Reader. The narrator could in fact come forward and present herself or himself to the reader in that intimate way and say, Dear Reader, I'm going to tell you about something that is going to amaze you, amuse you, enlighten you, and so forth.

To do that without irony was a goal for me, and it wasn't just an abstract or a theoretical goal, it grew out of a kind of frustration that I felt with the realistic convention of the author as merely a window into the world— a kind of Flaubertian presentation of the experience with the author out somewhere behind the clouds paring his nails so that there is this illusion of reality in front of you. And it *is* merely an illusion; you're aware of that as soon as one starts to write. Then it's in some sense an embarrassment, at least it was to me when I was a young writer first starting—I always felt embarrassed. And I mean it the way Emily Dickinson means embarrassed: exposed, and exposed for being false. And I felt uncomfortable in that relation to the reader and in that relation to language. This is all artifice, folks, I wanted to say, on the one hand; but I still want to tell you something, I still want to tell a story. I don't want to simply comment on the artifice and reveal the artifice, which seems boring after a point, and obvious and redundant, so why bother? So I did set out to kind of reinvent, for myself anyhow, a narrator that I could trust and that the reader could trust. It meant that I had to risk being didactic and pompous on the one hand or ironic and wry on the other hand and try to find something else in-between that I could be comfortable with. Each book has struggled with it in one way or the other and I think each has gotten closer and closer to a comfortable kind of narrator. *Continental Drift* probably comes as close as anything of mine published so far that has that presence in the book that I feel is not me but is a storyteller. And one that the reader relates to and trusts or doesn't trust, but deals with, and who is also not part of the story.

It's an invention; I have invented a narrator, in a sense, a person almost. A good metaphor for it occurred to me some years ago, a literal metaphor when I was in Jamaica and spending a lot of time in the back country with the Maroons, who are descendants of escaped slaves in the seventeenth and eighteenth century who set up villages there and retain many of the old ways of West African culture. Several of these villages, but one in particular, had a rather rigidly, effectively instituted and marvelous set-up: The chief had a person he called his mouth-man. And the mouth-man was very intelligent and articulate and had an extraordinary presence in public. The chief could be sort of dim and inarticulate and shy, but he had all the power. And the mouth-man had all the responsibility to speak. The chief could always fire the mouth-man if he wanted to or he could blame the mouth-man, sort of like our president's press secretary. The chief could let the mouth-man go, the mouth-man could rap on for hours and the chief was often as amused by him as everybody else. He was a rapper. I loved the idea. I thought, now that's what I want; I want a mouth-man, I want to be free to be sort of dim and shy in the background and yet have someone out there in the page taking responsibility for the story. So I *have* tried to do that, and I've taken some raps for it among readers who don't see the need for that kind of artifice, who are perfectly happy with "realism," and language as a window onto reality rather than language as a creator of reality. They have accused me of somehow having this intrusive narrator, as if I weren't conscious of having an intrusive narrator or hadn't intended to have one in the first place. Or they've accused me of being didactic. He's not that didactic. He's an explainer.

TR: Storyteller is what I kept thinking, the original meaning of storyteller.

RB: Yeah, it's very much a part of *Trailerpark*, it's a more artificial part of it than it is in *Continental Drift*. In *Trailerpark*, if you ever sit down and make a map of the trailer park you can see that there's one trailer that's never named or numbered. There are twelve trailers and one of them is never identified as having a resident, and that's where, presumably, the narrator lives—'cause he knows everything about everybody, the way he would only know if he had lived in the trailer park. He can tell the history of the trailer park back and forward in time, and he can tell all of their stories. He has no story of his own to tell, and you don't miss him. You don't miss his story or anything else. You don't miss his life. But he knows everything. So that's an artificial way of doing it. I was sort of happy with it but I felt it was a little tricky.

With *Continental Drift* I said, OK, I'll invoke a narrator the way you invoke a loa in Haitian Voudon. Which is to say, I'll allow myself, if I can, to be in a sense possessed; I'll let this voice speak through me, and it'll be of a specific character—the loa will be Legba who has the specific character of protector of children, guardian of the crossroads, figure that sees forward and backward in time, and so forth. This sort of fitted the needs I had for a narrator, and so that opening invocation is literally an invocation to bring into existence, into the book the loa Legba to speak for me, Russell Banks, through the book. That, too, has a certain amount of artifice and, well, it somehow frustrates me; I don't feel that's quite there yet either. But this book of short stories, [*Success Stories*] seems to do it differently.

TR: I was going to say that. In "Adultery;" the way it works at the end of that story is wonderful.

RB: Good, good. Yeah, it's somewhat different now. Each book does evolve in terms of formally trying to make this narrator more readily available to me and to the point where I can forget about it at some point, I can just do it. Just go out there and write the story; that's all I want to do. Just let the narrator tell it like that chieftain sitting back, let my mouth-man tell the story. That might come, too, from a kind of family background that essentially mistrusts language: rural New Englanders, working class. We weren't French or Italian or anything like that; we were these up-tight Yankees. My father was a grim and reticent, depressed man and my mother was a slightly hysterical woman—both of them had basically the same mistrust of language. Neither one of them believed anything useful could be said. Coming out of that background, there's an essential mistrust of the act of speech for myself, too, so that I have to create perhaps a stand-in for myself.

TR: Speaking of New England, there's often a character in your stories who is the wizard, a disguised wizard. And the wizard is usually extreme in what he says, or he's contrary or he's very ironic. My understanding is that wizards abound in New England, but I wonder if there *was* someone in your background who taught you this trait in a sense?

RB: No, no. There isn't any one person in my background, my childhood, or anything like that—and I don't think wizards are found in New England, I never found any anyhow.

TR: I meant that manner, that way of speaking.

RB: I understand. Yes, the wizard figure appears over and over. He's usually a man, an elderly man, out of a longing on my part for there to be such a thing as wisdom. I want to believe that there is wisdom, and so I try to evoke it in my work. And hope that I can make it available through the work, through a character. I can evoke a character who is a wise man. I like to believe in that, I want to believe in that. And to some limited degree I think that I've been able to evoke characters who prove the existence of a wizard. I've searched for wizards since I was a boy, and I've met a couple of individuals who somehow made me feel the search was not an utterly irrational one. They were figures who essentially, like the wizards in my work, I guess, saw clarity through paradox, could embrace contradictions, and had a language that would permit them to demonstrate that. So that's why, I think, they exist on the personal level. And also, they create in the work, I hope, a kind of tension, a kind of intellectual and spiritual tension in work that might otherwise be overtaken by a bleak materialism that I don't feel all that comfortable with. Even though I very much live in a material world and write about a material world, still, it's a material world that's always longing to exchange itself for a transcendent world.

TR: You've been writing for twenty-five, publishing for twenty years now, often concentrating on the American concept of success and the problems with that concept, the false promises. You are now what would have to be called a successful American author. How does that kind of success strike you?

RB: Like the man who ate his hat. I guess at several different levels, I'm not aware of it as success. Of course I'm not naive about it either. My life is not radically changed, not on a day-to-day basis; in fact, it's not changed much at all. I still do exactly what I seem to have been doing for the last couple of decades. It's more affected, by a long-shot, by my children having become teenagers and young women than it has by anything else. It's made me, I suppose, more careful, I necessarily have to be more careful about what I say and do, but not in any big way. Nobody pays that much attention to anybody. It's interesting to me because it's dramatized in my own life what has been a theme throughout my work, which is that I still view myself in the larger world the way I did when I was an adolescent. My view of myself in relation to the larger world is that of a working-class family: powerless people who look from below up. I'm unable to escape that. I guess one of my recurrent themes in the work is that one can't escape that—how one views oneself in the larger structure is determined at an extremely early age. The great delusion is that if you only can get success then you will shift your view of yourself, you will no longer look at the world from the bottom, you will look at it from the top, you will become a different person. That's the longing, for success is really not necessarily material goods, but in fact to become a whole new person, not to look at yourself in the same way. The *delusion* is that you can change through success, success will change you—it's the American dream—you can kill the old person and become a new one. In my own life I can see now, if I needed any further proof, that in fact I haven't become another person. I'm still stuck with and still view myself very much the way I did as a boy. Success can fool you into thinking that you're changed, of course, and one has to be on guard against that. I feel that it's been good for my work in that it's brought my work back into print—I like as large an audience as I can have. Why should I not want a large audience? Whether they like me or not, or understand the work or not doesn't matter to me. Give everybody a chance. I'm not sure I understand it or like it myself. But to get back to the point, it hasn't really changed me, to my knowledge, at all. I should hope not.

TR: You may still write some stories about people who want to succeed, to become adults, who are already adults?

RB: Oh, yeah. Isn't that wild. All of us, we're all groaning over that, if only I could become an adult. And then finally you discover like Bob Dubois, there's no such thing as adults. But if there's no such thing as adults, then there's no such thing as children either, really. Human beings are creatures who're different from either children or adults.

Interview with Russell Banks

Pinckney Benedict/1995

From *BOMB* 52 (Summer 1995): 24–29. Reprinted by permission.

PB: You spend a lot of time in Keene, New York, a rural community where you write, and at Princeton where you have an endowed chair. How do you make that double life work?

RB: Well, they're like different halves of being and they don't really work together. I have always lived a bifurcated life, and this is just another manifestation of that. I'm very fond of my life at Princeton but it has little, perhaps nothing, to do with my magical life as a writer. My life in upstate New York, even though it's a rural community on the edge of the rest of America, is much more a part of the country and has everything to do with my imaginative life. I do like dealing with people who are serious about ideas, either students or colleagues. Nevertheless, I know that's got almost nothing to do with the real world. And I live in the real world for most of the year.

PB: What we're describing is acting out in life your own psychological dividedness; most writers are profoundly divided. Some years ago we were out drinking and you said, if only your personal life were as ordered as your professional life.

RB: If my personal life were as ordered and consistent as my professional life has been, I would probably be a miserable, suicidal, withdrawn man. That's not something I wish for. I said that only in a frivolous, drunken way.

PB: Why did you choose to teach at Princeton, which is exclusively an undergraduate program, rather than a school with an MFA program?

RB: When I was young, there was much about me that was despicable. But there were a few things about me which were admirable and which I would like to maintain and retain into old age. And one of them was that a book or a conversation could change my life. I was still open to enormous changes at the last minute: the kids that I end up working with here are at that point in their lives. I'm an agent in the formation of their views on death, sex, marriage . . . So there's that opportunity. And then there's this incredible burden of responsibility because you can, in fact, do exactly that. But the tension between the two keeps teaching alive for me. I was never happy teaching graduate students because they're beyond that point.

PB: So what's your take on MFA programs? What's the value there?

RB: It keeps young writers off the streets.

PB: [*laughter*] And some old writers, too.

RB: As teachers, yeah.

PB: Do you talk to your students in a realistic way about what their professional prospects are?

RB: I talk to them in a realistic way about life, but not at all about the professional aspects of their life. I'm much more interested in dealing with sex, death, and class issues. One of the most important things that I learned early as a writer was to separate my work from my career and realize that they are two entirely different enterprises. I could deal with my career the same way I could deal with balancing a checking account. The work was something else. If I couldn't make that distinction, I was either going to be a very confused man or a very harmful man. Finally, what I can say about a writer's career is relatively little and relatively useless anyhow. So much depends upon luck and superficial social characteristics, the accidents of marketing and how they interface with the accidents of the surface of your work. That's nothing you can control: all you can control is manners—the tiniest part of a career. One thing that relates in this life to the larger writing life is that the danger for a writer who teaches is the same as for a writer who preaches, like John Donne or Jonathan Swift. You come to identify with the institution which is supporting you and its interests and ambitions, and that is absolutely essential to avoid. It's fine to be established and connected to a university as long as you continue to view it as an outsider and as long as you continue to feel that you are there under false pretenses. I could not have gone to Princeton, and my colleagues, Toni Morrison and Joyce Carol Oates, could not have gone to Princeton either, for gender, race, or class reasons.

Universities have become the main agent of patronage for writers in this country in the last twenty-five years. Real writers who are social critics, outlying figures, and loners are suddenly playing a corporate role. How can one do that and still maintain one's integrity and function adequately as a teacher of the arts? I believe you can only do it if you regard it as temporary and tentative, and mutually exploit the situation. The university is exploiting me and I'm exploiting the university, and I make no bones about it. That's the only way I think I can function.

PB: But you're tenured!

RB: Yeah, which means they've already started thinking about my death. [*laughter*] 'Til death do us part.

PB: That's right, it is kind of a marriage. You and I have been keeping in touch over the past couple of months through the Internet. Do you use computers to compose?

RB: I do about 90 percent of the time.

PB: And what's the other ten?

RB: Every now and then I get stuck and I'm frozen by it. It's so clean and it's so detached. I have become increasingly sophisticated and have internalized the process so that it's not really that different, no greater an extension from my body than my hand is. Yet every now and then I find myself locking up, and I have to return to the body in a more literal way and start writing out in long hand. My whole life I've had this tendency to close down and withdraw from my writing for various reasons, some of which I understand, some of which I don't wish to examine.

PB: Your books are sizeable books and they're not infrequent. I would have assumed that you were a five-thousand-word-a-day man.

RB: No way. That would be a day of great suspicion. And that's part of it, I grew up suspicious of language, suspicious of storytelling. I was raised in New England, in a Protestant, restrained, and reticent family which had a good many taboos, not in terms of their behavior but in terms of their linguistic expression—the description of that behavior. There was a master-story about the family, a cliché, and any attempt to vary the story or to tell different stories of the family was shot down. So telling stories and talking a lot were both a blessing and a curse for which I was marked. "Oh, Russell is telling stories again. Isn't he cute, but isn't he a pain in the ass." And that kind of ambivalence about storytelling I've maintained into my adult life.

So I've devised various means of overcoming this psychological disability, given my desires and my needs, this compulsion to go silent and simply observe from the outside and not comment, not describe, and not articulate in any way what I'm feeling or what I'm seeing, and that occurs in this most mechanistic way. I change the technical means by which I speak and shift back down to writing by hand with a fountain pen on lined paper. And when that doesn't work, I'll shift the medium and move to a regular typewriter . . . The computer is the most liberating because it is the fastest: I can sneak up on myself and write things that I would never dare to say or write if I had to write it out long-hand or if I had to say it publicly.

PB: Not too long ago, you were joshing Joyce Carol Oates about how in her latest novel, *What I Lived For*, she knows so much.

RB: Male underwear.

PB: Exactly. How does she know so much about men and mens' sexual attitudes? [*laughter*] Her comment was that there's this cultural knowledge that we all have . . .

RB: She's one of my dearest pals, but she was avoiding the question. What I think happens is that fiction writers' main gift is to extrapolate. It's not just the ability to tell a story. Seeing her father's shorts in the laundry at thirteen or fourteen—from that she could extrapolate the whole history of male sexuality. [*laughter*] The best fiction writers are the ones who can do that. Not the ones who spend their lives researching meat packing in Cairo, Illinois, but the ones who have the ability to take the tiniest clue, the tiniest piece of evidence, and from that read its history backwards and forwards in time. It's like taking a tiny bit of DNA and creating a dinosaur; it's like *Jurassic Park*.

PB: Here you are, in *Rule of the Bone*, writing about this homeless kid, a criminal who hangs out with bikers. You're extrapolating his life. Is it right for you to be writing about this kid?

RB: Well, if I didn't I wouldn't be using the gift that I have. Mark Twain was a middle-aged bourgeois gentleman living in Hartford, Connecticut, when he wrote *Huck Finn*; and he wasn't telling the story of himself as a boy . . .

PB: Do you know kids like your character?

RB: Oh, sure. My life was marginally like his in some ways, but that was in the 1950s. I've known kids like him too, but only briefly and superficially. It doesn't take much to find the common bonds and strands that tie us together, a middle-aged white guy and a homeless teenage mall-rat. We have much more in common than we don't have in common, when it gets right down to it. Part of it is in the genius of the American language. It's a democratic language. The language that we have available to us as American writers is a chorus of voices; it's not officially classified as upper and lower or middle, it moves in and out, it invades itself. It converts and alters itself on an ongoing basis. It's this big, crabby, wonderful, loving family of voices—the English American Language: southern, and northern, upper class and lower class, black and white, Hispanic . . . That's the beauty of the American language for writers—access to speakers comes through language, comes through voice. If you can hear the voice, you can speak in that voice, and then you can imagine the speaker. And for me, the access to *Rule of the Bone* was not through some sociological experience, but really through language. Once I had that voice in my ear, then I had the character in my heart. Journalists can deal with sociology; that's simple. The hard part is getting the heart of the matter or the heart of the character down.

PB: I remember hearing you say that a first-person narrator was like an interview with just the answers. That posits an interlocutor, somebody who's asking the questions. Is it you who's asking Bone questions?

RB: As I've gotten older I've imagined myself less and less as a ventriloquist, as somebody speaking through a character, and more and more as someone listening to a character. And I did think: I've got to listen to Bone and I've got to move around and rearrange myself, I've got to invent myself as the intimate, trusted listener, who is, in a sense, the ideal reader. It's an ego reversal. Only when I could do that, could I then begin to transcribe what Bone seemed to say. It's very concrete, and it began in a prison workshop that I was teaching in upstate New York, one of these boot camps where most of the inmates were eighteen- to twenty-two-year-old drug dealers. They were white and black from inner cities and suburban Schenectady and were bright, as bright as my Princeton students. They were really good at math, because to be a drug dealer you have to be good at math. And they had incredibly developed social skills, because to be a drug dealer, you've got to be a superbly gifted and practiced salesman. If you gave the SAT to those guys, they would be off the graph. So these were really brilliant guys—and so alive. Access to those voices was the opening for this book.

PB: This voice is really different from your other work. It's wildly funny in places, but it is a stark book in its circumstances. It would have been easy to make it a maudlin horror story, a freak show of contemporary America. But Bone's commentary is very wise and dry. He's not ironic, but in the distance between his perception and ours there is a comic tension, a comic energy. The tone of it—light's not the word. But there is a subtextual humor that I haven't seen in your writing before this.

RB: It's a violent humor. It's cold humor, survival humor. Bone knows the world. I was talking to some high school kids in Miami a couple of weeks ago and one of them said, "This is the first book that tells the truth about adults." And that's right, it's not about kids, it's about adults, about the world these kids are inheriting, about the people who have power in their lives. If the book has any lasting value and power, it's because it's the kid's point of view. Bone sees the lack of power he has, but with a gallows humor. It's a redemptive book, however Bone is triumphant in the end, spiritually and morally.

PB: Yeah, the final passage creates a morality that will last him the rest of his life, regardless of whether he is powerless or powerful.

RB: He is finally able to see the adult world realistically and with humor and not identify with it. He's still seeing: I am different, and I will remain different forever. He doesn't think he is excused of the responsibility to have morality. But he will never, never say, "I am they."

PB: That outsider stance has unraveled and undone so many people in your early work. They don't find redemption, there is no knitting back together of the various skeins of their lives. They just come apart. But Bone comes back together.

RB: There are several factors involved here. The other protagonists are adults, for whom in a sense the battle is lost. When their story begins the battle is over; they are who they are. Their destiny is closed.

PB: Is it predestination?

RB: No, but options are closed off very early in this country. Now options are being closed off at age eight, nine, and ten. When I was growing up they were closed off at nineteen, twenty, twenty-one. You become commodified, you become a part of the economy and a part of the system at that age. Bone is the first protagonist that I've had who was a kid, who still wasn't bought. And he has a chance to create a morality for himself freely and independently. He has an existential life still available to him that in two years you can't imagine him having. Bone is free because he is so young. And so he's not as trapped and not as tragically doomed as Bob Dubois in *Continental Drift* or Wade Whitehouse in *Affliction*. He is a free agent, and he recognizes that, which most fourteen-year-olds don't. So, if there is a redemptive element to the book, and I do believe he's triumphant in the end and is morally empowered, it's because he's young enough at the start to still have that option available to him; I would hate to have to write a book about Bone two or four years later, as a sixteen- or eighteen-year-old kid. It would be a different story completely. But at that moment, when he's on the cusp of adult life, he's saying, "If I do it this way, I'm dead. If I do it that way, I'm free. I might be lost, but I'm free."

PB: Bone's best buddy, a guy who is sixteen, he's already lost—

RB: He's an asshole. [*laughter*]

PB: He's not admirable. You named him after yourself?

RB: It's good to name a minor character after yourself. It puts you in the position of being a spear-carrier in the story and it takes you away from the foreground and into the background.

PB: So then it was conscious.

RB: Oh yeah, quite conscious. I named a minor character after myself to get myself out of Bone and move out any temptations I might have to over-identify with Bone, or to make his story my story. All that was neutralized by making his asshole pal named Russ have some of my worst characteristics.

Russ is a garrulous, fast-talking guy who's always got a plan, a way to deal, and he's also, of course, a Tom Sawyer. He's the slightly idiotic, conventionally smart guy. He knows how to deal with adults in a way that makes adults happy. Bone doesn't quite get how to do that, but he doesn't want to get it. But as a strategy for a writer it was useful for me to get myself out of the story.

PB: I had that thrill of recognition when I came across in *Bone* the school bus that in your novel, *The Sweet Hereafter*, was in a wreck that killed many of the children of the community.

RB: And in *Bone* it becomes a squat for homeless kids. A school bus is a very important image in American social life: it's emblematic. It's the first means by which we hand over our children to the corporate state, it's where they first lose the protection of their parents. It turned out to be central to the story. It seemed silly not to appropriate and use the same school bus that I had wrecked in *The Sweet Hereafter*, because in some ways the two novels are very related. *The Sweet Hereafter* is, in parable form, the dramatization of what I view as the loss of our children. That is to say, there has been an abandonment of children in our culture, so that we no longer feel any compunction about not protecting them. And it has occurred most dramatically in the last quarter-century and manifested itself in thousands of ways which we're only now beginning to recognize. By turning children into a consumer group we colonized and made them into little adults. We sexualized them, because that's the easiest way to colonize people, to sexualize them and then sell them the goods that will reinforce their sexualization. And we did this primarily through the means of television, which is the first time corporate America invaded the home. Up to then you could always turn a salesman away from the door. Now you can't. Now you turn on the television and the salesman sits down with you in your living room. A hundred and fifty-seven billion dollars worth of consumer goods were sold to children last year. We're talking only legal consumer goods, we're not talking tobacco products, or alcohol, or guns, or drugs. Just legal goods: sneakers, hoodies, clothing, makeup, video games, and whatever, sold to children.

PB: They make up a big part of Bone's world. He has this Homeric catalog, but it's video games, how can he resist?

RB: And in order to maintain a moral reality in the world he has got to resist that. The only way he can resist that is to become a homeless person, a marginalized person. If he's a regular kid, he is completely colonized.

In the past, we refused to sexualize children because we know that makes them vulnerable, we refused to allow them a role in the economy because that made them vulnerable, but somewhere in the fifties all those familial taboos were violated and broken, primarily by TV. And we ended up as a culture entering into the practice of auto-colonization.

We have devoured ourselves. We have eaten our future. Parents control—to such an extraordinary degree that it's shameful—and relate to their children overall on the basis of their being consumers and parents being providers.

PB: I don't mean it as a contradiction, but by making them into small adults we also infantilize them, it seems to me, well into their twenties.

RB: But that's always true of colonization. They're not cracked up to be adults, to be autonomous, free, and existential human beings. And really, from the point of view of economics, it's a self-renewing colony. The other colonies dry up or they get independence or have revolutions.

PB: I was going to say they get angry.

RB: Well, what do we have in front of us now? We've got a whole colony which is rebelling, which is refusing to play the game by our rules anymore. And so to go back to the early question of the school bus. *The Sweet Hereafter* begins with the school bus accident and the children's death, and then the story is about how a community lives without its children. I view that book as a parable: what is it like to live without your children? And then *Bone* is what it's like to be the child in a society that is trying to live without its children. To be an abandoned child, a homeless child, a child no longer protected, who has no sacred space in which to become a mature human being. The two books are meant to fit together. I think of *The Sweet Hereafter* as a German folktale, an allegorical novel, and *Bone* is a more realistic and first-person narrative. I'm retelling the same story but from the point of view of the kids who have been commodified and exploited. So much of what we see happening in Washington today with the "Contract with America" bullshit is the reaction to this delayed discovery that we don't have many kids who look or act like us. Why is that? The first response is to punish them for it. We're punishing our children for not being like us, because that's a way of not admitting that we have done something to our children that previous parents never did. Previous parents protected their children, gave them a sacred space, gave them time and room to become adults. Now we have "Toys R Us." I love that name, it's just diabolical. [*laughter*]

But we don't need to understand kids better, we need to understand ourselves better, our own nefarious methods and motives. We have to understand our weaknesses and fears and the degree to which we're manipulated by the culture of corporate America that we live in. We have to build an ideology in order to become moral and caring, custodial, protective human beings. To me, that's the great secret in American life, this betrayal and abandonment of the children.

PB: The American character is convoluted, complex, and multi-layered, and you've been taking it on book after book. The project you're into now concerns somebody who it seems to me is the ultimate adult. How does he fit into your exploration of the American tapestry?

RB: He's an archetypal figure, John Brown the abolitionist.

PB: Harper's Ferry, West Virginia, my home state.

RB: He's like the leader of every cult we've seen in America, going back for hundreds of years. Someone who with his force and single-mindedness stands in our child-like imagination for what an adult is supposed to be: clear. So the attraction to him is irresistible in a culture like ours. The fact that John Brown is the only white figure who is included in the pantheon of black heroes by black people but almost across the board amongst white people is regarded as a madman, is to me very clarifying about race in America.

PB: Hero and madman aren't mutually exclusive, are they? George Patton, Custer had a little bit of each . . .

RB: Yeah, but they don't articulate in their lives what Brown does in racial terms. W. E .B. DuBois said the problem of the twentieth century is going to be the race line. And the problem of the twenty-first century is clearly also going to be the race line. We're still there. A defining event that Brown led up to, the Civil War, was that same race line, and the fact that he's viewed in diametrically opposite perspectives, depending upon whether you're white or black, is very clarifying—not about Brown necessarily—but about America.

PB: And the book you're working on now is a novel?

RB: It's an intimate, private, personal novel about John Brown, the man. It's not about John Brown the historical image, although I'm very attracted to that.

PB: I've been hearing Brown's name a good deal recently, but in connection with Paul Hill, the guy who shot the abortion doctor.

RB: Well, the anti-abortionists are invoking his name in order to sanctify violence. It's a parallel between Brown in the 1850s as a radical abolitionist using violence against slavery, and the anti-abortionists in the late twentieth century who embrace violence on the same grounds—it's a clear, easy parallel to draw. Outside of Israel, there is no other nation created out of a moral necessity. Unlike say France, or England, or Russia, we have this moral destiny, which is biblical, and we seem forever doomed to play out our history in moral terms.

PB: We're a nation of Shakers and Branch Davidians.

RB: It's true. We still have this biblical mission to build the New Jerusalem. And not just simply to survive, the way France wants to, or survive and dominate the way England wants to. We want to survive as the City on the Hill. This is our basic religion, and in some ways it's how we entitle ourselves as citizens. We're not just patriotic, we're saved. That kind of patriotism is supra-nationalism. This creates a deep and profound conflict with our idea of ourselves as a nation that is a secular welcome wagon for every god-damned religion in the world. We have this deeply neurotic conflict which is bound to explode in violence every now and then.

PB: Tell me about Pottawatomie.

RB: Pottawatomie is historical material. But what I view it as, and what I think John Brown viewed it as, was the first example of terrorism committed in this country, perhaps the world. I believe John Brown went to Harper's Ferry with a certain amount of strategy: to begin from that point a guerrilla war which would be maintained in the Appalachians, running from northern Tennessee all the way up to the Adirondacks adjacent to the Underground Railroad. That was in some sense a fairly rational plan, and it might have worked had it been conducted in a certain way. It failed for various reasons, primarily because Frederick Douglass, at the last minute, decided not to join him. It's the next chapter in his life which is the most puzzling and wonderful chapter about him from the point of view of a novelist. The great puzzle for me is why John Brown, having lost very important elements which would have made Harper's Ferry the successful beginning of a guerilla war, nonetheless continued. He jumped from being a radical planner of a guerilla war to a martyr, consciously and deliberately. He knew he would not get out of Harper's Ferry alive. Puzzle one: why did he choose to become a martyr at that point? And puzzle two: why did he choose to martyr his children? He brought three sons with him, two died there, one escaped. And a son-in-law, and close devoted friends, people who followed him for years. What threw that switch is what intrigues me. What kind of hopelessness, what kind of idealism makes that possible? I can catch him up to that point. But then he steps off into space for me and I don't catch him. I don't know what he's talking about, what he's feeling, and that's the great moment for a novelist. That's where my novel focuses finally.

PB: I thought this was a really interesting sentence very early on in *Rule of the Bone*—it hearkens back to the opening of *Huckleberry Finn*—"This is nothing but the truth." It's very provocative to find that line in the beginning of a novel. What did you feel like, using that sentence as a prologue to a fiction?

RB: Of course, it's stated with a certain amount of self-deprecating irony. And it is a deliberate allusion to *Huck Finn*. And to *Catcher in the Rye*, which is in itself a deliberate allusion to *Huck Finn*.

I was trying to get down and let this kid have his story in an intimate, private, secret way, as you tell a story about your life. I imagine Bone as being where I have been in certain moments of my life, lying in a bed looking at the ceiling in the dark, with the person whom I loved next to me, either in the same bed or the next bed. It could have been when I was a boy or when I was a man, and the person in the next bed could have been a woman or a man or a boy, but a person who was also in bed looking up at the ceiling. And you start to talk at that late night hour, and you could lie, or you could tell the truth. And I just imagined Bone at that moment, lying there looking up at the ceiling deciding to tell the truth, even though it might be boring. He was willing to risk that. I wanted to clarify the relationship between the narrator and the reader, clear the decks and say, this is where I expect you, the reader, to be: it's dark and I trust you, and you're lying next to me and we're near sleep and I'm going to risk telling the truth.

An Interview with Russell Banks

Julie Checkoway and English 497/1996

From *AWP Chronicle* 28.6 (May/Summer 1996): 1–8. Reprinted by permission of Julie Checkoway.

JC: Let me put you on the speaker phone. There are about thirty people here with me; it's an old, old phone. I really appreciate your doing this.

RB: Well, I'm happy to do it, to see how it goes, because if it works, other people should be doing it.

JC: I agree. In fact, we have some professors here, observing to see if what we're doing is pedagogically sound. [*Banks's and students' laughter*] Is it freezing up there in Keene, New York?

RB: Yes, there's snow on the ground and temperatures in the teens, and I'm sitting here, I have a cabin, it's an old sugar shack used for boiling down maple sap into maple syrup that I've renovated into a studio that I heat with a kerosene heater. [*Laughter from students, Banks laughs*] I'm quite cozy, actually.

JC: Well, it's about sixty-something in Georgia. You're welcome here any time.

RB: Great.

JC: Russell, I'm going to go ahead and turn the phone over to the students. They've prepared lots of questions for you.

Shannon Lipe: Professor Banks, can you hear me okay?

RB: Yes, I can.

Shannon Lipe: I have a two-part question for you. In this course, we've read several reviews of *Rule of the Bone*. How do you respond to critics (like Jess Mowry) who say that Bone is not typical of a homeless child? In what ways were you concerned about realism in writing the novel, and how much of the writing of the novel was driven by a desire to construct a myth?

RB: Let's take the first part. Was that the piece that was in *The Nation*? To be honest with you, I didn't finish it. I read the first two paragraphs of it, and I saw where he was going and I caught the tone of it and I let it go. There were a couple of other reviews like that. There was one in *Time* also. Those were the two that I was most conscious of, *The Nation* in particular because I like the magazine and they had been very kind to me in the past and I'd hoped that the book might get into the hands of someone who could give it a serious reading and who could talk about it in a sympathetic way. Mainly, I guess I felt, at least from the little bit that I read, that the person had his own perspective and his own angle on things and he was writing as if he were competitive with me regarding kids, and that happens. Critics are often territorial, and they feel sometimes that a writer has encroached on their territory so that they write defensively, and I think that's probably what I picked up on right away, that he was writing defensively. I make a practice, really, of not answering reviewers or critics or correcting them, from my point of view, or even thanking them, although I'm grateful when they're thoughtful and when they are insightful. The fact of the matter is that writing and criticism, or writing and reading, let's put it that way, are such different activities that it is very difficult to learn much—from the writer's point of view—from criticism. In fact, I think I can learn more from watching a good carpenter or good cabinetmaker than I can from a literary critic. This isn't to say that literary criticism isn't a worthwhile activity; I think it is. But it's not necessarily useful to writers. I work very hard to keep myself free of any sense of a critic's being over my shoulder. You know, oftentimes when I do read them, I am astonished by their brilliance and insight and am grateful for it, but don't really learn a great deal from it.

And the second part of the question—that's a good question. I wasn't consciously concerned about realism in that I wasn't trying to write a type of novel, fit it into a pre-determined mode or aesthetic theory. I wasn't driven by that, nor did I particularly feel as though I was serving that in any way. I was trying to write what I think of as kind of a tall tale and trying to use the conventions of certain kinds of stories and storytelling in order to get at some deeper truths than you can usually get at through either the surface of realism, on the one hand, or the mythic structure, on the other. I was trying to do a little bit of both, but mainly because I tend to view the world that way. I tend to see the surface, the quotidian level of day-to-day life, and it tends to fall into patterns for me that I suppose afterwards might look mythic or archetypal, or something like that, but I don't set out to do that deliberately or have a particular plan in mind, or a mythic structure that I'm trying to plug into. It's just that oftentimes I see an individual life, like the life of a boy like Bone, the kids hanging out at the mall and so forth; I tend to see them as representative figures simultaneously as I see them as individuals.

I think that double vision, that bi-focular vision, is what produces the gritty texture on the one hand and, for lack of a better word, I guess, the mythic structure on the other hand.

John Beaty: This question goes back to your trying to tell a tall tale. There were several incidents in the novel that seemed almost contrived—similar to the incidents in the work of nineteenth-century writers like Dickens and Twain—like when the Ridgeways pick Bone up hitchhiking. Were you struggling with the issue of contrivance?

RB: I wasn't struggling with it. It's a lot easier, in a way, to keep coincidences out of a plot than it is to put them in, easier to keep on inventing and circling away from obsessive themes and concerns. No, I was trying to use coincidence for several reasons and in several ways. One was to remind the reader, at least on some level, maybe subconsciously, that this was not a documentary, that this was a consciously composed work of art, and the symmetries and coincidences were meant to both signal that and to implement that. You know, the parallel between the Ridgeways' house on the hill and the Mothership in Jamaica, and the various other figures that end up symmetrically paired and opposed to one another, operate in somewhat the same way that the coincidences do, I think. And I felt that I was at liberty to do that because I wasn't trying to present a documentary point of view here. I was trying to tell a story that is full of wonders and peculiar odd coincidences and symmetries.

JC: That seemed to be the problem that Mowry had in *The Nation*. He wanted Bone to be a documentary.

RB: That's right. That may be what was bugging him. That hit a couple of reviewers. It led them away from what I was doing. I wasn't trying to do some kind of social realist exposure of the underbelly of American society or something like that, although it's a worthy thing to do, and I suspect that there may be some aspects of the book which invite that reading, especially to people who may never have spent any time in the malls, although I don't know anybody who hasn't spent time in the mall. People over eighty, maybe.

JC: [*brightly*] Some people over eighty exercise in malls.

RB: [*laughing*] That's true. That's very true. My mother goes to the mall all the time. So maybe I shouldn't have said that. [*laughter*]

Jill Hall: So whose tall tale is this? Is it Bone's or yours?

RB: Well, it's his tall tale as far as I'm concerned. I worked very hard with this book to continually discipline myself to get outside of Bone's head and into a position where I was listening to him. I imagined myself as the person to whom he was telling the story. There are a couple of places there where he directly addresses the reader-slash-author, as I would think of it. At one point, you might remember, where he almost commits suicide, where he's gone home and has made one last attempt to return to his mother and step-father and then his grandmother, when he stands on the bridge and so on and he says "and this is the first time I ever told anyone about it." And there's another place later where he directly addresses the reader. In other words, he stops the narrative and directly confronts the reader. That's a way of organizing my own imagination, I think, so that I could keep myself out of it. But one of the reasons that I used my own name, for instance, for one of the own characters—for Russell—and also my own physical appearance and my wife's car [*laughs*], and we have a house very much like the Ridgeways' house, was in an odd way, a superstitious way, I suppose, of giving myself a little cameo, putting maybe particularly unattractive aspects of myself in the book, so that I wouldn't over-identify with Bone. It was a way of avoiding identification with him, so that he would be free to tell his story, and it wouldn't be necessarily my story and I would be free as a writer in the process of hearing him to hear things and discover things that I really didn't consciously know when I began to write. It's very much his story—in my mind. The voice, every now and then, I would find myself losing it, and it was like losing a signal on a radio, a distant signal and you had to fiddle with the tuner to bring it back in again and I'd have to stop and do that, and when I would lose it, when the voice would begin to sound a little bit more like my own voice, my own writerly voice, and not like his, that's when I would know that I was losing his signal. So I think of it very much as his tall tale. And yeah, there are a few "stretchers" in there, too, I'm sure. Although he's a totally honest human being, he's not above amusing himself with a little exaggeration. As you remember, when he's riding the bus with Russ and he's telling the tale of the lost tribes of Israel. So if he's stretching it there with a kind of dopey and easily fooled military guy, then you can bet he's probably stretching it here and there elsewhere, too, in the book. When he's talking to us.

Dana Siegmund: How autobiographical is the novel? How much of you is the character Russ himself?

RB: He's a little . . . let me see if I can put it another way, here. You know how in a dream people who appear to be strangers but have aspects of your own personality attached to them, how that's a way of depersonalizing, objectifying things in yourself that you're either ashamed of or don't like or are angry at or so forth? I think fiction writers tend to do that, too, oftentimes with villainous characters. Which is why you get that strange mixture of emotion where you know this is a character who is not particularly attractive but nonetheless the writer seems to really like him and you do yourself a little bit. Russ is not a particularly attractive guy, and he represents for me aspects of myself, of my personality, maybe when I was an adolescent, that I am ambivalent about, to say the least. He's garrulous, he's able to con people, he's got big plans all the time, he's a little slippery, and I know that that was an aspect certainly of myself when I was fifteen, sixteen years old. And I think that it was a way of externalizing, objectifying that. By the same token, there are aspects of myself, really, in almost all the other characters in this book. And it's typical, really. It's more pointed in some cases—physically I resemble Mr. Ridgeway, and to a kid like Bone I would look like the whitest man he ever saw, with a white beard and white hair and pink skin, so it's a physical aspect of myself that I externalized, extruded into the book. But on the other hand there are experiences that Bone has had and has in the book that parallel certain experiences that I had myself as a kid, his relation to his father, his lost father as it were, his fantasy about him being JFK and Bone being the son of JFK, mixed with the anger where earlier than that he imagined himself Lee Harvey Oswald; you know, that kind of split between the boy who imagines himself an assassin or a parricide, killing the father of his country, on the one hand, and the next minute he's imagining himself the son of that President. That kind of ambivalence, psychologically, is one I certainly experienced as an adolescent boy toward my own father. So those elements in your mind and your emotional life and emotional history and so forth are inescapable when you're writing a novel that you care about as much as I cared about this one when I was writing it. You're bound to get it in there. That's not at the same time, really, autobiography, is it? It's something else. Something, I think, maybe more useful, deeper, both for the writer it's more useful, and finally, I hope, useful for the reader as well, than simple autobiography.

Wendy Overman: We've had much speculation and discussion in class about the significance of Chappie's tattoo and name change. Why was it necessary for him to scar himself and change his own name? Many of us go back and forth and call him Chappie or Bone or Chappie/Bone.

RB: It's interesting what you said about people calling him one thing or the other. I think of him and refer to him constantly as Bone and sometimes forget that he had another name. I guess that's because I deal with him in my mind as he was at the end of the book, when he really had become his name, the name he had chosen. Let me think. The story really in many ways is about a boy who is in the process of inventing himself with very few resources available to him, cultural or familial or social resources, and so he has to make himself up out of the materials at hand, and they aren't very, well, by most standards very rich—I think they're very rich—but they're still the detritus of our everyday culture, modern American consumer culture is what he's doing it with. That becomes the terms he uses to, existentially, really, become a person and gain control and authenticity as a person. And the name-taking is part of that; it's a double-edged act. It's a rejection of the past and the given. And it's funny, Chappie is really a "chap," Chapman is what his real name is, which is a kind of Everyman's name, you know, an anonymous name in a way, even though it has a social gloss to it. You could see somebody from the lower-middle class giving their child the name Chapman because it sounds like he would go to Philips Exeter or something like that, or maybe go to Harvard. It sounds sort of upper-middle class. But he rejects that and he identifies doing that with Malcolm X rejecting his slave name and I-Man rejecting his name, and it's a very assertive act against the past to reject the name. And to take the name Bone, he does that for complicated but fairly rich reasons and imaginative reasons, I think, partly again identifying with Malcolm X, and Peter Pan. The name and the tattoo evoke both associations for him. The thing about tattooing, you mentioned that as an act of . . . how did you phrase it?

Wendy Overman: Scarring himself.

RB: Scarring himself. Yeah. I didn't think of it as scarring himself particularly, scar being the residue of a wound. I thought of it more the way I think of the reason a lot of kids get tattoos and/or earrings, body piercing, and so forth. A lot of that seems to me to be an expression of feelings that they have that there is nothing else they can assert any control over in their lives except their bodies, so they aggressively present that fact to you through the visible tattoos and body piercing and so forth. It's a way of asserting, "Well, I can't control anything in my life but I can control my body. It's my body." And even if it's a destructive act, or appears to be at least on the surface a destructive act, then it's nonetheless a kind of positive act because "I'm claiming control here. You can't control me here." And I think that's an age-old way for young people, particularly, who feel that there's nothing in their lives that they can control except their body for asserting that. In my generation we asserted that with our hair. I'm a sixties person. And we felt it was a way, not just of flying in the face of parents and getting them mad at us—which it did—but I think the initial thing was: "Well, I can at least grow my hair. That's part of my body. And that's what I have. I may not have control over anything else, but I have that."

Wendy Overman: Did you identify him with another character in litera-ture?

RB: I'm not quite sure I understand the question. You mean the tattooing and so forth?

Wendy Overman: Right.

RB: I wasn't trying to deliberately associate that act with characters out of literature, although he's obviously a descendant of Huck Finn. No, I really wasn't. I wasn't trying to point to any literary context, I don't think.

Judi Bartlett: Why is it that Bone has to go to the Caribbean to come of age? Are you suggesting that he must exit the geographical and social boundar-ies of the United States and embrace aspects of another culture in order to achieve maturity, to reject the "American way" in order to find himself?

RB: There is certainly that in the arc of his narrative out of the home, his trailer in Au Sable, into the school bus and on across the boat on Lake Cham-plain and the plane flight off into the other world, and then the Ant Farm and so forth. He certainly has gone about as far from small-town American bourgeois life as you can go in late twentieth-century America and still be on the planet. And I think that I did want to dramatize that theme, that the only way that you could save your soul in this consumer society is in some way of getting out of the society, abandoning its trappings and its clutter and its wreckage, really, the wreckage of the family and the wreckage of the community. He literally does do that. One doesn't have to do that, I suppose, go all the way to Jamaica to do that, but he does. So maybe it's a symbolic presentation of that arc. I'm not sure. I could have had him go to Haiti; I could have him go to lots of places. He could have gone into the inner city in New York. He could have gone to Schenectady, and I might have been able to tell the same story and make the same point.

Judi Bartlett: May I follow that up a little bit?

RB: Let me finish the thought a second more, though. The reason I had him go to Jamaica is very simple. I lived there in the seventies, and I've travelled back and forth there a lot over the years, and so I know it very well, and I had all the elements in my mind there that would allow me to tell the story. It was easier, in other words, in some ways for me to have him go to Jamaica rather than Schenectady.

Judi Bartlett: I just wanted you to talk a little bit about your choice to have Bone enter into his spiritual awakening through Rastafarianism versus Bud-dhism or another religion.

RB: Yes, there's that. And I also wanted to introduce the theme of race in the book. Because it seemed to me that it would be very hard to bring a boy, a white American boy in the late twentieth century, to consciousness without his becoming conscious of himself in a racial context, and I wanted to do it in a way that I understood it myself. And so his travels, both spiritual and political, and, I guess, racial, brought him, allowed him to encounter all three of those aspects of his reality, of his existence, through his connection with I-Man and the Rastafarianism in Jamaica, so that by the end he is able to have some kind of understanding of his own race and the power that goes with it and the meaning of it in a racialized world, which he wouldn't have otherwise.

Brent Andrews: Throughout the novel you depict societal norms and institutions negatively and seem to glorify the use of marijuana. Is this a conscious attempt to advocate the legalization of marijuana?

RB: Good question. [*Student's laughter*] I wasn't writing to advocate decriminalization, although I do favor decriminalization. I really wasn't taking a position on those issues. I was much more involved with how it seems and how it was experienced by a boy like, Bone in particular, but by a fourteen, fifteen-year-old kid, to try to look at the world from his point of view as much as possible. And I know from first-hand experience, as well as second and third, that fourteen, fifteen-year-old kids in his situation in life in America look at marijuana use very differently from the way people my age, probably people your age, even, look at the use of marijuana. It's really Bone's angle on marijuana, not mine. I happen to agree with him in certain areas. He's a lot more reckless than I would ever be. No, that's not true. He's a lot more reckless than I am today. [*Students' laughter*] But I do know that a kid like Bone looks at the use of marijuana very differently than a man like me, you know, a middle-class man in his middle fifties, looks at the use of whisky or wine, for that matter. I think that was more or less what I was after there. It was not an argument for or against the use of marijuana or the legalization of marijuana; it was just a fact. If you take Mark Twain's portrait of Huck Finn smoking tobacco, it would have been implausible if Mark Twain presented it in such a way that smoking tobacco was harmful to Huck or Huck believed it was harmful or was fearful of it or so forth or found it socially reprehensible. It was a perfectly natural and believable aspect of Huck's life that he would be smoking tobacco, and that he'd see smoking tobacco as a part of his recreational life. And I think it's the same thing with Bone; it's a big part of his recreational, and eventually, his spiritual life.

Brent Andrews: Do you feel that marijuana has a positive effect on informing his own personal code of values in the novel?

RB: I don't think so particularly. It had certainly an effect on inducing his vision, but so did fatigue and so did geographic and cultural dislocation have a big effect, so did the recent traumas in dealing with his father have an effect, so did the horrors of racism that he was coming up against have an effect on him. No, I just think it was one of the many elements in his life that gave him access to insight. He's also an imaginative kid and a bright kid, too, very alert. He makes different use of marijuana than say, someone like Russ. Russ uses it just to get high, to get stoned, and then he goes to sleep. So it has just a soporific effect on him. Whereas for Bone it has some other effect. But I think that's how he processes all his experiences.

Elizabeth Fogle: Earlier, you spoke of Bone's spirituality. I just wrote a paper on shamanism in *Bone*. In my reading of the novel, I noticed that I-Man functioned as a sort of shaman figure. How many of the shamanistic parallels were intentional?

RB: Well, quite a lot. From various levels, I guess. I certainly wanted him to encounter such a person and felt it was necessary that there be in his life someone like that, as there is for all of us, and since it couldn't be provided for him by his family and couldn't be provided for him in his own community, such as it was, it would have to come from somewhere else. And so he found it in the figure of I-Man, who is not an unmixed person. He's not idealized, I hope, because there's a dark side of every shaman, too, you know, there's a threatening and slightly ominous darkness that they bring with them as well; they're not all sweetness and light and careful instruction, and I wanted that to be there as well. So I am pretty conscious of structuring that into the book and into Bone's experience. Again, it's an experience that parallels some of my own when I was young, with various figures, not just one figure like I-Man. There were several people in my life who provided a similar role in my own personal life. I suspect most people, if they're lucky, go through that, have someone for whom they can be an apprentice, and it can turn out not to have been a self-destructive relationship, not a destructive relationship.

Andrea Stewart: I was wondering if there's a reason why the abuse of Chappie is sexual. If it had been any other kind of abuse, would it still *work*?

RB: I think it would have had a different story to it, a different kind of force to it, if he were physically beaten. Is that what you mean?

Andrea Stewart: Yes, sir.

RB: That kind of abuse would have had a different effect on his personality, and he would have had to deal with it and come to grips with it differently. But the sexual abuse is not the central force in his life, the way I look at it or the way he looked at it. I think he understood it was important, very important, and it defined his relationship with Ken, certainly, and early on his sense of his self-worth was considerably diminished by it, and in Ken's presence he felt ashamed, as he said, "all doughy," and worthless, as though he had some shameful secret. And he had to finally probably come to grips and deal with it over the course of his life. You must remember that this is a tall tale and it's foreshortened, all the experiences of a lifetime compressed into one year. I mean, I would never want to go through in one year what that poor guy goes through. But his experiences of his stepfather are meant to be paralleled with Evening Star. She is actually quite kind to him and gentle to him sexually. And he puts off for quite a long time any kind of sexual encounter. You know, Russ is always trying to get him to go along with him, and there are various occasions where he could certainly have, a kid his age and his circumstances, sexual encounters. He is oddly virginal—not odd to me—but given his circumstances, he's unusually virginal and withholding of himself sexually. And it isn't until finally he's with someone who is really rather gentle and protective of him that he's able to make a sexual connection. So there is meant to be, I think, a connection between the early abuse and the later sexually liberating experience that he has with Evening Star.

Jill Hall: Can you comment on Bruce's homosexuality in the novel and Bone's response to it? By the end of the novel Bruce has become a kind of Christ figure.

RB: Well, kids like Bone on the streets seem to me to be a lot—I don't want to say blasé, but they're a lot less analytical, certainly, and less threatened by sexual misbehavior or sexual aggression. They tend to see it more clearly, I think, in terms of economics and power than to see or deal with the psychological aspects of it. Take the way he deals, for instance, with Buster Brown. He just sees him, he has certain rules, and that's that, and he realizes what's going on very quickly and doesn't judge it particularly. What he really judges Buster for is his treatment of Rose and his use of Rose. But he doesn't judge him sexually. He says, "I just saw him as an old gay guy who was hitting on me, blah, blah, blah," and he deals with it on that level, and I think that's true with Bruce, too. As far as Bruce's sexual aberrance goes, and he is aberrant, because he's violent against homosexuals even as he's picking them up in bus stations, and Bone sees the connection between the violence and the attraction, which is true of a lot of homophobia, that it's aggression addressed against a version of you or a suspected view of oneself. Bone sees that, but he doesn't judge it particularly; he just sees Bruce as a person who has his own hang-ups, I guess, and can deal with that and the consequences of the hang-ups. He doesn't judge the hang-ups in any way. So my thought was, that's fairly normal to me. I mean a lot of kids tend to view it that way. And as a result, I didn't see any particular connection between Bruce's sexual neurosis and Bone's relationship to his stepfather, which was so devastating to him in many ways, because of the refusal of his stepfather to in any way protect him or respect him as an individual, but just to use him as an object. That's what he's dealing with there, most pointedly. Bruce really doesn't deal with Bone as an object; he sees him as a person and is amused by him and he likes him and he respects him in his own whacked-out way. And I think that's why Bone is drawn to Bruce and remembers him with great loving kindness at the end of the book.

Katherine Jones: Is Bone at the end of the novel on his way to acting as an I-Man or shaman to others? What type of person would he be ten years from now?

RB: That's an interesting question. It's come up before. And I'm delighted by the question, because it suggests that he's become real enough so that people can imagine his life outside the novel, his having a life beyond the novel, which is an author's hope and dream, that you can come up with a character who has that kind of reality for people. I can imagine various states for him down the line. And I'd love some day to return to him and find out what he's doing; although, I think, I know better than to try and write a sequel. I don't think I will. Bone has got all the tools he needs to lead a mature and loving life by the end of the book. First of all, he has control over his economic life. He has a skill; he's a cook now; he can cook vegetarian for twelve-stepping rock-and-rollers. And he's able to love other human beings in imaginative ways, and he's able to see that they have a reality, like those two young children on the boat; he's able to see into their lives and imagine them fully and not just see them as objects. So he has that. And he has a clear sense, and a firm and tested sense, of what's right and wrong. He has a morality. If you have a morality and you have the ability to love someone and have control over your own economic life, then you're a very powerful person in the world. So I think of him at the end as a very powerful person, even though he's only fifteen years old and he's living in a boat in the Caribbean somewhere. So I wouldn't mind running into a kid like him down the road somewhere and hanging out with him for a while and sharing some adventures for a while.

Finding the Melody: An Interview with Russell Banks

Rob Davidson and Fred Santiago Arroyo/1996

From *Delicious Imaginations: Conversations with Contemporary Writers*. Ed. Sarah Griffiths and Kevin J. Kehrwald. West Lafayette, IN: Purdue UP, 1996: 222–48. © 1998 Purdue University Press. Unauthorized duplication not permitted.

FSA: I once heard you say, in relation to *Huckleberry Finn*, *Catcher in the Rye*, and your writing of *Rule of the Bone*, that one of the major problems a writer will have is the relationship between vernacular and voice. I was wondering if you could talk about this process.

RB: I think I was describing the process for myself. Finding by ear, really, the particular line of music that's carried in the American vernacular, which is an almost infinitely flexible linguistic medium. Perhaps other languages have the same flexibility and range, but I don't know them well enough to say. But it seems to me that American English, from the mid-nineteenth century on, has a widening range of expressive modes in the vernacular voice. Twain taps into what was there already in a way that no other white writer had before; he taps into, among other tunes, African-American speech patterns, that particular melody in the American chorus, I guess is the way I think of it. The way I experience . . . and then increasingly other melodies chime in as the century wears on and into the twentieth century. And now in the late twentieth century, there are a dozen or more melodies that are still there, running: the Eastern European Jewish and the African-American lines have become the increasingly dominant modes.

We can almost tell by reading the newspapers when there's a new voice or a new melody entering the American vernacular because everybody wants to legislate it out of existence. There's the fear of Spanglish right now, for instance. I mean, you don't pass laws against what people *don't* do. You pass laws against what people do do, and so if they try to pass laws against Spanish, then it must be because people are starting to speak a lot of Spanish and it's invading English in a way, so we better legislate it out.

But I think what I was pointing to there was that a young writer coming along today—and it doesn't matter whether it's a Latino writer, or an African-American writer, or an Anglo writer, or even a Francophonic writer from the northern-tier states—but one of the tasks he or she will face is finding the melody that speaks to his or her own material, the material one is trying to write about and to approach on an intimate level. And it can't be approached linguistically until one can find that melody. And it's the beauty of American vernacular English that it contains within it so many different chords. You can't play them all. You're going to have to find the one that registers an intimate relation with your own experience and material. So I think that, for young writers, this is a tremendous possibility, but it's also by the same token a difficulty.

I mean, when Hawthorne picked up a pen to write, there wasn't any question in his mind about what voice to use. It was ready-made. Somewhat the way, I think, Oxford-educated Englishmen feel, even today, when they pick up the pen. But what about an Irish writer? What about a Scottish writer? What about a Nigerian writer? What about an Anglo-Canadian writer, or an Indian-Canadian writer? Or an Indian-American writer? Or someone like Cristina Garcia, a Hispanic-American writer? They have to listen to language very differently, in a way, in order to find that intimate voice, that authentic voice.

But this really is a way of complimenting and praising, I should say, American vernacular English, because it raises the question for us in a vital and important and continuing way. As I said, I don't know enough about other languages, but my limited experience with them is that it doesn't occur with the same intensity and complexity as it occurs here.

FSA: If you speak so strongly about the question, about the "vitality," about the "complexity" and "praising," it seems to me there's the possibility that art can be lost because we have laws saying, "What are we going to do with these immigrants that come in?" When, instead, art could celebrate all the different vernaculars entering the language, and we could see who we are through them. I mean, that's storytelling. We need the multiplicity and these possibilities, but there are so many obstructions.

RB: Yeah. And of course they're based on fear. Fear of the other. You're never afraid of the other unless you don't know who you yourself are. I think that those who are afraid of the other in the form of fear of immigration now are afraid not for economic reasons—although they may couch their fears sometimes that way—but really because they don't know themselves who they are, and they're threatened by that, by the influx of the other. It's the old story: "Most of them are dark-skinned people. They're coming from Asia, and they're coming from Africa, and they're coming from the Caribbean, and they're coming from Mexico. That's scary. We're white people, aren't we? Aren't we? Aren't we?"

RD: How do you see the role of the writer in relation to that? I know, for example, in an essay entitled "The Politics of Imagination," Bob Shacochis discusses some of the resistance writers can encounter when they write about a class, gender, race, or sexuality other than their own. Specifically, there are critics who question the validity not to mention the motives of a white, male North American writing the story of say, a poor Afro-Caribbean woman like Vanise Dorsinville in *Continental Drift*. Have you encountered such resistance? How would you respond to such critics? Also, perhaps you have some thoughts on the obligations that writers have in this regard.

RB: Actually, I've never really taken much flack for that, for writing about people who weren't like me, who were either female, or were black, or were non-American. I mean, a Haitian peasant woman is about as unlike me as you can probably get. But I never really have taken much flack for that, even from Haitians. In fact, the book is quite widely read, to my delight, by Haitians in French, and it has been written about in fairly detailed ways in the Haitian literary press and is taught in courses by Haitians in universities. So, I feel at ease about my own work in that regard.

But the question arises, "Well, okay, so how come they aren't offended?" Because you do risk offending people when you appropriate their experience and claim to speak for them, or at least appear to speak for them, when their experience is clearly radically different from your own. And I think that the guiding rule I've had in my own work has been to know my own limits, and to know what I don't know, in other words, and then to try to do my homework, essentially. To overcome, or to deal with those limits and to push them back by several means. One is simply to just do some research. Just go and find out and ask somebody who does know. And come to know someone like that personally. To address the situation, in other words, to address my own limits. First to identify them and then to address them. And also to find ways of writing about people who are unlike yourself that are non-appropriational, which also reflects your knowledge of your own limits, so that in the case of Vanise Dorsinville, I didn't tell her story from her point of view, I told it from outside. Because I know how people like

Vanise—taken as a sociological type—act and how they sound and how they look because I've spent a lot of time in the Caribbean and in Haiti and in Miami, in the Haitian community, I know how they look to a white man on the outside, and that's what I'm representing on the page. It's not how it feels to be looked at by a white man from the inside. But that's a technical decision, or a formal decision that I've made in the writing which reflects an inner decision, or an inner observation, about my own limitations. An agreement with that. So in doing that, I've avoided what Shacochis identifies as, I think, a problem.

It's not really a problem. It's a condition, and I'm not sure that Bob is thinking real clearly about that. I admire his work greatly, but I think he's a little defensive about it. As a result, he makes large and assertive claims about the artist's prerogative and this, that, and the other, which I don't particularly find very helpful or insightful, necessarily. But I think I know where he's coming from. And I admire his scale and the broad focus of his lens. I like the way he expands to include as much as possible in his tale. He's very unusual in that regard amongst American white male fiction writers, and I admire that. He and Robert Stone and Don DeLillo and half a dozen others . . . But you run out of names pretty fast.

FSA: The other day, you talked about the three parts of process a writer might consider in approaching a subject. Could you discuss these again?

RB: I was speaking earlier about language, actually, a quality of language. This grew out of my writing, well, before I began the book and was researching. It's really a long historical novel based on the life of John Brown. As a result of entering that world, I ended up reading a lot of mid-nineteenth-century diaries, letters, primary texts from middle- and lower-middle-class people, white and black, and finding a quality of language in there that's very difficult to identify today in casual writing, in intimate, casual writing like letters and diaries and so forth. A kind of clarity and muscularity in it, and an authenticity in it that's much remarked upon, for instance, in the letters and diaries that Ken Burns used in his Civil War documentary. Or that you see in the great masterpiece of American prose of that era, Ulysses S. Grant's memoirs. Or as you see in Twain full-blown from early on, and certain other writers, the non-literary writers, the non-salon, non-parlor writers. And in thinking about it, I asked, "How come it was so goddamn good?" It's sort of like New England architecture of the seventeenth century. How come it was so goddamn good? It still looks beautiful. And how come jazz was so good so suddenly with so many people in New Orleans from 1890 to 1920? What's going on there? It seemed like everybody could do it. I mean, a carpenter in

Duxbury, Massachusetts, an ordinary guy without any architectural training, could go out and build a church. And, you know, two hundred years later it still looks absolutely, stunningly beautiful. How come? How can a people be so smart?

And I think Americans, in language terms, were that smart in the middle-nineteenth century—and without any formal training. Usually the educational level might be third to eighth grade, the equivalent of that, but they would've been schooled in the Bible, and they would've been schooled in Milton and Shakespeare, and Jonathan Edwards and the Puritan Divines, Benjamin Franklin, a few things like that. The Constitution, the Declaration of Independence. But outside of those texts, that was pretty much their exposure to literature and language. So how come?

It occurred to me that there were three things operative then that are not necessarily operative now, or are only rarely operative now, when a writer sits down to write, whether it's a personal letter or a novel. The creative triangle. And the first point was that, in relation to language, the writer believed that he or she had something to say, really believed in the worth of what was to be communicated through language, whether it was what happened at Shiloh or what happened in berry-picking season in Amherst, Massachusetts, this year, or what happened when mother died. They believed that they had something to say.

The second was that they believed that they had enough education and enough facility with language that they could convey what was of worth to them.

And then the third point was that they believed that the person to whom it was directed, their reader, would understand it. So there was a three-point connection through language that was whole and solid and trusted. Trust, I think, is maybe the key. Trust the subject, trust the medium, and trust the recipient—the person to whom you're communicating.

When you feel that as a writer, today, or anytime in your life—when you feel those three points operating at all times, those three cylinders or whatever working together, in harmony and unison—then, in a way, there's no problem with writing. You write way over your normal ability as a result. That's a very rare state of mind to achieve. One I think we all, in some ways, try real hard to find. It precludes certain levels and kinds of writing, however. It probably makes it difficult to be ironic.

On the other hand, you read Lincoln's speeches and they're loaded with complicated irony. He's as ironic as Borges. His public speech given in Chicago in 1858 is a rebuttal to an earlier speech of [Stephen] Douglas's, and it's just cutting. It flays Douglas into pieces. It's a thousand cuts. It's brilliant. And he's just speaking ordinary American speech, he's just writing, yet it's incredibly flexible.

I just think it's one of those high moments in American linguistic history, one that corresponds to New England architecture of the seventeenth century and the development of jazz in New Orleans, where an entire people seem to be able to do a very difficult thing with ease. And it kind of astonishes me to look at it, and I must say it makes me somewhat envious.

RD: The "creative triangle" idea is very interesting. I assume this is why a number of your books begin with a kind of justification of the narrative. For example, on the first page of *Rule of the Bone*, Bone states, "the truth is more interesting than anything I could make up and that's why I'm telling it in the first place." *Continental Drift* begins with an invocation of the "mouth man," or Loa, which really frames our reading experience, pointing to the vision that's necessary, and the anger. And Rolfe, the narrator of *Affliction*, explains a number of times throughout the novel why he's telling his story. Are these prefatory statements and justifications the means by which you establish that authority for yourself as a writer?

RB: I think it is. I think that's a good point. Because I don't live in the mid-nineteenth-century American vernacular, and the triangle doesn't operate quite as effortlessly and naturally as it seems to have operated for them. Yeah, I probably need, in order to obtain that security, certain kinds of devices to set the narrative up, and what I might be doing there is establishing that kind of linguistic intimacy with the reader, that trust, by more-or-less literary means. I think you're right. I think back to the "Invocation" in *Continental Drift*. It really was a way, for me, of establishing a relation to an imagined reader that got me and my insecurities and my trepidations out of the way and substituted them for a muse, in a way. Maybe the invocation of the muse, the tradition of that, is a way of doing that, of taking the narrator, the writer, the author/narrator, out of the picture and filling his or her mouth with a different voice that's more authentic than the writer's. I use the invocation of a Loa, a voudon spirit, to fill the mouth of this poor old white man and get him out of the way and tell the story. But that, of course, goes back to the beginnings of literature, that process. But I think maybe psychologically that's what's going on. The same thing with the device of the indirect narrator in *Affliction*. And Bone clearing his throat in the beginning and sort of establishing, you know . . . you come through the door and now he's establishing who he is in a way that basically is designed to build trust in the reader and in himself, and to test the possibilities of the language he's using to make that connection.

RD: You've said that each book you complete "clears the space" and allows you to see the possibilities for the next book. There seems to be a progression, at least as I see it, in the development of your narrative voice since 1985. Briefly, *Continental Drift* is told by a first-person "mouth man" who, having been invoked, steps back and relates the story in the third person. Much of *Affliction* is related in the third person, though the reader is aware the story is told by Rolfe, a first-person agent-narrator compelled to create the narrative for personal reasons. Rolfe, however, does "intrude" at numerous points. *The Sweet Hereafter* is narrated by a range of four different first-person voices, and then—and maybe I'm overdetermined in this—in *Rule of the Bone* you move to the first-person storyteller's voice.

Broadly speaking, then, it seems your aesthetic, at least since 1985, has been marked by a movement toward the true storyteller's voice: the intimate, colloquial first-person.

RB: It is an interesting progression. One I'm not conscious of, particularly. Or wasn't during the process. But I can see, by the same token, how in those four books the narrator becomes, let's say, less problematic, or less self-consciously problematic. Just using those as examples.

The formal apparatus, or structure of the book, becomes more willed and overt in a funny way, and less straight-forwardly linear in its presentation, and in the unfolding of the narrative. So it might be that the formal apparatus is doing the job of the earlier, self-conscious re-arranging of the narrator in, say, *Continental Drift,* which then proceeds to have a very linear narrative and a very primitive kind of alternation of locale. It doesn't change point of view, it changes geographic locale, and the two stories converge. That's a very primitive kind of storytelling once you eliminate that frame.

Affliction is a little more intricate formally because it's an indirect and unreliable narrator talking about a third person who's not present, and is moving through time and is gathering various kinds of evidence, selected from various sources, in order to construct a narrative in a fairly artificial way, if you take that book apart. To the even more, in a sense, artificial structure of *The Sweet Hereafter*, where it's four narrators, four points of view picking up and continuing the story over, again, a straight-forward line of time. To *Rule of the Bone*, which has a very simple—on the surface of it—straight-forward three-part narrative structure in three acts, and moves through three different locales, but by the same token has such an intimate and deliberate and,

I think, obvious intertextual connection to *Huckleberry Finn* that it almost can't be read without it. Nor do I want it to be read without it, particularly. It's meant to be in a call-and-response relation to *Huckleberry Finn*.

And so in a deeper sense, perhaps, that's the most artificial book of all four of those books. Even as the narrative flow and the point of view seem more casual, the structure of the book becomes less casual and more formalized. I don't think that's obvious to the casual reader, but I do think it's there. And what we're talking about here are not literary tricks, we're talking about why a book might take the form that it does. And what I think we're saying is that it seems to take the form it does because of the nature of the writer's relation to the thing written about. That has shifted and changed to some degree, and as it does, different technical means arise for expressing that.

FSA: I can't sense that the "Envoy" and the "Invocation" in *Continental Drift* are chronological in the process of the writing of the book. Technically, I wonder if you actually wrote them first. *The Book of Jamaica* has a similar thing for me. The first part feels the most done and developed, as if you had to write the other parts before you could go back and write the beginning of the book to lead the reader in and make it authentic.

RB: Didn't happen that way, actually, in *The Book of Jamaica*. I wrote that pretty much in the order that it appears. It has four sections, and moves through, basically, four different points of view with the same character. I think it starts in the first person past tense, in a kind of straight-forward memoirist point of view, and then shifts in a way that is meant to correspond to the shifts in consciousness and increasing detachment that the narrator has on himself and his own experience. So it's meant to follow that progression, to parallel and to amplify the psychological and spiritual moves that the protagonist is going through. I wrote it exactly in the order that it appears. Actually, the same thing is true of *Continental Drift*.

It's not true of *Affliction*, however. *Affliction* I tried first to write from Wade's point of view. I wrote about 150 pages and realized that I simply couldn't get the kind of sympathy that I felt for this character if I let him tell his own story, because of who the character was. The way in which he would have to tell his story, given who he was, would be such that it obviated any genuine sympathy for him. The kind of sympathy that I, myself, felt for him. So I had to invent another point of view to tell the story. As it happened, the themes that I was working with—of alcoholism and violence, of domestic violence and its continuation through generations—if you think very deeply about it, as I was doing, you begin to realize there's an equal and opposite reaction to this kind of trauma. One is to repeat it in a compulsive repetition reaction, which is what Wade is undergoing and struggling with. And the other is to withdraw from the fray entirely and refuse to engage that trauma. Which is what Rolfe is doing. They become mirror images, almost, of each other.

And so the failure, in a way, of the first narrative approach led me to consider alternative narrative approaches, and that in turn led me to a deeper understanding of the subject matter itself, of the material that I was working with. I really had to go back to my own relation to what I was trying to write about, which was that of a very sympathetic relation to a man that most people would dismiss as a brute and would put in jail in order to protect other people. Yet I had this passionate sympathy for him, this love of him, and so I had to go back to that in order to find the technical means for telling his story.

FSA: In every one of your books there is a great amount of choice, of inclusion and exclusion. I guess I was thinking there must be a lot of process for you, like you're writing hundreds and hundreds of pages and then starting to see where you're going. But it almost sounds as if you have to find the rhythm, in relation to the creative triangle, and then you see your form.

RB: I have to mediate my work through a great deal of thought and reflection. I don't work real fast. I work in spurts and binges, it seems, but over time I really don't work real fast. It takes me at least a couple years to do a medium-sized book, and it doesn't matter what my external conditions are. A couple of years a book, unless it's a real big long one like this last one, and then it takes more time. But I know that it doesn't just pour forth the way it does with some writers.

On the other hand, I don't just make a plan and keep to it, and just doggedly go ahead and pursue it all the way to the end. I start to play and see if I can hear the melody and if I can I'll keep playing until I can't hear it anymore. If I can't, then I stop and listen and rethink my relation to what it is I'm writing about. I do believe, at bottom, that's where all my problems as a writer arise. They arise in terms of my relation to what I'm writing about, and that's what I've got to always go back to and stop and think about. What do I really, really feel or think about this situation, this person, this condition, et cetera? And try to be as honest as possible. I really do have to approach it that way. As I would any kind of important personal relationship. It's like that. How do I act toward this person? Well, it depends on what I really think about this person and feel about this person. What does this person mean to me? My behavior becomes relatively clear once I understand that.

Well, writing is behavior, and once I understand my true relation on the deepest level to this thing written about, then my behavior becomes fairly clear and apparent to me, the appropriate behavior.

RD: In a 1987 interview in *New Letters*, you said that yours is a family background that essentially mistrusted language. Speaking of your parents, you stated: "Neither one of them believed anything useful could be said." In what ways was your decision to become a writer a reaction to growing up in that kind of environment? How has your knowledge of that kind of environment, and your relation to that material, shaped your writing?

RB: It's kind of a two-pronged question, I guess. My family were working people, and had been poor and uneducated beyond high school for generations, but they were very intelligent people, and people of painfully delicate sensibilities in many ways, but they deeply mistrusted language because I think they felt they had been lied to for so much of their lives, and because they felt no great sense of their worth in the world. Therefore, anything they had to say would not be of great use to anyone in the world. They felt ignorant. You know, people say, "Oh, I've got nothing to say," and, "Nothing interesting ever happened to me," or they think, "Oh, I don't really know how to talk good," or, "Well, nobody's gonna listen to me, anyhow. People just gonna use whatever I say to manipulate me, or to hurt me, or take something away from me." It's a sullen withholding of self, which is sometimes the last resort a poor person has. I think that was the emotional and linguistic context in relation to narrative that I grew up with.

How that affected me as a writer is complex because it's probably given me a sometimes handicapping self-consciousness about writing, which has in some ways led to an analytical relation to my own writing, where I tend to analyze it and try to make myself conscious of the process more than a lot of writers feel the need to. I think I do it out of a fear of being betrayed by my own impulse to tell stories—exposed or manipulated. I still have some of that sullen withholding of myself, despite a compulsion to explain and talk and tell stories, which is a childhood habit. Or as it was thought of at the time, the habit of lying. "Russell, you have the habit of lying. And stop explaining everything." [*Laughs.*] So it was there early, you know.

But writing was a way for me, as I grew older, to see that it wasn't a bad habit. This desire to explain everything to everybody wasn't a feeling of superiority or something. In fact, it was based in a delight in language itself, in the texture and rhythms and possibilities of words, and the sheer playful, sensual pleasure in language itself that was driving a great deal of that. And the kind of imagination which organizes chaos into narrative, which loves symmetries and doubles and pairings and coincidence, and so forth, and loves to connect . . . loves causal relations . . . loves things which seem unconnected . . . it was a mental agility, and also desire. So I think that that's what was working and made me uncooperative with the sullen withholding business . . . The badger backing-into-the-cave-and-facing-out mentality of my family background. My siblings, for instance, are not really storytellers at all, and their relation to language is much more defended and consistent with the family's, as is true with almost everyone else in the family. I think it was this other, contrary impulse that bucked that.

But there's still a tension and an ongoing kind of dialectical relationship that exists in my life between the two poles of wanting to withhold and defend and protect myself through silence, and wanting at the same time to tell stories, to explain, to use language as an entry point for experience of the world. It's an ongoing dialectic and it takes different forms. One of the forms it takes is, perhaps, this undue self-consciousness about narrator and point of view.

FSA: In a way you're explaining it like . . . we have a big thing in America about whether a writer is "authentic." So working-class writers hold a certain kind of stature.

RB: Today, yes. Our brief moment in the sun, right? Take it, man. The sun is shining, let's do it.

FSA: From my own personal experience, from what you've just explained, this is the type of authenticity that I actually feel in the work, and it tells me that it comes from the type of background that you're talking about.

The other day, a police officer came up here [*into Heavilon Hall*], a woman, and another writer friend of mine, a woman, said, "Boy, that police officer smelled so good. I never smelled a police officer like that." And she said, "What do you think of police?"

I said, "All through my life I've been terribly afraid of police because I was always brought up that you are in your house, silent like that, and you wait for them to come up to the door and knock and say, "We're here to take away your TV and your couch."

For the beginning writer this is something that really troubles me. Sometimes it's the inability to write on the page. You want to work really hard but one day someone could just come and say, "No. We're going to take this all away." I'm thinking about this in relation to minority writers and working-class writers, as if they can only write about their experiences, and those experiences are only autobiographical.

RB: But what you describe is the occasion that evokes the emotions, the presence of a cop on the floor here inside the building—what matters is not the presence of the cop, but the emotions that the cop evokes. What I was describing, what was important, wasn't necessarily the class conditions that I grew out of, but the psychological conditions that were created by the class conditions, and that's where the authenticity lies. It lies there. So it isn't the subject matter . . . I mean, I'm not limited to writing entirely about blue-collar people for the rest of my life. I haven't been a blue-collar person since I was twenty-five years old. And you're not limited to writing about Puerto Ricans, or your parents' lives. But it's the emotions that grow out of your having shared that life with them that validate your writing. That's what you have to connect to, and that's what you have to be conscious of as a writer. The core of your own emotional life. That's the hardest thing.

What the media would love you to do, what the marketing people in the publishing industry would love you to do is write about, you know, your Puerto Rican parents. That's the day we live in. "We need some really good stories. Male Puerto Rican. A young writer. Boy, this is great." They want the sociological parts of it so that they can book you into *Oprah*, and so forth.

But it isn't the subject matter that's going to give you the authenticity that you sense and love in other writers. It's the emotional authenticity.

FSA: I think, for you, you're aware that you're doing a lot of formal things. Even in your very first book, some could say the emotional honesty was being pulled back.

RB: Right. Withheld. Definitely.

FSA: But you still feel that in the work . . .

RB: But, you know, that raises a question, too. A sort of literary-historical question for myself. My earlier work is much more self-consciously formal, and was identified early on as metafiction, and so forth. I look back on it, and I think in some ways I'm still just as formalistic a writer as I was at twenty-five; it's just not that obvious anymore. What I was doing then was learning my craft.

If you're a young poet, the best way, the fastest way to learn your craft—if you don't know anything about writing poetry—is to write formal verse. To learn formal verse and then to interiorize it. For me, this was absolutely necessary, given the anxieties I was just describing, which are "background anxieties." I came into writing feeling very insecure about the formal means of communication available to me, my ability to master them. So I spent a longer time, perhaps, and a more conscious and deliberate time, learning to write. Learning the formal modes of exposition and narrative.

I was sufficiently insecure about my own ability to tell the truth in narrative that I had to do it in this very deliberate, overt way. Only when I became more secure about it could I start to feed into these forms, the emotional reservoirs that I'd been holding back. I could let them move in, because I was enough in control of the narrative forms that I could trust them to carry it. Increasingly, I think with each book I've felt stronger that way, to let more and more into it. It has to do with a growing trust in my own ability as a craftsman.

RD: One of the pleasures of reading *Rule of the Bone* was finding all the connections to your previous works. Characters and locations from *The Book of Jamaica, Continental Drift,* and *The Sweet Hereafter* become important elements of *Rule of the Bone.* It struck me that it's important to you to construct, if you will, a kind of literary community amongst your own works. But it's not a Winesburg, Ohio, and it's not a Yoknapatawpha County. It's New York, New Hampshire, Florida, Haiti, Jamaica, and the Caribbean. It seems important to you to create a "global village," as opposed to a small, enclosed area like Faulkner or Anderson wrote about.

RB: Well, there are two kinds of connections. One is accidental and strictly circumstantial, and the other is conscious and deliberately imposed upon the work. The fact that most of it is set in the far northeastern part of the United States, or the Caribbean and south Florida, is due mainly to the accidents of my birth and travel and youth. I mean, I know more about that part of the world than I know any other part of the world, so it's inevitable that that's where I want to set my fiction, because I can see it more clearly as I write. I can visualize it. I know how the light falls on December 15 in New Hampshire, and what time the sun sets, and so forth. And I know what it smells like and looks like in south Florida. So I can invoke those sets, if you will, those locations, with ease. I gotta go to Utah and stay a while and figure it out, if I want to put something in Utah, in Salt Lake City.

The other kind of connections you're talking about, sort of recycling certain images from one to the other, like the school bus from *The Sweet Hereafter* reappearing in *Rule of the Bone,* or the boat, the Belinda Blue from *Continental Drift* reappearing there also, and even a character, Avery Boone, the captain of the Belinda Blue reappearing in *Rule of the Bone* at the end, and even the distant relation of Wade Whitehouse appearing . . .

RD: And the Maroons . . .

RB: Yeah, the Maroons come back in again. Part of that is very simply explained, I think. For me as a writer, those images haven't been exhausted yet. The possibility of their continuing to resonate is very real, and there are other dimensions of those images that I don't feel have been exhausted at all in the previous narratives, their previous fictional uses. So I bring them back in order to explore them further, just as a poet would, and continue to explore them and hope that I can get to the ground with them, and then if they're exhausted move on. In the case of the Belinda Blue and the school bus, these were both vehicles that were vehicles of death and terrible dismay and pain in their respective original appearances.

And yet, they're both also a boat and a school bus. I mean, there's another side to both of these images, and I knew that, and I wanted to explore it further. To see if the boat could be used for purposes of salvation or redemption, or if the school bus could become an Edenic place of innocence. Certainly that's true of my experience. I'm not afraid of boats. And school busses raise feelings of alarm in me and great pleasure at the same time. I see a school bus going down the street and I say, "Oh my God, that's terrible. All those kids are in there in one place and the kid who's driving is probably stoned." And on the other hand, I'm thinking, "Look at all those kids. They're happy. They're going to school, they're waving at me out of the windows." There's innocence and pleasure in it.

Sometimes I do feel that the books, some books, do bear an intimate relation to one another thematically or otherwise. In the case, say, of *The Sweet Hereafter* and *Rule of the Bone*, these books are very linked in my mind. They're both about the loss of children, something which I feel very passionately about, and which I think has occurred most dramatically without our even knowing it in the last half-century in this country, in this culture. And the first is about that loss in a parable form, from the point of view of the adults. And the second is about that loss, also in a parable form, from the point of view of a child himself. I wanted to link them together that way, and to point the books both backwards and forwards to each other, because the one is, in a sense, in my mind at least, incomplete without the other.

RD: That's interesting, because one of the things that stood out for me when reading those two books was that Nichole Burnell and Bone are both children, but they're resourceful and imaginative in remarkable ways that some of your adult protagonists aren't, like Bob Dubois and Wade Whitehouse. The children have a leg up—they're capable of affecting real and lasting change in their lives. You feel like they're going to make it. This isn't true of some of the adults you've written about; their lives are sometimes quite bleak.

RB: That's true, and Nichole Burnell and Bone are both at that last possible minute where the future is still opening out. They're both fourteen years old and the world is still ahead of them, and they're not as helpless as their younger siblings—as is Rose in the case of Bone, and the younger kids who surround Nichole Burnell. Bone and Nichole are at that heady moment in early adolescence where they're conscious of a larger world, they're at the doorway of the larger world, and they aren't totally in the power of the adults that surround them, even though the adults that surround them are still attempting to control them and to keep them in their power. Nichole Burnell's father, for instance, and the lawyer, Mitchell Stephens, are trying to use her for their own purposes—sexual and economic and so forth, which are intimately linked in the world and the ways in which we deal with children. In Bone's case, that's certainly the case as well, with his stepfather and, later on, with his real father.

So they're both at that wonderful moment of possibility, and the world threatens to close in on them any minute. And so, in a way, I guess, with both those characters, more consciously and deliberately with Bone than Nichole, I was trying to explore how you could keep the world from closing in on you if you were at that moment in your life. What's possible? If you think about it, if I kept Bone in upstate New York, and kept him in the malls and on the streets and so forth, the world would start to close in on him pretty fast. If he didn't get the hell out of there and go to a place where he could gain some power and control over his life, then he was probably doomed. I think that's one reason why I took him out of there. I did not want to let go of him, that boy. I really loved that boy, and I wanted him to keep moving. And also, I wanted to see what life looked like from outside, the life of bourgeois American consumerism, a world in which children are viewed primarily as commodities, a world defined by racialism, and so on. I wanted to see how it looked to Bone from outside, and test him. And that was a way to do that. To take him out of it. Anywhere, but out of this world.

I could have done it by taking him other than to Jamaica, but that comes back to what I was saying earlier about the serendipity of my own experience. I know Jamaica. I didn't have to work very hard to do that. I understand that country fairly well and the connotations that would prevail for a kid like that, and so forth.

This is just an aside, in a way, but the origins for Bone go way back. They go back to 1989. My wife and I were in the Caribbean and we landed on Nevis, a tiny dot of an island. Part of Nevis-St. Kitt's. I mean, it's really a dot. I think it's like fifteen miles across, total, with a little landing strip about the size of this table. There was a little wind-blown, cinder-block airport, a one-room airport, where one guy—the same guy—carries the bags from the plane, puts them on a little open counter, and then goes around and gets on the other side and then takes them through the counter. [*Laughs.*] He becomes another person. You know those kinds of airports in the Caribbean? I love them. [*Laughs.*] And we were standing there, my wife and I, kind of getting oriented, trying to think of where we were going to go, what we were going to do, trying to figure whether to get a car, and we saw these two little white American kids, couldn't have been more than fourteen or fifteen years old, standing there. And there was this one old, beat-up pay phone there, and they were trying to call their parents in California. These two little guys. And they had these matted dreadlocks on. They'd got their hair into these fabulously grotesque white-boy dreadlocks and they were covered with self-inflicted tattoos, all these Rastafarian tattoos. Big lions that say Jah Lives and stuff like that on them, all over. [*Laughs.*] And they were wearing short-shorts and cut-off T-shirts so they could really show you their tattoos on their pink, sun-burned skin. They were so touching to me. They were trying to figure out how to get home, and they couldn't remember their parents' telephone calling card number. They were at the end of the planet, out there. And I just thought, Oh my God, how did they get here, who are they, these poor little guys? [*Laughs.*] And those kids stuck in my brain. I didn't see them again, but they stuck in my brain.

Some many years later, when Bone started to appear to me, that image of those kids kept coming back to haunt me. In some way I wanted to get him there to re-write that scene in some way so that it wasn't the sad, pathetic scene that it really was, but was something else. A corrective, in a way.

And then that late scene in *Rule of the Bone*, when Russ appears, I was thinking Russ is the kid that I saw in Nevis, that loser, that total loser asshole fantasist, "Oh, wow, I'm going to get me some good dope and a lot of black women." [*Laughs.*]

RD: For Bone, that's a kind of epiphany for him, he quickly realizes . . .

RB: "I am not that." [*Laughs.*]

RD: That's nice. That's what's so ironic about the use of that scene. It became something quite positive.

RB: Yeah, he knows he's changed. It's an old-fashioned recognition scene.

RD: I was going to ask you about the West Indian language. I really admire the accuracy and grace with which you get it on the page. Do you have any particular difficulties writing it? Or is it the kind of thing that, after having lived in Jamaica for two years, doesn't really present a problem? Also, how did learning to write and think in West Indian English inform your own North American English? I've found that it's done amazing things for me as a writer.

RB: Well, you've lived there yourself, so you know how it forces you to listen to your own English differently. Anytime you're surrounded by people who are speaking English but speaking it very differently from the way you do, you hear your own voice. You can't hear it when you're surrounded by people who speak just like you. Southerners don't know they speak with accents, you know? Living in Alabama, I could only hear *my* accent tinkling. And I think it's the same when you get into the English-speaking Caribbean, where you're hearing what's clearly and wonderfully English, but it's dramatically different from your own. So much so that it takes a while to understand it, almost as if it were another language. I found that wonderfully exciting and terrifically enlightening about my own English.

But so far as using it and representing it on the page, it was very difficult, because of the way written dialogue slows down speech—you can only read it as fast as you can say it when you see the words. It's very difficult to represent with the conventions of written dialogue, the pacing and the shifts of inflection and so forth, in Caribbean speech. I've never been really satisfied with the way I've gotten it on the page. But I don't know of any other alternatives, either. I've read a lot of different versions of it. Going back to Peter Matthiessen's *Far Tortuga*, which is actually very accurate, but by his insisting on spelling words the way they sound instead of spelling them the way we know they're conventionally spelled, it flirts with dialect. Bob Shacochis is very good at it. When I read Bob's West Indian patois, I hear it. And I think that's what I had to look for, a way to represent it on the page so that the reader could hear it when reading it, which involves a kind of self-conscious translation. There's no way around it, I think, for an American Anglo reader. You really can't get around it. You're stuck with the notational conventions of fiction writing, to some degree.

Also, I didn't want to make too big a deal out of it, after all. If I could find ways of putting it on the page such that the sensitive reader—the reader with a good ear—could hear it, and the reader without a good ear wouldn't be led to condescend to the speaker in any way, then I'd be happy. But that's a bit of a compromise.

RD: Do you write, then, with a North American audience in mind? Do you view yourself in the Homeric tradition—as a North American writer "bringing home the news"? Or do you view yourself as participating in a kind of new literature of say, the entire Western Hemisphere? Essentially, is yours an American voice, or a voice of the Americas?

RB: It's a question that I don't ask myself and so therefore don't really have an answer for. In the process of writing it certainly never occurs to me that I'm writing for any sociologically identifiable group, racially or even linguistically. My work is now widely enough translated that I'm aware that there is a foreign audience, a non-English speaking audience for my work. There's been enough information back from them to me so that I know they're there. But I'm not conscious of them in the slightest when I'm writing, anymore than I am of writing for one gender or the other. It's just not part of my thinking when I'm working.

But I'm not, on the other hand, blind to the fact that after completion of it, I can look around and see that, yes, this is a sociological fact of my life, just as all the other sociological facts or information or data are part of it. The fact that I'm male, white, and American, et cetera, and of a specific generation are true conditions of my life. They're not, however, conditions—or at least I'm not conscious of them as being conditions—when I'm writing. It's only when I'm not writing that I'm aware of it, and then I can appraise it and take issue with those who might appraise it differently, or learn from other people's perspectives, vis-à-vis sociological considerations.

I don't think I represent any particular, or am the voice of any particular segment of American literature. I'm merely a paid-in-full member of a generation of writers that came to socio-political maturity—that is, left the family, left adolescence, and entered adult life and the larger public world—in the sixties, and whose view, whose sense of self and sense of values, and maybe even sense of the enterprise of writing, are informed by that passage and the conditions that prevailed at that time, just as the so-called "Lost Generation" of writers was informed by the experience of World War I, or the post-war generation of American writers—Mailer, Jones, Styron, et cetera—was informed by having gone through that same passage during World War II. One could find similar conditions for any generation of writers. There is a period where you enter the larger world from adolescence, and it's like a crucible. Things get formed there, values and relations and sense of responsibilities, a sense of history and what's meaningful in the larger world, and that informs you for the rest of your life. That's how you, in a way, become a generation. Where were you when you were in your early twenties and late teens? What did you share with everybody else in that period? It isn't decades you share, it's socio-historical events.

For my generation, it really was the sixties and the social conditions of that time, and as a result I think, as a generation of writers, and we're talking writers who probably run from their late forties, the sort of the leading edge of the baby boomers, to my age, maybe the middle-late fifties somewhere. It includes most of the prominent writers—DeLillo, Robert Stone, Joyce Carol Oates, John Wideman.

RD: Toni Morrison?

RB: Toni Morrison is a little bit older and I think there is a difference there. I do think that there's a cutting-off point, and she's in her sixties and she really came through the previous decade. The crucible for her, I think, was the fifties.

I think as a group we tend to be more aware of the possibilities for fiction, or for art generally, to connect to the larger world, because we as young men and women felt that was a possibility, and even a necessity. To connect to the larger socio-political world. To put our private lives out on the public line. I look across at my colleagues and peers, and I can see that it is an abiding and continuing desire, and it guides the work to a considerable degree.

So in that sense I feel a member of a generation, though I don't think I speak for anybody but myself in that generation. I might find a lot of strong disagreement amongst my colleagues and peers with regard to that last statement, but we'll see.

FSA: Even though you put yourself in that generation, I think that some of what Rob asked about that—maybe not being a voice of the Americas—but there is a specific way that you look at the world, and way that you look at fiction. And it's hard for me to find it in other American writers. So that sometimes it seems to me "un-American," whatever we think it means to be American.

RD: Almost a sense of exile.

FSA: Yeah, I've used that. I don't like to use that only because we might think that all writers are exiles—but in a nostalgic way. But in your work it's more like an anger, that I am outside of this stuff.

RB: Yeah, marginalized.

FSA: You've been talking about tracing the lives of writers, to learn from them. Well, how do you feel about this? It's interesting. You're at Colgate, and you leave and you go south and, you said, you just kind of "woke up" in Florida. [*Laughter.*] Then you went to the Caribbean, then you went to Mexico. And lately you've been relating to us that you're about to leave Princeton and spend more time in upstate New York. And then you told us you're getting an apartment in Montreal. As if you've come full circle around back to a place. How do feel about that? Is it comfortable to go back around that way? The American vision would be to go from east to west. To be linear. So the way you're looking at it is a bit different.

RB: Yeah, it is. I've moved north and south, that's true, and not east and west. The east-to-west flow of the American imagination over the last couple hundred years really took its impetus from the east-to-west flow of culture from Europe to North America. And Anglo-European-dominated culture would naturally imagine its continued progression and momentum westward. But as American culture has evolved in the latter part of the twentieth century, that now has weakened, the current from northwestern Europe to North America has become more diffuse and weak. In a way the flow has changed, to Hispanic-American and Caribbean-American culture moving north and south. You can see it. It's not just reflected in the culture and language, it's reflected in the economics, too. What is NAFTA all about, after all? We're not making economic alliances with the seven nations of Europe, we're making them with the half-dozen nations of the north-south axis.

And so I think there has been a shift in the late twentieth century in all important ways. The politicians are always the last to know. It's the businessmen and the artists who identify it first. And since the businessmen have a much stronger lobby than we have, they can make it into law.

My life has, I suppose, reflected that to some degree. From the actual physical locations or locales that I've placed it in, as well as my own imaginative progress. In recent years, well, starting really in the early seventies, I became increasingly engaged by Latin American and Caribbean literature and history. And I've always been engaged by Canadian history and literature, partially through familial connections. My father's family and my father were Canadians, and I lived on the border of Canada as a child. So it was a viable and real presence in my life. Canada wasn't just this big gray space north of the United States. It was a real place, and real people lived there. Some of them were related to me. My father flew the Canadian flag outside his house in New Hampshire until the day he died. A funny little pathetic gesture. Dad's got the old maple leaf out, I used to think. He's tuning in, you know, he's watching the hockey game. [*Laughs.*]

So the north-south orientation, to me, is a coherent one, and not aberrant, particularly. It makes perfectly good sense for me, and it seems to be an integrated orientation in terms of where my literary culture is concerned, in terms of my political values.

I mean, when I got a Guggenheim in 1975, I didn't go to Italy. It never occurred to me to go to Italy. I went to Jamaica. I rented a house in the country and moved my kids down there and we lived there for a couple years. The kids went to school locally. That was the most exciting thing I could think of doing with my Guggenheim. It never occurred to me to go to France or

England or Italy. And I think increasingly that's what happens with writers, too. It's more interesting to go to Guadeloupe, man. Or go to Peru and find out what that's all about.

So I don't see it as anything particularly perverse or aberrant. Nor does it make me feel in the slightest like an outsider or exile or running against the current, particularly. This mentality is not unfamiliar to Latino-American writers. And I think it's not that unfamiliar or uncomfortable for African-American writers, either, that north-south axis. It seems perfectly natural and obvious. Toni Morrison has got a lot more in common with Carlos Fuentes and Gabriel García Márquez than with the novelists of Eastern Europe. She's got much more in common with Derek Walcott than with Seamus Heaney. You can see it because the themes and the history and the day-to-day life that she's dealing with are going to be amplified and informed by the work of someone like Derek Walcott. This is true for me and it's true for, I think, most American writers now.

FSA: That's the thing. That's the earlier answer to say that exile or "away from the current" is to be defensive about the thing that is just you. But it's still quite different than mainstream America.

RB: True.

FSA: I like following maps like that. Writers are raised to believe that if you go out of the particular, then you'll go to some kind of universal. And it seems that you were already going south. You were meeting the immigrants before they started to cross. You were already going out into that big world picture, meeting them halfway. Going out into that big thing that brought more back into your particular, and now you're going back to it that way.

RB: One of the things I like about Montreal is that it's the city in North America most like Miami. The linguistic and cultural collision that goes on there between French and English is very like the collision that goes on in Miami and south Florida between Spanish and English, and it's also racially mixed in many of the same ways. The black immigrants in Montreal are all from the French colonies, Martinique, Guadeloupe, Haiti. Or they're from French West Africa. The great colonial return. I love that. And it's in Miami you've got the great Latino and Anglo-Caribbean return to Miami. Miami is a city I've loved since the day I first arrived in '59. I felt like Balboa in the Pacific when I got to Miami. I thought, "Whoa. Wow, this is something. This is going to change my life."

Montreal had some of the same impact on me as Miami did and for some of the same reasons, because of this wonderful collision which, of course, horrifies most people. But I find it a fascinating and wonderful moment in history, when cultures and languages come rubbing up against each other like that. They can't get away from each other. They're marrying each other. And their kids are falling in love and they have to work alongside each other. Those are great moments in the history of a culture. And in these two cities you can see it with great clarity.

It happens for various mundane reasons that Montreal is close by, and I can get to it easily and know it fairly well, and Miami is a long ways away from where I've been working, et cetera. Actually, in some ways, despite the weather, Montreal is a more livable city. It's not such an automobile-driven city. I can imagine growing old in Montreal. It's hard for me to imagine growing old in Miami without a chauffeur. [*Laughs.*] But in Montreal I can walk down the street with my cane tapping and go to my favorite little bistro and have my table waiting for me. [*Laughs.*]

FSA: There's something integral in the work that's mirrored through all of what you're talking about. And that's a complexity that, I think, too many people are afraid to cover. And that was what you said about, "Look what I did last summer." The writer goes to the place and it's, look what I did last summer. And you don't have that.

RB: No, that's true. I'm not sure what it is that drives that part of my life, especially as it relates to writing. I just think that the writers I have loved the most were writers who were willing to take big risks. They were willing to risk being wrong about a lot. I wouldn't be satisfied with myself as a writer if I didn't risk being wrong about a lot. And to do that, you've got to take yourself out of what you know intimately and privately and into what you don't know and what's public and confront it. Deal with people who are much unlike you. I've just felt that necessity as I've gone along. I suppose it does, in some ways, start with liking some writers more than others and their having moved me. And wanting to imitate them. I want to be like them. I want to be like Mike, you know? Only I want to be like Herman. [*Laughs.*] So it's kind of a mimetic act, using your life in that way. But I really don't think I could have it any other way. It wouldn't seem worth doing. The price you have to pay to spend a lifetime writing books is too high for it not to mean something, not to matter.

RD: In his essay "The Literature of Place and No Place," novelist William O'Rourke has written that "Writers may wonder where they are coming from—the effect of place on their work—but they are also concerned with where they are going, what sort of place their work might have in the culture" (*Signs of the Literary Times* 34). What sort of place do you envision your work having—or creating—in our culture?

RB: I don't really "envision" it, but I might have a hope, a desire for it to play a role in the culture that's essentially the role of the storyteller, in a very primitive sense of what a storyteller is in the tribe. Which is to tell us who we are, and where we came from, and what are the limits of our power. To tell us what we can legitimately control and what we can't control. This is what storytellers have done since the beginning of time, since they were invited to come in and sit beside the fire and were tossed a joint off the slain mammoth. You can eat, but not until you tell us a story first. What you gonna tell us? Well, you're gonna tell us where we came from, who we are, what are our responsibilities to one another, what's our kinship relations, and what are the extents of our domain. So everything I do as a writer, I think, is, in some ways, an attempt to do that in contemporary terms. And if the work has value to the culture at large, then that's where it will obtain its value.

Human beings are the only species that have to constantly re-learn what it is to be human, to be itself. We have to constantly learn it over again. Every generation, every human being has to learn what it is to be human. No other animal, no other species has to do that. Storytellers have an essential role in the process of teaching us over and over and over again what it is to be human.

So that's really all I . . . "That's really all." Yeah, right. That's a rather grandiose ambition. But that is probably, in the sense of your question, the way I understand it.

Russell Banks:
The Art of Fiction No. 152

Robert Faggen and Barry Munger/1998

RF & BM: You began to write in the 1960s. How did that decade influence you? Did you meet any notable figures?

RB: Yes, I met Kerouac. It must have been 1967, a year or two, at the most, before he died. I got a call from a pal in a bar in town, The Tempo Room, a local hangout: "Jack Kerouac is in town with a couple of other guys, and he wants to have a party." I said, "Yeah, sure, right." He said, "No, really." I was the only guy in this crowd with a regular house. So Jack Kerouac showed up with a troupe of about forty people he had gathered as he went along, and three guys whom he insisted—and I think they indeed were—Micmac Indians from Quebec. Kerouac, like a lot of writers of the open road, didn't have a driver's license. He needed a Neal Cassady just to get around; this time he had these crazy Indians, who were driving him to Florida to be with his mother. They all ended up crashing for the weekend. He had just received his advance for what turned out to be his last book and was spending it like a sailor on leave. He brought with him a disruptiveness and wild disorder, and moments of brilliance, too. I could see how attractive he must have been when he was young, both physically and intellectually. He was an incredibly beautiful man, but at that age (he was about forty-five) the alcohol had wreaked such destruction that it left him beautiful only from the neck up. Also, you could see why they called him Memory Babe: he would switch into long, beautiful twenty-minute recitations of Blake or the Upanishads or Hoagy Carmichael song lyrics. Then he would phase out and turn into an anti-Semitic, angry, fucked-up, tormented old drunk—a real know-nothing. It was comical, but sad. There were a lot of arguments back and forth, then we would realize, No, he's just a sad, old drunk; I can't take this stuff seriously. Eventually he would realize it himself, and he would back off and turn himself into a senior literary figure and say, I can't take that stuff seriously either. Every time he came forward, he would switch personas, and you would go bouncing back off him. It was a very strange and strenuous weekend. And very moving. It was the first time I had seen one of my literary heroes seem fragile and vulnerable.

RF & BM: Was Kerouac an early inspiration?

RB: Kerouac was very important to me for a lot of reasons, though not necessarily for the reasons that he was inspiring to other folks. But for a working-class New England kid who was, for the most part, an autodidact, reading Jack Kerouac, a writer of clear significance, was very liberating—liberating both in literary terms and in sexual terms, as well as in social behavior. He gave me another way to think and walk; validated my life so far and my hopes for that life. I never actually wanted to write like Kerouac; I never wanted to write about what he wrote, particularly. But there was a rough personalism and expansiveness in his work that had gone out of favor at the time. Kerouac reinvoked a Whitmanesque perspective and texture; he renewed the old barbaric yawp, which was very exciting and inspiring. To me, it was something new, although that rough personalism is, of course, a very strong, old current in American literature, with its headwaters in Whitman and Twain. In the twentieth century it got blocked by the power of the Hemingway, Faulkner, Joyce models and the High Modernists' affection for formalism. But there was also Dreiser, Steinbeck, Sherwood Anderson, Richard Wright, and Nelson Algren. I think Kerouac reinvigorated that stream, opened it up again. I think that's what happens with a young writer: a single figure, who may not be major in any way, can help you rethink and re-view writers that otherwise you would have dismissed or feared.

RF & BM: Do you remember the first writer who really bowled you over?

RB: Whitman. It was in my late teens, and I suddenly realized that was the kind of writer I wanted to be. Not the kind of writing I wanted to do, but the kind of writer I wanted to be: a man of the people, but at the same time writing high art. It was the first time I had the sense that you could be a writer and it would be a lofty, noble position, yet still connected to the reality around you. You didn't have to be Edgar Allan Poe, or Robert Lowell for that matter. Whitman was the first figure of that sort.

RF & BM: Do you make a distinction between highbrow and lowbrow literature?

RB: The distinction between high and low culture depresses me, dividing all culture like Gaul into high, middle, and low. It's a very comforting way to think about culture, so long as you think of yourself as highbrow. I think it speaks to, and speaks out of, anxiety about class, especially in the United States, as people from the lower classes begin to participate in the literary arts and intellectual life in an aggressive way. Then folks start claiming there is high, middle, and low culture, so know your place, please, and stay there. I don't think it would have made much sense to Whitman. Some of the distinctions between high and low culture wouldn't make much sense to someone like John Brown of Harper's Ferry, for example, who thought that Milton and Jonathan Edwards were as available to him as penny broadsides.

RF & BM: Did you sense that anxiety when you started to write?

RB: I sensed that the culture was run by people who went to Harvard, Princeton, and Yale, that it was run by upper-class white men. I don't think I was wrong. Pick up an O. Henry Award anthology or any poetry anthology from that era—there may have been a few Jewish guys from Columbia—and that's it. But pick up an O. Henry anthology from 1996, the contributors come from everywhere—white men, women, African-Americans, Asian-Americans, Native Americans. But in the fifties there was no way you could think about culture as something that was not run, not the product of, and not consumed primarily by that small group of white male graduates of Ivy League colleges.

RF & BM: Given this, you were hardly encouraged to become an artist early on?

RB: No. No push in that direction whatsoever.

RF & BM: Where did it come from?

RB: I think it came in by the side door. When I was a kid, the first evidence of any special talent that I might have had was artistic. I had a good hand. I could draw and paint, and I loved to do it. It was physically satisfying, it provided escape and a kind of sexual pleasure. It got me attention, too—praise from teachers, strangers, from my family. "Isn't he amazing. Can he play the violin too?" That sort of thing. I was a kind of prodigious curiosity to people. As I got into my middle teens, I thought, That's what I want to be, an artist! I think that allowed me to separate myself from the conventional expectations for a bright kid from my class.

RF & BM: What were those expectations?

RB: From others, probably to get a scholarship and go to college and become a lawyer or a doctor. The goal was to get into the middle class: make some money, marry a nice girl, buy a house, and settle down. I already had started to imagine for myself a life that couldn't meet that set of expectations, which I think is why I left Colgate after eight weeks. Colgate was then a preppy, neo-Ivy school for upper-middle-class white boys, and I was sort of an early affirmative-action kid. It was a good program, a wonderful program for most. For me it wasn't. I was so out of it on the social surface and at the psychological depths that I felt I had no choice but to flee. I stole away in the night, literally. Hitchhiked my way out in a snowstorm with all my belongings in a backpack. I hitchhiked as far from that little network of expectations and pressure as I could get. I headed off to Florida to join Castro.

RF & BM: You wanted to join Castro's revolution?

RB: Why not? He was a heroic figure. He was a Robin Hood figure for a lot of Americans at that time—you didn't have to be radical to imagine him that way. It was pretty easy to picture myself at his side. He was, in some ways, the good father. I only got as far as Miami. By that time Castro was marching into Havana and didn't need me anymore. Also, I realized I didn't know quite how to get from Key West to Cuba, and I couldn't speak Spanish.

RF & BM: You dedicated *Affliction* to your father. What was he like?

RB: He was violent, and alcoholic. He abandoned the family when I was twelve.

RF & BM: Did you ever reconcile with him?

RB: Yes, I did. In my late teens I sought him out and even lived with him in New Hampshire for a while and worked as a plumber alongside him until I was twenty-four. I remember a talk I had with him when I was trying to write at night—stories and a novel and so forth, trying to invent myself as a writer while being a plumber. I remember talking to him about it, at one point saying, "Jesus Christ, I don't want to do this, I hate plumbing." He looked at me with puzzlement and said, "You think *I* like it?" I realized, My God, of course not. What was he then? Around my age now, and he had done this all his adult life. He was a very bright man, talented in many ways. But he grew up in the Depression and when he got out of high school at sixteen he went right to work to help support the family. No matter how bright he was his life was shaped entirely by those forces. I'll never forget that moment.

But it was always a testy, anxiety-ridden relationship on both sides. It wasn't until I was in my early thirties that I began to feel at ease with him. I vividly remember a perception that transformed my relationship to him. He had given me a Christmas present—a cord of firewood. Typically, it wasn't quite a gift. I had to go pick it up at his house. The wood was pretty much frozen solidly into the ground when I finally arranged to get over there. It was snowing, and I was out in the yard kicking the logs loose and tossing them into my truck. I was pissed off, goddamn it, he could have given me something smaller, or he didn't have to give me anything, instead of this damn wood! The old man was in the kitchen watching me. Finally, he put his coat on and came out and worked alongside me. I was working pretty furiously, ignoring him, but after a while I looked over at him and saw that it was very difficult for him. I suddenly saw him as an old man, and very fragile. We reversed our polarity at that moment.

RF & BM: What were you writing at the time?

RB: I was working on *Hamilton Stark* then. I wonder if the book and that reversal of polarity are connected in some way, the power shift. Probably there is some real connection to it. There *is* a wonderful intelligence to the unconscious. It's always smarter than we are.

RF & BM: Your personal mythology looks like part of the American mythology—the young rebel setting out for the territory ahead.

RB: What happens—at least this is what happened to me, and I suspect it has happened to a lot of writers—is that there comes a point when the work starts to shape your life. Early on, you intuit and start to create patterns of images and narrative forms that are bound to be central to American mythology. If you start to plug the imagery and sequences of your personal life into these patterns and forms, then they are going to feed the way you imagine your own life. Before long, writing will turn out, for the writer, to be a self-creative act. The narrative that early on attracted me was the run from civilization, in which a young fellow in tweeds at Colgate University lights out and becomes a Robin Hood figure in fatigues in the Caribbean jungle. That fantasy is a story for myself. It also happens to be a very basic American story, as well as a basic white-male fantasy. A wonderful reciprocity between literature and life evolves. It seems to be inescapable.

RF & BM: When did you notice the impact of the mythology of your writing on your life?

RB: With *The Book of Jamaica*. That book leaves the protagonist at the end stunned into self-recognition by his confrontation with what people call the "radical other." Having gone through the same experiences, literally and imaginatively, that the protagonist in *The Book of Jamaica* experiences, I began to live my life more consciously and aggressively in racial and class terms, laying the ground on which I stood a few years later when I wrote *Continental Drift*.

RF & BM: How did that play out?

RB: After living in Jamaica and writing *The Book of Jamaica*, I accepted that I was obliged, for example, to have African-American friends. I was obliged to address, deliberately, the overlapping social and racial contexts of my life. I'm a white man in a white-dominated, racialized society, therefore, if I want to, I can live my whole life in a racial fantasy. Most white Americans do just that. Because we *can.* In a color-defined society we are invited to think that white is not a color. We are invited to fantasize, and we act accordingly.

RF & BM: *Rule of the Bone* invites comparisons to *Huckleberry Finn.* Certainly I-Man makes us think of Jim.

RB: Well, Jim is not the only black man in white man's literature. Toni Morrison talks about that shadow in *Playing in the Dark.*

RF & BM: Do you think Morrison is right in seeing American writers as essentially parasitic of the African-American experience?

RB: I didn't take it that way at all. I took it to be a description of an American literature that persists on unconsciously including the African-American presence while at the same time denying it a shaping role, and she argues that the denial of that presence proves, not the absence of the African-American, but his presence, a presence that makes itself known mainly through denial. I thought her attempt to assert that was in the end healing and inclusive. To write a novel that claims to be, or intends to be, about the American experience and yet does not consciously include the African-American presence in some way is to lapse into a kind of pathological denial.

RF & BM: What drew you to Jamaica?

RB: Serendipity. I had a white Jamaican friend who directed me there and helped me rent a house, first for four weeks and then a year later for six weeks. Gradually my interest in the history of the region exfoliated, until I found almost all my intellectual interests being nurtured there; so when I got a Guggenheim in 1976 and had the opportunity to take off from teaching and travel and live someplace for a year and a half, instead of Italy or France I went to Jamaica.

RF & BM: *Continental Drift* reveals a wealth of knowledge about Caribbean language, history, religion. Did the research begin then?

RB: Yes, but I wasn't planning a book at the time. I was just following my nose, and what began as a curiosity became a continuing interest and then turned into an obsession. The more information I got, the more I wanted— my obsession extended out into the entire Caribbean, including Haitian religion, history, and culture generally. I found myself living for long periods out in the bush in Accompong, reading and working on my own in isolation. It was a deliberate withdrawal into another world. I accumulated most of the material that later became *The Book of Jamaica.* I wrote lots of stories too, most of *The New World.*

RF & BM: How do you make the decision to work in the form of short story as opposed to the novel. Are they continuous forms?

RB: No, they're very discontinuous. For me, they each bear greatly different relations to time. The novel, I think, has a mimetic relation to time. The novel simulates the flow of time, so once you get very far into a novel, you forget where you began—just as you do in real time. Whereas with a short story the point is not to forget the beginning. The ending only makes sense if you can remember the beginning. I think the proper length for a short story is to go as far as you can without going so far that you have forgotten the beginning.

RF & BM: Do you outline or make sketches of novels?

RB: With novels, yes. Not with short stories. Usually, with a novel, I have a pretty good idea of the arc of the narrative and its breaking points. I know if it's going to be a five-act or a three-act novel, or to drive right through to one place or require a reversal, come this way for a while, then reverse and go that way. I do work that out. I also have a short-term outline that covers the next fifty or sixty pages, which I keep rewriting as I work. Of course, it's all tentative; I can change it at will as new ideas, plot turns, characters appear and develop. The trick, I suppose, is to find the point between control and freedom that allows you to do your work.

RF & BM: Do you find when you are writing short stories you must have that keynote?

RB: With a short story, I never know where I'm going until I get there. I just know where I entered. That is what comes to me: the opening, a sentence or phrase, even. But with a novel, it's like entering a huge mansion: it doesn't matter where you come in, as long as you get in. I usually imagine the ending, not literally and not in detail, but I do have a clear idea whether it's going to end with a funeral or wedding. Or if I am going to burn the mansion down or throw a dinner party at the end. The important question—the reason you write the novel—is to discover how you get from here to there.

RF & BM: When you started writing *Continental Drift*, you saw Bob Dubois's demise?

RB: I saw the boat, the collision of two worlds, and the people drowning. In both cases, Bob's and Vanise's, I began with a dark and stormy night in Haiti and a dark and stormy night in New Hampshire. I did know that they were going to end up together at sea in a boat, that the Haitians were going to drown and Bob was going to have to deal with that. I didn't know the meaning of it, but I trusted that the meaning would be acquired through getting there. The journey itself would be the truth and meaning of the ending. As in life.

RF & BM: Suffering and blame are important themes in your work. How did the title *Affliction* come to you?

RB: It came from Simone Weil. I felt that every other name for it, like domestic violence, or male violence, if you want, or child abuse—those terms were too reductive and simplistic and weren't descriptive, finally. They didn't describe the condition the way the word *affliction* did, which implies something greater than a disease, but still a disease. It has a moral dimension, too. An affliction is a blood curse, in a way, a blood disease. I wanted all of those associations. I couldn't get at the condition without a metaphor that was large enough and suggestive enough to handle it. I needed a religious term, almost.

RF & BM: What kind of religious upbringing did you have?

RB: New England Presbyterian. But more the culture than the actual religion. My family was not deeply religious, but we did go to church regularly and Sunday school and so forth, up until I was about fourteen. I think a sensitive kid doesn't need to be heavily indoctrinated in order to have a very elaborate, lasting, and powerful set of responses to stimuli like that.

RF & BM: You associate Protestantism with capitalism.

RB: Who doesn't? It's a great explanation for greed—the devil made me do it! And success—the Lord blessed me with it! As well as failure, or poverty. The whole idea of the free-market system having some kind of great, Darwinian logic to it is wonderfully Protestant. You are either touched by grace or you're not—if you're not, there is nothing you can do about it, and nobody is to blame or obliged to help. Except God or Satan.

RF & BM: There is a great scene in *Rule of the Bone* where Bone burns the spider. I thought of Jonathan Edwards's sermon "Sinners in the Hands of an Angry God."

RB: It comes out of Edwards, pointedly. It's a vivid image for me. But it also comes out of *Huckleberry Finn*—a scene where Huck burns a spider in a candle flame, very early, at his father's cabin, I think. When you are writing fiction, you try to write it as deeply as you can, so you have to go to the images that have power for you personally.

RF & BM: The school bus is a powerful symbol for you.

RB: The school bus is a very powerful image to me. I'm not sure why. I'll probably keep on recycling it until it no longer has resonance for me. I think that is what poets do. Perhaps less overtly, novelists keep going back to images that retain power for them and recycling them, reusing them in another context, coming at them from another angle to see what they suggest from there. In that sense, I was trying to take what had been a vehicle for death in *The Sweet Hereafter* and see if it could possibly be a source of life for Bone. It took doing. But as you can see from my collection of toy school buses, it's still an obsession with me.

RF & BM: Absolutely!

RB: Some are antiques, and from all over the world. The school bus is a layered, multifaceted image. It is instantly recognizable to every American. It is associated, at least for me, with the first time you give your children over to the state. From the child's point of view, it is the first time he leaves home and goes out into the larger world. It is the connecting cord between the family and the outside world, and has both positive and negative implications.

RF & BM: There is obviously a difference between your sense of childhood and J. D. Salinger's.

RB: Salinger believes in innocence, and I don't think I do. He wrote obsessively about the fall from innocence, or the threat of it. I have a hard time imagining such a thing, mainly because I don't think that I believe in innocence. Salinger thinks of childhood differently than I do, as if the main threat to childhood is knowledge of adult life. Whereas I think that the main threat to children has more to do with power, adult power and the misuse and abuse of it.

RF & BM: Because childhood isn't innocent?

RB: Right. Even Froggy in *Rule of the Bone* isn't innocent.

RF & BM: And the girl in *The Sweet Hereafter* who survived the bus crash, Nichole, she isn't innocent?

RB: She's enraged, far from innocent.

RF & BM: Getting even is all right?

RB: It can be liberating, and empowering, as it is to Nichole. For Bone, I think the point of his anger is simply in taking power back from his stepfather.

RF & BM: That happens in *Affliction*, too.

RB: That is the pathological extreme—the abuse is so pervasive and long-lived that it has been transferred from the abuser to the abused. The victim's great conflict is how to avoid becoming an abuser himself.

RF & BM: How do you avoid it?

RB: Well, the book isn't a handbook, it's a novel. But the two brothers, Wade and Rolfe, can be seen as equal and opposite reactions to the same conditions. Rolfe manages not to inflict on others the same violence that was inflicted on him—but he does it by withdrawal and an absence of connection. Whereas Wade doesn't keep other people safe from him; he has relationships, an ex-wife, a lover, a child—he puts himself into the fray of life. But the story isn't meant to be a twelve-chapter recovery manual. It just allows you to imagine your life differently than you might have otherwise. There is a kind of obsessive return in some of my work, as in *Hamilton Stark, Afflic-tion*, and *Rule of the Bone*, to an abusive, patriarchal figure. Certain stories, too, return to it. Put simply, because I was able to write these novels and stories, I think I have managed to live a different story than the one I was given by my childhood.

RF & BM: What do you think are the dangers of associating writing with therapy?

RB: Bad writing is the basic danger. It's also a lousy way to get therapy. But if you submit the material of your life—all the materials, not just the conscious materials, but all your obsessions and dreams and your dimly apprehended intuitions of the world—if you submit those materials to the rigorous disci-plines of art, then you are going to end up with a clearer story about some-one other than you than the one that is about you. You can use your own books in the same way you use anybody's books . . . to inform your life about the person who inhabits it. I think the reason you write, after all, is to inform your own life with a book that is made out of the subconscious materials of that life.

RF & BM: There is something else that comes up again and again—some-body who is trying to figure out a conspiracy or a crime. Certainly in *The Book of Jamaica*, certainly in *The Sweet Hereafter*. Is there a tension for you between having a solvable mystery and a sense that things just happen?

RB: There is a mystery at the center of all the books . . . for many reasons. One is simply that it provides the engine that drives the book—it provides a quest, the quest for knowledge, in most cases, for information. I suppose, too, at bottom I must believe that the oldest question, What is the secret of the universe? is still worth asking. And I must believe that there is, not just a question, but also an answer. So the books are an attempt, each time, to find the answer. The mystery in the book, the literal mystery that might exist in the plot of the book, is really a metaphor for the other, deeper quest that the author is engaged in. Remember that great Borges story "The Aleph"? Each time you sit down to write, you hope that this will turn out to be your aleph. This will be the story that decodes the universe for you. So you will never have to write again.

RF & BM: Do you often long for that?

RB: With every novel or story.

RF & BM: If you wrote that book, would you be content to stop and not respond to the pressures of having to go out and fight the bear to prove that you are the great hunter?

RB: I like to think so. Essentially, you're asking me if I no longer had to write, for whatever reason, would I then feel obliged to continue to write fiction in order to sustain the career? I don't think it would happen. One thing I have complete control over—my writing; the other thing I have no control over—my career. Writers often get confused about the two and tend to treat the one as if it were the other. They think they can control their careers and can't control their work.

RF & BM: How did your career, as opposed to your writing, begin?

RB: I was slow to find a publishing home. I had written a first novel at twenty-one, twenty-two, and then wrote another at twenty-four, twenty-five. For the second first novel, I had an agent, and she sent it to Random House, and they bought it. I was amazed. But just as the manuscript was about to be set in type, my editor, Steven M. L. Aronson, left Random House to work for *Playboy*, leaving my book in the lap of some poor, overworked junior editor, who probably didn't like the book anyhow. I asked a couple of writer friends, older and more experienced in these matters, what I should do. They said, "Well, your editor is gone and nobody has picked up his support for you. If you force them to publish it, they will, but without an editor to champion it, the book will die. Withdraw the book and sell it somewhere else." Which I did. Of course, then I couldn't sell it. I bet fifteen publishers turned it down. Maybe, I thought, I should take another look at this book. I reread it. It turned out to be quite a terrible novel. So I called my agent and said, "Let's just park this one and I'll start my public writing life over again." She said fine—this lovely, understanding woman, Ellen Levine, the only agent I have ever had. She was just starting out then, too. We have more or less grown up together.

RF & BM: You are prolific.

RB: Depends on whom you're comparing me to. I have been able to work fairly steadily over the years. Every eighteen months to two years I can have a book finished, usually. It hasn't been troublesome for me, but I want to say I know it is the exception and not the rule for writers. Also, I have been blessed with loyalty from my publishers when my audience was very small, so I could keep on keeping on in my own way, without feeling as though if I didn't write a book that got on the best-seller list, I would lose my publisher. I was allowed to mature as a writer in solitude and anonymity.

RF & BM: How did you afford to do that?

RB: Well, a combination. My ex-wife's family had money and they paid for my college years in Chapel Hill. And I worked as a teacher from 1968 on, starting at the University of New Hampshire. The other day at Princeton, some of us were talking about our writing students, and Toni Morrison said the first job of a writer is to get a job. Absolutely right. I had jobs as a plumber, a department-store window decorator, a shoe salesman and, after college, a teacher. Teaching turned out to be the best way for me to make a living while I wrote books that didn't sell. It was better than any other kind of work I had done because I could organize and control my time better. And no heavy lifting. You can save your best energies for your writing. After about ten years, I reached a point where I could live off my writing and didn't need to teach. But I saw then that, actually, I like teaching and am pretty good at it. It situates me in a community that is serious about ideas and engages me in an interesting and continually changing way with young people. So why not continue doing it? Princeton has been willing to accommodate my needs well enough, so that now I teach only the spring term and pull away for eight months and hide out at my place in upstate New York. I have always led a bipolar life. Maybe it's a way to externalize interior conflicts that I grew up with and continue to be controlled by. My life these days is split between the very privileged, genteel world of Princeton, New Jersey, and a small Adirondack village in upstate New York where unemployment is about twenty percent in the wintertime. But I'm comfortable with that back and forth. I don't think I could do just one or the other and feel comfortable emotionally. I feel stabilized by being able to do both. I think you end up identifying with any community that you live in continuously, whether a monastery or a company town or a university or a corporation, and in some way I've managed to avoid ever living in one place long enough to identify with that place or the institution that shapes it. Both in the university and up north, I feel that I am, if not a saboteur, certainly a mole, a spy. Which is a healthy way for a writer to view himself, I think.

RF & BM: As in the end of *Continental Drift*, to help destroy the world as it is?

RB: Not very subtle of me, was it? Well, it is a tradition, after all, ending with an envoi to send your book out in the world to give it an explicit, literal task. But, yes, I have felt like an outlaw when in a university context. But I also know very well that, like most writers who teach, I am essentially parasitic there. As soon as the university's economic interests and mine don't coincide, they can rub me off on the nearest rock without any trouble. But for now, an institution can make good economic and pedagogical use of the fact that Joyce Carol Oates is here, Toni Morrison is here, I am here.

RF & BM: That's quite a cluster.

RB: A cluster bomb.

RF & BM: Do you have a lot of interaction with the others?

RB: Joyce and I are very close friends, and Toni and I are good friends—I won't say that we are close friends, because I don't see her as much since she lives mostly in New York, but we work closely here in the creative-writing program and African-American studies and we do see each other socially quite a lot.

RF & BM: Do you ever share work with them when it is in progress?

RB: No, but we do try out notions and ideas on each other—ideas and notions concerning writing, other writers, other books, about the bodies politic, about the world that surrounds us. They are people whose ideas and opinions I value highly, so that is an enlivening and enriching part of being there. The personal relationships, as well, are valuable to me, because it is not a competitive scene. I don't think any of us feels particularly competitive with one another.

RF & BM: E. L. Doctorow also taught at Princeton. Did you know him at all when he was there?

RB: I came to Princeton after he left. Ed Doctorow is one of those writers I most look up to. Of that generation, he and Grace Paley are the two who stand out for me as models. They are exemplary figures, really, both in their lives and in their work.

RF & BM: Several of your books have been made into films.

RB: I've written a script for *Continental Drift*. Two other books are also in development, as they say—*Rule of the Bone* and *The Book of Jamaica*. And *The Sweet Hereafter* came out in 1997 and *Affliction* will be out later this year. In those cases, I signed off on them and let others do it. For a fiction writer, writing screenplays can create certain occupational hazards.

RF & BM: Such as?

RB: Well, cocaine for one! No, getting big money in short bursts for little labor can hurt you. And working closely with people who see the world in terms of the movie industry can affect you in a negative way. You can't identify with any institution.

RF & BM: When you are getting into a voice, whether it be the narrators of *The Sweet Hereafter*, or Rolfe in *Affliction* or Bone, what decisions do you make about tone? How do you sustain it? Is there a sense in which that person is still an emanation of yourself?

RB: When it has worked—and I can't ever be sure when it has and when it hasn't—but when it's felt like it was working, which is pretty much the case throughout *Rule of the Bone* and also, oddly enough, with the female narrators in *The Sweet Hereafter*, Dolores and Nichole, it felt not as though I was speaking through them, like a ventriloquist, but rather was listening to them and transcribing what I was hearing. I was listening to a voice; occasionally, the signal would get weak, and I could, as it were, adjust the tuner and bring in the signal again and begin to transcribe again. Obviously this is a complicated process. It's not simply opening your ears up, because you are simultaneously broadcasting and receiving. But while you are engaged in the process, your attention is fixed on the listening part and not the broadcasting part. When it doesn't work is when my attention has shifted to the broadcasting part. I know I am speaking figuratively, but that's how it feels. In the case of the male narrators in *The Sweet Hereafter*, I felt that I was more focused on broadcasting and speaking *through* those characters than listening to them—and their voices don't seem as authentic to me. Maybe the less a character is like me—female characters, a teenage boy, and so on—the easier it is for me to write as a listener and not a speaker.

RF & BM: At the risk of seeming too mysterious, where do the voices come from?

RB: It is sort of mysterious. But I think we all at times have buzzing in our heads a whole range of voices, some of them heard early on and retained, some of them taken from the ether, the broadcast ether. I mean it literally. I can hear John F. Kennedy's voice in a second. I can hear my father's voice; I can hear the voices of people I have met only once on the street. So I think the voices are buzzing around in an aural memory bank, and you can tap into them the way you can tap into forgotten visual memories. It's analogous to the way in a dream someone who is long dead or from way back in your childhood, someone whose face and voice you can't really call up, suddenly comes back with great clarity and vividness, as if the dreaming self has a more powerful memory than the conscious self. I think writers, to a greater or lesser degree, have the ability to tap into their aural memories more effectively, more directly than the average citizen. I probably overheard the voice of a kid like Bone somewhere along the line and, in a sense, recorded it. Maybe it's a mix of several tracks. I don't know.

RF & BM: When you were writing *Rule of the Bone*, did you feel that there was a dangerous line between listening and broadcasting, or that Bone would seem too intelligent for someone his age?

RB: It didn't worry me particularly. Kids are much smarter than most adults give them credit for being. I don't think there is as sharp a difference between children and adults as, again, Salinger believes—except in terms of power. Who is to say that the inner life of a child is less complex or intelligent than the inner life of an adult? You can remember yourself at fourteen: you were able to say incredibly complicated, subtle things when you spoke to a trusted friend; you could move deep centers of meaning straight into speech and could communicate those meanings with ease and precision. But you couldn't do it very well when you had to speak to someone who was threatening to you, like an adult. The tricky part in that book, for me, was to imagine myself as the trusted friend and listener, so that Bone could become articulate.

Many of my characters are drawn from people who—to the world at the large, the reading public let's say—are perceived as inarticulate or mute altogether; but who, given the chance to speak, turn out to be quite able to address and describe their lives with clarity and intelligence. At bottom, I really believe that people are not more or less inarticulate by virtue of their age or education or class: what makes you inarticulate is a feeling of threat. And it is generally true that poor people and children feel more threatened than rich adults and, surprise, the people who feel least threatened turn out to be the people we think of as the most articulate—rich, white men.

RF & BM: Do characters tend to come first when you are planning a novel?

RB: It's very difficult to generalize. If you had asked me that question in my thirties, I'd have said that the narrative form comes to me before anything else. Later on, in my forties, I would have said character, definitely characters first. A few years later, I'd have said no, actually voice—narrative voice, language—comes to me first. It has varied over the years. I don't think it has evolved, just changed. I tended to grasp at form more immediately in the beginning, when I was still learning my craft and consequently was more conscious of, and anxious about it. Then in the middle years, I was coming to important understandings of basic relationships—my parents, my wife, my children, my friends. Now I think I'm much more interested in listening and language. Not abstractly so, but humanly so. I'm more interested in the act of witnessing, more engaged by it—a result, perhaps, of being more confident in my ability to organize and control and develop a formal apparatus that will carry the story sufficiently and efficiently, more confident and secure in my ability to maintain loving, gentle, continuing relations with other people. I feel free to turn my attention to other things, and what I have been most anxious about in these recent years is my ability to listen to and understand the lives of people who are different from me—people who don't live the way I live and don't have my privileges.

RF & BM: Would you agree with the critic who said of you: "Banks began his career divided between a common life subject matter and an experimental style. Subject has obviously won out, and Banks's liberated energies have gone into the forging of a straight-on technique."

RB: It's essentially true. It's descriptive, but not very analytical. What has occurred is that the formal aspects are less apparent than they were—I didn't know how to make them less apparent when I was younger. I don't think the work itself is less formal.

Another thing vis-à-vis that perceived shift is that I became a writer without having a clear sense of entitlement. I didn't know any writers. It wasn't a trade I could imagine myself into very easily. So in order to do it, I felt I had to reject a lot of my background and the circumstances of my youth, and willfully learn the techniques of fiction. In my early years as a writer, I was a lot more self-conscious and deliberate in my attempts to acquire craft and at the same time somewhat apologetic about what I knew about the material. Over the years that aggressive approach to craft diminished at the same time as my defensive relation to the content. As that occurred, the work began to appear more assertive in terms of content, and more self-confident.

RF & BM: In your novel about John Brown were you interested in creating a hero?

RB: I am interested in the whole question of the possibility of heroism, especially in a secular age and especially in a democratic society. There are two things that are ongoing perplexities for me: First, Is there such a thing as wisdom? And second, Is there such a thing as heroism? I want there to be both, but I am not sure that I believe they exist as human potential anymore. At least, I am not sure in what terms they are available. Those are the truths I am trying to find out: the truth about wisdom and the truth about heroism. That quest takes different forms. For example, in *The Sweet Hereafter*, I was interested in whether you could locate heroism in a community rather than in a single individual—whether some of the conventional notions about the characteristics of heroism could be distributed across a broader spectrum. The four main individuals in the story are unable to resolve the contradictions of their experience—the contradictions inherent in loving somebody and knowing that we all die soon and there is no afterlife—and they do not behave heroically as individuals. But as a community they are able to resolve those contradictions; they do it by means of public ritual, in which they simultaneously appoint Dolores, the school-bus driver, as the scapegoat and forgive her for the school-bus accident that killed their children, which their ragtag American religions and their legal systems couldn't do for them. That is what I was working towards: trying to create a consciousness large enough to absorb the human contradictions of the situation.

RF & BM: How did you get interested in John Brown?

RB: A short ways down the road from my home in upstate New York is the home he lived in and maintained for the longest period of his life. His body lies moldering there today. But I first got interested in John Brown in the 1960s in Chapel Hill, when I was reading and taking very seriously the literature of the New England Renaissance. His name repeatedly appeared in association with them—the transcendentalists' Che Guevara, a romantic but violent figure who, in a sense, acted out their deepest political fantasies. Certainly he was a romantic figure for me as well—he had acted out some of my own neoabolitionist fantasies of the sixties. Then he faded from my consciousness for a long period, until I settled in upstate New York and learned that his house and grave were down the road. The ghost of John Brown returned to haunt me. About the same time, events like Waco, Ruby Ridge, the militia movement, the radical anti-abortionists started making headlines—all of them invoking his name to justify violence. Certain parallels became pretty obvious to me, and I realized how significantly he figures in the old American weave of violence, politics, religion, race. All those strands cross him, yet the nearest John Brown Boulevard is in Port au Prince, Haiti, and there are no schools named after him, no stamp honoring him—even though he is regarded, certainly by African-Americans, as a hero of the first order. James Baldwin and Malcolm X placed him even higher than Abraham Lincoln. But white Americans generally regard him as mad, at best, and criminal.

RF & BM: That split is revealing about America, isn't it?

RB: The irony is that it is Brown's own race that regards him as a criminal. Anyhow, all of these forces converged to draw me into his orbit. He is an ambiguous figure, morally ambiguous. He had a ferocious, charismatic presence and from early in his life he deeply impressed people not easily impressed—Frederick Douglass and Harriet Tubman, people normally very skeptical, especially of an energetic white man. The defining actions in his life, however, are in some ways inexplicable. He didn't just sacrifice himself, remember, he sacrificed his sons as well—he took two sons to certain death and would have taken a third, who escaped, and two sons-in-law, and all those other young, idealistic men who died at Harper's Ferry. He knew they were going to die there. The book is an attempt to deal with that mystery. And with another mystery: Nat Turner might be the first true terrorist in American history, but John Brown became the first deliberate white terrorist in American history when he calmly executed five pro-slavery civilians in order to "spread terror." For no other reason. They were selected at random. There is not much difference between him and an IRA bomber. I wanted to understand that—the mystery of terrorism.

RF & BM: Did you find yourself wanting or able to justify Brown's violence?

RB: Neither. I'm his creator, not his defense attorney. It's a novel, not a trial transcript; and Brown is a fictional character in the novel, not a real person. I wasn't trying to write his biography.

RF & BM: How did you arrive at the title *Cloudsplitter*?

RB: It's the translation of *Tahawus*, the Algonquin name of the Adirondack mountain we call Marcy today, which is in full view from John Brown's farm and burial place in North Elba. Besides having been old Brown's favorite sight, or site, it seemed a useful metaphor, both for Brown's career and for his son Owen's task-in-hand, which is to clear away, or split, the clouds that surround his father's actions and character.

RF & BM: How did you decide to make John Brown's son Owen the narrator?

RB: You can't stand too near the heat of a character like John Brown. It scalds you. To see him as other than an icon you need the distancing that a weaker character provides.

When I was still researching the novel and hadn't worked out a way to tell the story yet, I came across an endnote in a 1972 biography of Brown by Richard O. Boyer that referred to the research materials of a previous biographer, Oswald Garrison Villard, which had been gathered early in the century when several of Brown's children were still living. So I went up to Columbia and pulled this material from the rare books room—seven dusty boxes of material—and found interviews made by Villard's assistant, a Miss Catherine Mayo, with three surviving children. Reading the interviews, I started hearing the voice I wanted for my narrator—the writing voice, not the speaking voice, of an old man born probably in the first quarter of the nineteenth century, looking back half a century to the events that defined his life. It was one of those moments when you know you've got something very basic very right, a moment that stops the whirl in your head and lets you plunge into the writing. Owen had been with Brown at Harper's Ferry and had escaped and lived to tell about it, except that he never did tell about it. He escaped through the abolitionist underground and surfaced after the war as a shepherd on a mountaintop in Altadena, California, where he died in 1889. The perfect narrator. For the purposes of storytelling, I let him live on till 1902, long enough to be interviewed by Miss Catherine Mayo and then to write the letters that make the novel.

RF & BM: Did you have models of the epistolary novel in mind?

RB: Not specifically. We've inherited the biblical epistles, of course, and the great eighteenth-century English epistolary novels, which are based—even if satirically—on the classical writers' use of it. Then they get based on each other, so that by our time it has become more than a literary form—it's practically a genre. You almost don't need models. You need a structure—my narrator, his psychology and the occasion of his telling, gave me that structure, but the form drops whole from the genre, the tradition of the epistolary novel.

RF & BM: Why does Owen not mail the letters?

RB: He intends to, at least at first. But before long he realizes that it's the writing itself that is important to him and that he is not so much interested in setting the public record straight as he is in telling, and in that way learning, the truth—the personal, private truth of who and what his father was and who, in turn, he is himself.

RF & BM: Does your approach to John Brown differ from other major versions in American literature?

RB: Do you mean those by Stephen Vincent Benét, Thoreau, Melville, Hayden, and so on? To them, I think, he is an icon, larger than life—a bearded, emblematic figure used mainly to express the authors' passionate feelings about race, slavery, injustice, religion, and martyrdom. To me, he is just an ordinary American workingman of the mid-nineteenth century, radicalized by the inherent conflict between his conscience and his historical circumstances. He is the last Puritan and the first modern terrorist—it's the terrible logic of that transition that fascinates me.

RF & BM: Are you concerned with the ethical impact of your characters? Do you worry that a young person reading *Rule of the Bone* would be inclined to follow Bone—chuck it all for reefer and split for Jamaica?

RB: Wouldn't be the worst thing he could do. But the book really isn't about kids, it's about adults. Just as *Huckleberry Finn* isn't about kids. What I think upsets adults when they read *Huckleberry Finn* is Huck's portrait of adults—their chicanery, hypocrisy, cruelty, violence, racism. That was instructive to me in thinking about Bone. What I hoped was that when kids read *Rule of the Bone*, they would see themselves and the book would confirm and validate their view of adults. Just as when you read *Huckleberry Finn* for the first time at fourteen or fifteen, you say, Yeah, man, adults suck. And because it's told in such a smart and funny way, for the first time you don't feel guilty or fearful for holding that view.

RF & BM: I read somewhere that the Ridgeways were portraits of you and your wife.

RB: No. The Ridgeways themselves certainly are not based on me and my wife. You sometimes introduce *aspects* of yourself, consciously and unconsciously, into a book. It's inescapable. There are a couple of places where, in a minor way, I inserted aspects of myself and my wife. It's a way, I think, of depriving us of major roles. Bone's best friend is named Russ, a garrulous wise-cracking, bullshitting schemer; I know there are times certainly when I was a kid, when I have been just that—a garrulous, wise-cracking, bullshitting schemer. If I could put myself over there in that corner of the book, then it was less likely that I would inadvertently let myself slide into Bone, or some other important part of the book. Same with the Ridgeways. In that case, I slipped in the bourgeois snob aspect, another unlovely side of myself. It wasn't just being coy or seeding the book with obscure references; but I think it served a useful purpose by giving a minor character my own name and giving myself a cameo, as it were, I was able to keep my head clear about who Bone really was—it helped me know that he was not me and his story was not mine. Paradoxically, it helped me stay invisible.

RF & BM: The question of invisibility comes up over and over again in that book and, of course, in American literature.

RB: I think the question you are raising here is more about authorial invisibility than, say, Ralph Ellison's use of the term. It is something I strive for, mainly because I have treasured it in other writers. Its absence in Hemingway makes me uncomfortable in ways that reading Faulkner, to keep to the same generation, does not. But authorial invisibility is extremely difficult to achieve, because to give the work any real heat and power you have to go straight toward what matters to you personally. You have to deal with what really is a life-or-death issue for you. Because of that you are inadvertently, almost inescapably, going to end up becoming visible in the book. So you have to discover and impose on the text a means of keeping yourself out— you have to keep catching yourself in the glare of your own light and then getting the hell out of there.

RF & BM: How do you manage the day-to-day stuff of writing?

RB: It has changed over the years, much as my life's circumstances have changed. When I was younger and had young kids, I wrote from ten at night till two in the morning and then got up in the morning and got the kids ready for school and went off to my teaching job. Now that I am in my middle fifties, happily I have a lot more time but, unfortunately, I have a lot less energy. In the mornings, I go down the hill to my cabin—an old, renovated sugarhouse that I've used as a studio for the last eight years—and crank it up and work until I start to get stupid, or at least start to feel stupid. Actually, I feel stupid rather quickly, but usually it's perfectly obvious that I *am* stupid after about four to five hours.

RF & BM: Four or five hours is quite a bit of writing.

RB: But when you are working well, it goes by so fast. You look up and, My God, it's one o'clock and I'm hungry.

RF & BM: Do you try to keep on a regular schedule?

RB: I try. I am able, most of the time, to work several days a week, although now and then I take a day or two off for a short holiday or to come into the city on business. But generally I work every day and then hold the afternoons free for everything from hiking in the mountains, to doing laundry, to answering letters, to editing, to paying bills.

RF & BM: Do you get a lot of letters from readers?

RB: Seems to me a lot. Enough time goes by and enough books end up in print—people will pick one up and read it and have that old impulse, and I think it's such a wonderful impulse, to write back to the author. I do like that, and I try to answer eventually. It's only polite if someone has taken the time to write you a letter. Also, a lot of times it's somebody in prison or a kid or someone who's had a really fucked-up life and says, Thanks a lot, your books sound just like my life. You have to answer those, no?

RF & BM: Do you write on a word processor?

RB: I love the word processor. I grew up with wet clay and a stylus. Consequently, I don't think the computer has had the same impact on me as the sense of rhythm and pacing and language basically formed in the stone age of writing technology. Also, from the beginning I've found that I have to sneak past that internal censor who basically wants me to shut up and be silent, and the best way for me to get something said has been to move real fast. The faster I can write the more likely I'll get something worth saving down on paper. From the very beginning, I've grabbed onto any technology that would allow me to write faster: a soft pencil instead of a hard pencil, ballpoint instead of a fountain pen, electric typewriter instead of manual and now, working with light on a screen rather than marks on a page, I find that I can noodle and doodle and be much more spontaneous. It doesn't mean that I don't go back and rework and rework and rework.

RF & BM: You do a lot of revising?

RB: Oh, I do! Much more revising than I used to do. Because it's much easier with a computer.

RF & BM: What about reviewers?

RB: I have gotten irritated here and there, especially when the reviewer seems not to have read the book I wrote and complains because it's not some other book—sometimes an earlier book of my own, as if I were supposed to be cloning my books instead of writing them. But only mildly irritated. I tend to avoid the negative reviews anyhow. Positive reviews help to sell the book, of course, and they feel good—they're better than a stick in the eye—but I've learned over the years that any book, when it is first published, is forced to fit into the gestalt of the moment. Whatever the popular perception of the moment, whether in literary terms or social terms, the book is forced into the gestalt and media vocabulary of that moment. So it takes about five years, at least—if the book can stay in print that long and get circulated and read—for it to be seen in its own terms. When *Rule of the Bone* was published, there was a flurry of literary interest in *Huck Finn* and a flurry of media interest in child abuse and homeless kids; consequently *Rule of the Bone* was read mostly in those contexts. But years from now, if the book should be so lucky as to stay in print, it will be seen and read on its own terms. It will be easier then to know what the book is about. That is when I'll care what people think of it. Just as I care now what people think of *Affliction* or *Continental Drift* or any of the earlier books.

RF & BM: It's a broad question, but has the determination to keep writing had an effect on your home life?

RB: Oh, definitely. My married life would have been worse if I hadn't been a writer. I don't think my being a writer has ever had the slightest negative effect on my domestic life. In fact, I think writing has channeled my self-absorption and selfishness into socially and domestically constructive forms of behavior.

RF & BM: Who is the funniest writer you've ever met?

RB: A lot of writers are unintentionally funny. But intentionally? Joyce Carol Oates. You might not think so from her work, but she is incredibly, slyly funny, a brilliant tease who pretends not to be funny at all. We recently had dinner and she kept me laughing all evening—little things, sly little darts in and out. She especially likes to tease men, I think, and does it very effectively. By the end of the evening, your shirt is covered with blood and you don't remember being wounded once. Actually, she plays a role in my life that nobody else ever has played—the older, scolding sister. I get to play the bad, younger brother. It's comforting in some ways for both of us, and enjoyable. You recreate those basic roles over again with your friends—sibling and parental relations and so on—and carry them on into the rest of your life.

RF & BM: Have you ever had a knock-down drag-out fight with another writer?

RB: I've had some serious disagreements with other writers over the years, but they never reached the point of verbal or any other kind of violence. Not that I know of, anyhow. I take great pleasure in the gift of friendship, when it's given; I value it very highly and try to live up to its responsibilities. I have managed over the years to have many friendships with writers that really nurtured and sustained me. With Joyce, of course, and Paul Auster, Michael Ondaatje, and a half-dozen other novelists; the poets Charles Simic, Bill Matthews, C. K. Williams, and Dan Halpern; and another poet, in Boston, Bill Corbett. He's a great man and he has been a dear friend for more than thirty years. When you reach a certain age, the friends who have carried you through thirty years of work and the accompanying insecurities and fears—people you have relied upon to reality-check everything from marriage to money to your basic political and religious beliefs—those people are irreplaceable and absolutely invaluable. I've been very lucky to have had a dozen or so such friendships.

RF & BM: Then you are not working in total isolation?

RB: No, not at all. Not at all in isolation.

Interview

Rob Trucks/1999

From *Glimmer Train* 32 (Fall 1999): 18–39. Reprinted in Trucks, Rob, *The Pleasure of Influence: Conversations with American Male Fiction Writers*, West Lafayette: Purdue University Press, 2002: 233–56. Reprinted by permission of Rob Trucks.

RT: I guess with the recent publication of *Cloudsplitter*, the most obvious question to start with is, Why John Brown?

RB: Well, I think that's a question you can ask about any novel in a way. Why a school-bus accident? Why a fourteen-year-old mall rat? Or, Why a white whale, Mr. Melville? And you're going to get a similar answer from most writers, because there's a braid of reasons. There's rarely, if ever, just one reason, if you look at it honestly and try to understand it, or try to speak about it honestly.

I can say that, on a personal level—this is one strand in the braid—Brown was in my life in a vivid way when I was in my twenties in college in Chapel Hill in the middle sixties, because he was sort of an emblematic figure like Che Guevara. Very much like Che Guevara. He was a man of action whose ideals one could identify with. And his picture would be up on the wall of the SDS office or the SCLC office, and he crossed those racial lines that a lot of us white kids were trying to cross during that period, trying to do it in a thoughtful and respectful and committed political way. He was also, at the same time, uniquely connected to the literary figures that meant a great deal to me then, and still do. Which is to say the mid-nineteenth-century New England writers—the Transcendentalists, Thoreau and Emerson and so on. I loved Melville's poem about him, and even lesser poets like John Greenleaf Whittier wrote about him. So he was a figure who was a part of my literary constellation, too. In addition to being a part of my political and social constellation, he was part of my literary constellation. And unique in that regard. So Brown was there at the beginning, but I was a kid and I couldn't have imagined writing about him—although at the time I couldn't have imagined but *did* write about Simon Bolivar and other historical figures without much hesitation. But somehow I couldn't imagine him. I couldn't get to him.

And then he kind of faded from my conscious mind. But in 1987 Chase and I bought a house that was going to be a summer house, and it's turned out to be our year-round house now. It's up in the Adirondacks in the northeast corner of New York State, just south of Canada a little ways, south of Quebec, and it turned out he was buried up there. Not only was he buried there, but so were eleven others who were killed at Harper's Ferry, or executed afterwards. He had lived there longer than he had lived anywhere else, and had run an underground railroad stop there. And there had been a settlement of black families, of freed slaves and escaped slaves, living on land grants that they'd been given by a wealthy New York abolitionist.

So his presence, in this ghostly way all of a sudden—I mean, really, it was almost like his ghost was in the woods, and also him physically. That area, since most of it is state forest, is not that different from the way it was in the 1840s and '50s visually, and I could walk through the woods and over those hills and even alongside many of those old roads, and know I was in John Brown territory. So he was physically present, and it didn't take me very long to begin to imagine his life there in that period. And I had been doing some local history research anyhow. I was kind of getting the background, really, of what turned out to be Brown's life. So it wasn't a very complicated move for me. That's the personal linkup.

Then, as I got (sort of superficially and tentatively) into the material of his life and the era and the whole abolitionist movement, pretty soon I began to see that he's a really mythical figure, and his story is a major American myth, a historical myth. I really wanted to understand that and see it freshly. I mean, this is why so many poets and novelists and dramatists and even movie makers have gone back to that story. It isn't because of the personality of the man. It's really the arc of his life, and the end of it, and the obsessive quality of it, and the fix that his life has on race, that drives people back to it again and again. As long as race is a central part of our historical narrative—and it is and will continue to be for a long, long time—then you go back to Brown and you try to reconnect with him and re-understand that.

So there was that, which is a kind of a literary and maybe even social or historical connection to Brown. Then I realized that for nearly twenty years in one way or the other, certainly in at least four books, I had been writing about the African diaspora from the white point of view. That's another great and continuously retold story, but it's been told almost exclusively from the African-American perspective. Yet it's a big white story too. It's a big part of white history on this continent, in this hemisphere, the African diaspora, because we white folks obviously participated in it, and to the greatest degree caused it, benefited from it, and have suffered from it as well. I realized that I've had this sort of obsession with it over the years. I've come back to that story, have been fascinated by that story. You know, the Caribbean in *The Book of Jamaica*, and the Haitian extension of it in *Continental Drift*, and certainly a big chunk of *Rule of the Bone* deals with it from another angle. Brown is central to that story because his story deals with the most dramatic episode in it, in a way, outside of the actual fact of slavery itself, the commencement of slavery itself. So for literary reasons, I suppose, looking at the body of my own work, I thought this was a necessary thing for me to do.

RT: There's been a recent trend towards the large, historical work. Thomas Pynchon, Don DeLillo, and yourself, three white male Northeastern writers in their fifties, have all published large, historical novels in the past couple of years. *Cloudsplitter* is twice as long as any of your previous works, and it took you at least twice as long to write it. Was this something in your mind where you needed or wanted to write the Big Book and John Brown was the proper topic, or did Brown come first and necessitate a sizable effort?

RB: I think the latter. I felt the desire to write this particular book about John Brown, or a novel based on the life of Brown, more accurately, and, of necessity, it would be a long, dense book. The historical narrative—for me anyhow, at least to do it in a realistic way—required a great deal of space, and I didn't want to just focus on one episode or aspect of Brown's life. I felt that I needed to cover quite a bit of time, at least twenty years, and that required me to fill out a lot of space. Also just the density of detail and background and material which would not be familiar to most readers, and it being a historical fiction displaced by a hundred and fifty years from the time of its composition required me to explain a lot. I needed a lot of space, so I think those were all factors.

Actually you've put your finger on an interesting phenomenon, really. A number of novelists in their fifties are writing ambitious, historical novels, and that's of some interest to me, and I think that it probably has to do with a couple of factors. Something that's true, certainly, for the three you named, and you could add another half-dozen. Charles Johnson. Jane Smiley's got a novel coming out right now that's about the Kansas wars. John Wideman had a historical novel a year or two ago set in Philadelphia, in the antebellum era. You could come up with a number of writers in my generation who are writing historical fiction, and I have a feeling this is in response to a culture-wide mindset—or a culture-wide confusion might be a better way to say it—a culture-wide confusion about what it means to be American. And for a novelist, that question will send you back in time.

In the late twentieth century we are extremely conscious of ourselves, as a people, of being hyphenated. We're Asian-Americans, African-Americans, Euro-Americans, Native Americans. We're hyphenated. To the left of the hyphen we know what we are—Euro, Afro, Asian, or whatever. What we don't know is what really is embodied to the right of the hyphen. What does that mean? What do we share? Why bother to call ourselves something-American, anyhow? It's historically true, at least for Americans, that when people are unsure about what it is to be themselves, their novelists start writing historical fiction. In the 1830s and '40s it was not that clear what it meant to be American. Fifty years after the revolution you could ask, Why aren't we British? Well, politically we're not, but really, Why aren't we British? And so Hawthorne writes *The Scarlet Letter* and you have Cooper and you have Irving and the major novelists, both South and North, of that era, writing historical fiction. And I think there's something like that going on now. There's a certain kind of confusion and lack of confidence in what it means to be American, and novelists are essentially, at bottom, mythmakers—mythmakers with regard to social identity, the tribe's identity. I mean a storyteller, basically, is creating, always, a myth about what it is to be whoever you are in this tribe. Why are we in this tribe and living in this corner of the planet instead of some other?

RT: Your fiction of the past seven or eight years has been told with a more conventional narrative than your earlier work. I'm thinking in terms of form and structure. *Hamilton Stark*, for example, had a unique form, a unique structure. Does the historical fiction, as a form, dictate in any way the structure of the novel that you have to write?

RB: Well, *Cloudsplitter* is basically an epistolary novel. That's the form, and the structure of it is the arc of the life of John Brown. See, I think of form and structure as two different things, almost as if one is exterior—form—and one is interior—structure—which grows out of the material that you're writing, the necessary pressures that the material puts on the narrative structure, the narrative itself. The novel is in some ways a sum or a record of the tension between the interior—structure—and the exterior—form—and the limits of both. And I had the structure of it, because I had the material of Brown's life in hand. I could have put a different form on it. It could've been a *bildungsroman* told by Owen Brown about growing up, in episodic ways. I could have used the same form basically that I used with *Rule of the*

Bone, or I could have done it with four different narratives as I did with *The Sweet Hereafter*, that form, that choral form. But it seemed to me that a more intimate—and yet formalized in terms of rhetoric—mode for telling the story was the epistolary, so I elected to use that. I made that choice for lots of different reasons, but in some sense it just kind of happened. It just was there and seemed to feel good and feel right and so I used it. It wasn't all that conscious a process.

But to go back to the early part of the question, it is true that one reads my earlier work with greater awareness of the artifices of fiction. They're worn almost on their sleeves. You're very aware of it. But I don't think that I've had any particularly dramatic shift in my writing life over the years from that early work, whether it's *Hamilton Stark* or *Relation of My Imprisonment*, particularly. It's just that I think I've become more skillful at hiding the form and less insecure about it, and so what was an exoderm has in some ways been absorbed into the text and made invisible, or less visible, to a more scrutinizing, analytical eye, maybe.

When I was a younger writer I was acting out of some insecurity, and therefore tended to need to prove to myself and my reader that I understood the traditions and the forms and the formats of fiction, of modernist and post-modernist fiction, and so I was asserting it more than I feel the need to do now. But in some ways, you know, an awful lot of the overt aspects of any work of art are telling. They tell us what the artist is insecure about, in a way. What you push in the reader's face is very often what you're least secure about. And as you grow more secure about it you think about it less and you have less necessity to assert it. Your trust is there and you don't have to worry about that.

RT: Do you feel any insecurity looking back on those books?

RB: Well, not particularly. I mean, obviously I would write them differently today, but I think they have their own essential identity and qualities. They're just different qualities than the work I'm writing now. I don't think they're less or more, necessarily. I have a sense that all my books are failures and that none of them are finished, they're just abandoned. That's a commonplace, almost. Most writers say that, one way or another, and mean it, too. But what that means is that you can't then put your work in a hierarchy. You can't value one more than the other, because they're all failures in that essential sense, and you have to look at them that way and forgive them.

RT: So there's no particular work that maintains a softer spot?

RB: Oh yeah, but that's for reasons outside the text itself. Like, I have a great sentimental affection for *The Relation of My Imprisonment*, and it has a lot to do with the fact that nobody wanted to publish it. At the time I wrote it I was publishing at Houghton Mifflin, and they didn't even want to look at it or think about it, and then later at HarperCollins, after I had published *Continental Drift*, they didn't want to deal with it. They said, Well, if you want to go ahead and do it with a small press, you can do it. You won't be violating your contract, and so on. Like it was a big favor. Like, You want to go and play around on the side? Go ahead. And they condescended to it, so it was published first, serially, in about six issues of a wonderful, mimeographed, stapled-together, Lower East Side magazine called *United Artists*. Bernadette Mayer and Louis Warsh were the editors. And then an editor at a small, wonderful press in Los Angeles who had followed the serialization picked it up and published it in a small, very handsome edition. And then it was a different thing. Later, when Ballantine brought all the paperbacks out in uniform editions, they picked it up, so it came out as a nice trade paperback, and now it's in the HarperCollins Perennial Library, their trade paperback. So it's had a nice history, you know? It's sort of like the outcast that managed to come in from the cold, so I have an affection for it for those reasons if no other.

RT: While we're on the subject of *The Relation of My Imprisonment*, do you feel any pressure to write commercially viable fiction? Would someone at HarperCollins hemorrhage if you wrote *Relation, Part Two*?

RB: They'd publish it, but they'd hate the idea, and they wouldn't offer me a big advance, that's for sure. But any pressure I have to write commercial fiction, or fiction other than that which is driven by a personal obsession, comes from me, myself. I put it on myself, or would have to put it on myself, because my own personal-obsession fiction gets published. I mean, it's a different position for a younger writer who's just sort of worried and trying hard to get his or her work in print. They may think, Well, maybe if I just shade it this way or shade it that way then I can get it published, but there are no assurances that it's going to reach print. I mean, I have at least that, assurance that it's going to reach print. I don't have assurance it's going to sell, or be popular, or that critics are going to like it or anything else, but at least I'm pretty sure I can get over that first hurdle. I can get it into print in any number of ways, and that's been true, you know, for a long time. So that doesn't put pressure on me. After that it becomes a desire to be loved by as many people as possible. You never know the degree to which you're immune from that desire. And you need an immunity, because it's like a sickness, that desire. It's a sneaky sickness and it gets sneakier as you get older and more popular. In a way, it becomes more insidious. It can really creep in without your being aware of it, because other people, they're stroking you.

RT: How conscious are you of the reader when you're writing? Were you more conscious with this book?

RB: I'm not conscious of the reader particularly. When I'm not writing, I'm conscious of the reader certainly, and conscious of my career, as we call it, but I'm not conscious of the reader when I'm working. I've worked very hard since I was young to separate my career from my work, because the career is the part that I have no control over, or very, very little control over, and it's got nothing to do with the work. It's like managing, you know, a mutual-stock fund or something like that. I don't know enough about it to do it, so I don't. Let somebody else do it. But the work I know a lot about. I'm the only one who knows about it. Nobody else knows about my work but me. Not even my wife knows what I really want to do, or what I really want to say, or what I really feel or intuit. I don't even know what it is half the time until it's there. But that's where I can do something and can control things, and so when I'm there I don't think about audience at all. When I'm not there, I do think about audience. Sure, I think about it. I'm not going to play some kind of faux naive. I think about it and I think I've been reasonably cautious and careful and knowledgeable in my handling of my career, but I can say with confidence that I don't think about my reader at all when I'm writing. That would be death to the writing, for me.

I write books that have an effect on me, and that's the main reason why I write, for how they will affect me. Not thrill me, although I hope that will happen, nor move me, but so that it will make me a more intelligent person, and maybe even, if possible, a more decent person. Writing *Cloudsplitter*, for instance, made me more intelligent about a number of things: about race, about relations between fathers and sons, about sex—Owen, after all, has a sexual identity that plays a significant role—about the interweaving between sex and race in America, about American history. It just made me more intelligent about those things, because I put myself at open-ended risk in the writing of the book, and that's what the book's about. That I'm working within the disciplines of an art means it may connect with other human beings in a way that resembles the way the writing of it connected to me.

But after the book is done and out, then you look around. I mean, I can take a look at it. I'm a somewhat educated reader of this book, and I can look at it somewhat from the outside and I can see, Yes, this will appeal to certain people. Or not. If you don't already know something about American history, for instance, this book is going to be troublesome. I have a French publisher and an Italian publisher and so on, and they look at this manuscript and they say, Well, I don't know. Maybe we need a glossary. We don't know a lot of this stuff, and who a lot of these people are. And that's a way of considering your reader. I think in those terms I do consider my reader, after the fact, in a kind of demographic or sociological way. And I suppose, naturally, I want the book to be popular. I want the book to reach as many readers as possible, for various reasons, some of them venal and some of them not so.

RT: Do you know which of your books has sold the most?

RB: Over the years *Continental Drift*, because it's taught the most, but with the initial publication it didn't sell very much. It's just that over the years it kind of settled into a comfortable role within the culture, generally, so that an awful lot of people under twenty-five have read it. They read it in school, or their friends told them to read it, or something like that. But the initial publication didn't sell very well. In terms of initial publication, then, I would say probably the most recent, *Cloudsplitter*, but before that it was *Rule of the Bone*. Each book has sold more on initial publication than the previous, but some have greater staying power. Some are stronger as backlist books.

RT: I know there's not a direct relationship between sales and quality, but do you find any significance in those numbers in terms of learning about your audience? Do you understand why each book has done what it has in terms of sales? Are you comfortable with *Continental Drift* being your best-selling work? I would imagine that *The Sweet Hereafter* is quickly catching up.

RB: Well, actually, I was just about to say my agent called me earlier and she had some sales figures over the last few months for *The Sweet Hereafter*, and it's gone through the roof, but that's obviously because of the film tie-in. It happened to be Oscar week, and it got a tremendous amount of publicity for the previous couple of months. Fine Line was advertising the film, but they were advertising it in terms of the book often enough and sometimes playing my name up as big as they were playing up the director's name. What's that got to do with quality? That's just the luck of the draw, the accident of a film being made, so I don't think there's any correlation between quality and numbers. There may be a correlation between the quality of a book and its staying power, its ability to continue to be read for no reason other than it continues to speak to people's lives in an ongoing way. People continue to read *Rule of the Bone*. That seems to be largely because younger readers talk to each other and pass it on. It has a real life with kids now.

RT: Do you think the primary audience for *Bone* is younger readers? I did find a copy in the young-adult section of the New York Public Library.

RB: That's great. I think the New York State Education Board has just approved it for being taught in public high schools, which pleases me immensely. Probably it's natural, and a continuing audience would be younger readers who would connect to Bone and would feel that their lives, in many ways, are validated by the book and affirmed by the book. That would be great.

RT: How conscious were you of *Huck Finn* when you were writing *Rule of the Bone*?

RB: Totally.

RT: What term would you be comfortable with? Is it an homage?

RB: It's an homage and a critique. There's an intertextual dialogue that I was trying to set up and participate in with *Huck Finn*. Definitely it was there.

RT: Well, I know the connection wasn't accidental. I mean, the words "light out" do appear at the end.

RB: Absolutely. It's throughout. I want to not only bow down before *Huck Finn* but also to argue with it and to point out, by similarities, the differences between Twain's world and Banks's world, the 1870s and 1990s. He's a middle-aged man writing about a teenaged kid, obviously an adolescent version of himself, and I was doing something very similar these many years later. It would be absurd for me to even begin to write a book about a kid like that without first giving more than a passing nod in the direction of *Huckleberry Finn*, and then going on—by noting the similarities, by seeding the book with plenty of similarities to note that there's a big difference in our worlds. I mean, the world has changed in dramatic and frightening ways in the intervening years.

RT: In what sense are you arguing with *Huckleberry Finn*?

RB: I only mean that figuratively. I think that basically what I mean is, not arguing with it, but adding to it. That's a better way to think about it. That book establishes a tradition in American literature that most writers participate in, consciously or not, and I was conscious of participating in it and wanted to extend the tradition into the late twentieth century, because there's so much in the book that's still valid and applicable. It's a great, classic work of art. But all the best stories, *The Odyssey*, *The Iliad*, have to constantly be retold, can be constantly retold. That's what we mean by classics. They can be retold. Not just updated, but retold so we can hear again and recycle, apply again to our lives with fresh eyes and ears, the essential insights and power that that tradition holds.

RT: This certainly wasn't the first time that you worked from a specific literary reference. I'm thinking that *Trailerpark* is a response to *Winesburg, Ohio*, and that the short story from *Trailerpark*, "Black Man and White Woman in Dark Green Rowboat," came from Dreiser's *An American Tragedy*.

RB: Naturally those are important points of reference for me in the writing of the story and of that book, but there are others as well. *Trailerpark* is in some ways a response to my reading of *The Canterbury Tales*, too, and *Dubliners*. There are various levels of response in, I think, any work of literature. You don't write in a vacuum. You participate. That's one of the great, satisfying things about being a fiction writer or a poet, an artist of any kind. Nobody's dead. You participate in the tradition. You become one with these books, and these texts become part of your immediate daily life, and so you enter into that conversation and hope you become part of the chorus in the course of writing the book. It's inevitable. It's inescapable for me. I've been a compulsive reader since my youth, since adolescence, so how could I not end up having a conversation of that sort? Having my work be a response to the works, the books that I've read?

RT: Can we go to either a short story or a novel and talk about the particular process?

RB: Actually there's a double source for the short story you mentioned, "Black Man and White Woman in Dark Green Rowboat." Well, not source. It responds to Dreiser, certainly, in terms of the psychology of the characters, but it reverses and plays with it so that the victim is the man, in a sense. But also it's a response to a Hemingway story in how it's structured. So the psychology, in a way, and the erotic component of it comes out of Dreiser, but certainly the form of the story and the arrangement—one might even say the architecture of the story—comes out of "Hills Like White Elephants." The physical positioning of the characters and the movement of the boat, when they turn and so forth, is very much learned from Hemingway. I mean, I learned how to do that from Hemingway, how to dramatize by moving the characters around physically in relation to each other and in relation to the landscape. Where they are in the lake and in the boat is all very carefully orchestrated or choreographed, and I didn't know how to do that until I read Hemingway's stories.

RT: When you sit down in front of the keyboard, have you just finished reading the Hemingway story, or are you working from some distant memory?

RB: Usually I'm working from memory, and what's retained. I read like a writer and what stays with me is often what has resonance for me as a writer. It might be a false memory, too. It often is. If I go back and reread it, I say, Well, it wasn't like I remembered it at all.

RT: But if it gets you the story . . .

RB: Right. It's what I needed from it. So it isn't necessarily a close reading by any means. It's associational and sometimes it's intuited, and it's strong enough or raises questions for what I really was responding to, that I'll go back to the text. I did that with *Cloudsplitter*. As I was nearing the end of it I was hearing certain tones, you know? I'd orchestrated these various pieces, and I was starting to hear tones that were reminding me of tones at the end of *Moby Dick*. And I wanted to get it right and I remembered that there's a beautiful diminuendo ending to *Moby Dick*. That was how I remembered it. I didn't remember it as like the great, cataclysmic ending. There is a cataclysm and then there is a diminuendo, and I was remembering that and that's what I was reaching for. I was starting to hear the necessity for that. Coming down from Harper's Ferry I thought, There has to be a diminuendo. It can't just sort of be like, That's all, folks. There has to be a follow-through. I was orchestrating it almost musically in my mind, so I went back and read the last forty, fifty pages of *Moby Dick* to see how he did that. Really, it was pacing I was looking at, and the rhetoric, to see how the rhetoric kind of cooled down, and how the narrative became more direct at the end, and how the whole voice was lowered. And I studied it consciously, but I was led there by what I deeply remembered, not having read *Moby Dick* in twenty-five years, so I think it operates that way, too. Sometimes you will go directly back to the text and see how it's done, but you're led there because you have this memory of it. You're led there because what's unfolding on the page is leading you there. It's in response to what's unfolding on the page.

RT: Was "The Guinea-Pig Lady" the first story written for *Trailerpark*?

RB: Yeah. Actually, they were pretty much written in the order they appear. That book is more orchestrated than it looks. It's more formal than it looks. I remember planning it out very carefully, the order in which the stories would be written.

RT: You knew it was going to be a book before you wrote the stories?

RB: Yeah. That one I definitely did. I had a cast of characters, and I was trying to structure it, in some ways, like an opera. All of the characters appear in the first story. All of the characters appear in the end story. Also, each of the characters assumed a role in my mind as a member of the tribe—the warrior, the magician, the fool, and so on. The mother, the virgin, the initiate. Merle Ring, the fisherman at the end, is the magician. And the guinea-pig lady is the fool, and they're both at the extreme outside of the community, but they have the greatest power over the community, too. So those pieces and those relationships were worked out in my mind. I don't remember, at this point, what the exact details were, but I do know that they all had roles and I was trying to write a novel that wasn't a novel, but that was, in an important way to me, a portrait of a community.

RT: Which is not all that dissimilar to your attempt with *The Sweet Hereafter*.

RB: Exactly. I think it's much more successful in *The Sweet Hereafter*. I was trying to avoid having a hero. I was really playing with the whole idea of having a hero by avoidance. Can you write a novel without a hero?

RT: Can you use the term protagonist in the same sense as hero, or do you have to stay with the classical term?

RB: I think you can say protagonist. A single, central figure. What James called the emotional center of the narrative. A single person where all values are tested. Any action which occurs is important in so far as it affects that character. And so *Trailerpark* is kind of a crude attempt to do what I think I did much more successfully in *The Sweet Hereafter*, but in *The Sweet Hereafter* I gave up the ambition of making each of the separate parts stand alone and satisfy the needs of drama in the short story. *Trailerpark* is a very schematic book in a way. Sometimes maybe too schematic.

RT: This question probably puts too much pressure on memory, but when you talk about writing the story sequentially so it's still familiar, there's a certain amount of time that it takes to write each chapter. Was there a relationship in the time it took to write each of the chapters?

RB: There's literal time and then there's writing time, and they're different. They really have different clocks. However long it takes me to write a certain section of a book is no indication of how long that section of the book is. It's the same thing with *Continental Drift*. All of those sections are approximately the same length. Some of them may have taken me a week to write and others may have taken two months, but for me that's the same amount of time. It's the same amount of imaginative time.

RT: You took a break when you were writing *Cloudsplitter*. Is that the first time it's ever happened? That you put something aside?

RB: Yeah. I think so. I think I probably have stopped before in the middle of a novel to write a short story now and then.

RT: How far were you into *Cloudsplitter* before you took a break?

RB: I think I was probably two-thirds through *Cloudsplitter* when I pulled away from it and wrote *Rule of the Bone*. Then I went back to *Cloudsplitter*, and then the last third I went through pretty fast. I did a lot of revising and changing after that, but just getting it down went pretty fast.

I think I got bogged down and scared of *Cloudsplitter* in some ways, because there was just so much material to organize and to structure into a coherent and compelling story. What to leave out, what to put in, how much to allow myself to digress, controlling the pacing. It was hard work. Harder work than anything I'd tried before. It's as good as I can do now. I learned a lot and maybe I can do better next time, but I was certainly working as hard as I could.

RT: It wasn't a choice to pull away from it? It was something that had to be done?

RB: Well, you know, it didn't work quite like that. I didn't want to go away from it, but it was just as well and wise that I did. Sometimes your sleeping self is a lot smarter than your waking self, and I just thought, Well, I'll stop and write a short story about this kid, because I was really getting into these kids and the kid's voice, and I was getting into that world, being seduced by it. And I said, Well, I'd love to tell this funny story about this kid stealing his grandmother's coins and using it for dope, and then he doesn't know it until they're all gone because he stole one or two at a time. The story appealed to me, the setup with the kid, the kid's voice. I could hear that, because I really like kidspeak. So I wrote the story, what became the first chapter of the book, as a story. And I said, Wait a minute. This is more than that. This is opening up a whole world here. This is just a door. This is just a way in. It's not a very good short story, but it's really a way in to a larger world that I'm fascinated by, and a character I really, already, love. I've only been with him for ten or fifteen pages and I already love him. So that's when I decided to go ahead and see how long it would take me. John Brown was going to be around a long, long time anyhow.

RT: There was never any doubt that you would go back to *Cloudsplitter*?

RB: No. Never. I never thought of abandoning it. I just knew it would be there—I'd already done too much work and I was too committed to it to fear that I wouldn't finish it. But then when I got into the other book, I realized, Boy, it's a good thing I'm doing this, because I didn't know what the fuck I was doing for a while there, for the last six months, on that book. And maybe I'll know when I go back, freshened by this. And it was true. It was the case. When I got back, I was freshened by it. But I didn't deliberately pause and look around, put down *Cloudsplitter* and say, Now what do I really want to write while I'm waiting around? Really, I just got kind of seduced. It was like a little love affair or something.

RT: You've been involved with several film projects recently, and that obviously takes a lot of time and energy and attention. Is it a distraction? A welcome opportunity? How does it fit in with your fiction?

RB: Well, I think of it as a temporary engagement and not a distraction at the moment. I realized when I finished *Cloudsplitter* last May that I'd been really working hard for a decade, without a break, and that I needed a break. I was tired. I was kind of bone weary. So I decided just to try a few different things, and I had the opportunity to get involved in these film projects, to write the script for *Continental Drift* and to help produce *Book of Jamaica* and *Continental Drift*. I've learned a lot over the last couple of years, over the making of *The Sweet Hereafter* and *Affliction*, about how a movie gets made, and I liked it. I was interested. I am interested in how a movie gets made. It's also one of the few ways a writer can keep some control over what the movie ends up being. I certainly plan to do that this year up to a certain point. I mean, I don't think this is a continuing thing.

RT: But you've been on fiction break since last May?

RB: Yeah. I wrote a text for a book of photographs by a man named Arturo Patten who does the author's headshot for *Cloudsplitter*, but he's mainly known as a portrait artist in Europe. He's not known here, although he is becoming better known. His work is being exhibited now more. Anyway he did a collection of photographs of all the citizens of a small town in Maine, and I loved them. They're just real formal, renaissance-style portraits of these country people, and they're just beautiful. It turned these people into universal types without condescending, without sentimentalizing them. They're just beautiful portraits, so my French publisher wanted to do a book of them and asked me if I'd write the text, and I got into the pictures. Now HarperCollins is going to do it here, and it'll be out next year.

And then I'm doing an opera libretto. I've done most of the background work and blocked it out, and I'll try to write that over the next few months, once I come in off the road. But the movie stuff, you know, if you sit around worrying about the movie stuff, you go crazy. It basically takes time in fits and starts, so it'll be like two or three days where I'll work and be all involved in it, and then there won't be anything going on for a week or ten days.

RT: Is it that easily controlled, where you know when the breaks will happen?

RB: Well, sometimes the work comes unexpectedly, but most of the time I know about it in advance. A lot of it's just yak, yak, phones and stuff, and meetings and bullshit. I don't want to direct a movie. I had fun writing *Continental Drift*. I might write another one along the way somewhere. Egoyan and I are talking about doing something together, an original screenplay that he would direct. It's an interesting thing for me to do. I love films and I take them very seriously. I grew up in the era when it was clear that films were capable of being high art.

RT: Do you expect the same satisfaction with your participation in these film projects as you get with fiction, or does the fact that film is a collaborative effort diminish it in any way?

RB: It doesn't diminish it. But it certainly alters it, and I'm probably not temperamentally suited to collaborate, except as a temporary engagement. In a continuing and permanent way, I can't imagine it satisfying me enough. I need to be in control of everything as much as possible.

RT: Do you know when your fiction break will be over, or will the film projects dictate that?

RB: I'll probably go for another year at most. I've already got a novel that's starting to boil up in my mind, and I imagine that'll put everything else on the back burner. There'll be a point in which I just say, Okay, enough of this shit. Now I've got to write fiction. I need to get this story told.

RT: I know it goes against all sorts of rules and superstitions, but can you tell me anything about that novel you have in your mind?

RB: Oh yeah, I don't have those superstitions. I want to write a novel about the Liberian Civil War of 1991. I want to follow the diaspora to its logical conclusion, which is Liberia in the 1990s, the last chapter in the African diaspora. I want to write that. Then I have in my mind a fifth novel, if you think of these as a cycle of novels about the diaspora from the white point of view. This would be the first chapter, a historical novel dealing with the slave trade, set in West Africa in the seventeenth century. I'd love to write about the slave trade, the beginnings of the diaspora. Then I could put together, in my own mind, *Book of Jamaica, Continental Drift, Rule of the Bone, Cloudsplitter*, and the Liberian novel. I'd have a sequence of them that would make sense to me, and that would probably exhaust the subject for me.

RT: Will this be a large book?

RB: I don't think so. I don't think so. I don't imagine it that way. I can't imagine it that way. It'll be a very personal book, a white woman telling the story. The story of a white woman, a nice white liberal, who goes to Africa as a Peace Corps worker in the seventies. A woman my age.

RT: You love the research, don't you?

RB: Yeah. The research is the most fun. That's other worlds.

An Interview with Russell Banks

Chad Trevitte/2000

From *The Carolina Quarterly* 52.3 (Spring 2000): 103–26. Reprinted by permission of Chad Trevitte.

The following people were also present during this interview: Brian Carpenter, George Hovis, Becky Morphis, Laura Mielke, Julius Raper, and Joseph Flora. Their questions contributed significantly to this interview, and they have been retained here.

CT: Many of our readers may not know that you were an undergraduate here in the sixties, and that you were highly involved with a group of young poets and writers. What was the environment here like for creative writing, and what experiences from that time would you regard as important in your development as a writer?

RB: Well, I think it was different. I say "I think" because I'm not really very knowledgeable about the nature of the literary life here today. But I think that the literary life for college students on campuses generally around the country is different than it was in the middle 1960s here in Chapel Hill.

In this way, particularly. We were, like any young writer or beginning writer, reading omnivorously and taking what we read very personally, and we were naturally being fed texts by the English department over at Bingham—the classics. The classic American, classic British, classic European literatures were being placed in our hands and we were reading them with passion and, I think, with a great deal of intellectual energy. But at the same time we were also reading and taking very personally the new American writing that was coming out of San Francisco and New York and other places—by and large, in the small presses and literary magazines of the Beat, Black Mountain, and West Coast writers. Robert Bly's Sixties Press up in Minnesota; George Hitchcock's Kayak Press at the University of California at Santa Cruz; Leroi Jones's Totem Corinth Press in New York; the City Lights Press—these publications were not on the syllabus. They weren't even in the bookstores, and so they were more or less brought back in suitcases and bags from New York or Washington or L.A., and passed around like contraband and hovered over.

So it was like a bipolar literary culture: one that came out of the academy that dealt essentially with classical literature (I can't remember any contemporary writers being taught at that time in the classroom), and then there was the contemporary writing—writing by writers who were just maybe fifteen to twenty years older than we—that confronted, challenged, and was opposed to the texts we were getting in class. There was this kind of dialectical relationship between the streets—the literature of the streets as it was felt—and the literature of the classroom. That was very good, I think. It empowered us in many ways and forced us to think our way through the classics from that perspective; it also forced us to deal with the literature of the streets and to try to evaluate it from the point of view of the classics. It was a very reciprocal relationship that was very fertile, I think, as well as enlightening. And we would seriously argue and bring that back into the classroom; I think in many ways it was probably a difficult time to be a teacher at Chapel Hill and at many universities dealing with that crew.

It happened also in that period that there were a lot of writers here who had gifts and ambitions to match each other—and that's really the case: one usually has one or the other and not both. Robert Morgan was here then and a good friend, William Matthews the poet was here, Leon Rooke was hanging around the corner, and Max Steele had come in at that time. Actually Reynolds Price was across the way over at Duke and he was just a couple of years older. So there was this gathering of writers and poets and people who—if later on they didn't become writers and poets—certainly at that point had a strong desire to become one. So their engagement with literature was very much that of a writer at the time. I think that was probably different from the way it is now—at least that's what I gather from having met with the writing students and so forth. That sense of entitlement, really: that we were going to go out there and re-make American literature. It was obviously slightly overweening, but nonetheless that's how we felt. We were going to be the next generation.

That's one of the reasons why we ended up founding literary magazines and small presses ourselves. They were so important to our education—it gave us a sense of our own historicity in a way, and then we could go out and participate in the culture in that way ourselves.

CT: It certainly seems to relate to your two experiences: your work as an editor for the *Quarterly* and your decision to start *Lillabullero* as a sort of alternative to the *Quarterly*.

RB: They're interestingly connected, I think. After a year or so on campus here we managed to identify each other. We ended up in the same classes, we ended up hanging out at the old Temple Room down on Franklin Street and at Harry's—and you end up at the same demonstrations, you know. Through all that stuff you get to know each other and you find out who all the poets are and who the young fiction writers are. There weren't creative writing classes at the time; there was one small group that Jessie Rader taught, but other than that there weren't any creative writing classes, certainly not like there is today. So we ended up getting to know each other, and a small group of us felt that *The Carolina Quarterly* was very much an expression of the academy—that half of the two, or that pole of the two; we felt that it was a part of the establishment, part of Bingham. We thought, "These guys don't know anything," and that they weren't reading anybody except people who (it looked like to us) were Southern writers for one thing, and formalists for another. So we wanted to storm the barricades of *The Carolina Quarterly*.

You had to be interviewed in those days by a publication board, and I know that's not the way they do it now. Well, we had to cut our hair and our beards and put on a suit jacket and a tie and go over to Graham. There was a small group of us, and we put forward a kid named Ray Kass to apply for the interview. He was a painter, and wasn't a writer or poet. But he made a good appearance, and we figured, "Well, Ray's clean shaven and he looks good and he really speaks well," and I think he had a sports coat. So we sent him over and he interviewed with us, and he was going to appoint me as fiction editor even though I was a poet, and it was Bill Matthews I think who was going to be the poetry editor. So we took over one issue, and we published everything we wanted to publish. We got stuff from all over, and it was shockingly different from what they had been publishing. So they immediately took the magazine away from us, and started conducting interviews again to replace us.

And then we said, "Well, damn it, we'll start our own magazine." We knew that there was a multilith press up on the second floor of the Y, so we went over and talked to Anne Queen at the Y who allowed us to set up an office and use that press. It was me, Newt Smith, Doug Collins, Bill Matthews, and David Mallison. David and I were the slightly older undergraduates, and the others were all PhD candidates here. So she said we could run the press; what we didn't know we faked and lied about. She said we could do it if we were willing to print something like ten hours a week. So we said sure, and we ended up printing our magazine there and stapling it together. I remember we didn't have a collating machine so we had to collate it by hand—and we got so sick of doing that. Newt got a key to one of the buildings up near the Y that had a collating machine in it. We had to carry over all the printed pages under cover of darkness into the building, sneak up the stairs, and pull down the shades and turn on the lights and run the collating machine all night until we could get the magazine collated. Then we would carry it back in the morning to the Y where we would staple it together and start shipping it out and selling it.

But that was an interesting event because it did grow out of that opposition to the traditional—as we saw it—and conservative *Carolina Quarterly* and English department. As it turned out, the English department was a lot less conservative than we thought. In fact, once our magazine *Lillabullero* started to appear, they became very supportive of the magazine. Forrest Reid and Max Steele were around then, and Charles Wright was teaching here then, and Dan Patterson, O. B. Hardison—they were all very supportive. I mean they dug into their pockets and gave us some money to develop it, and they contributed work too. Hardison gave us some poems, and I remember publishing Patterson's Shaker music drawings that he had collected over the years. So then, in an odd way, it built a bridge back to the English department, which was very satisfying and interesting.

CT: Was it at that time that you were beginning to move into fiction, or were you strictly working with poetry?

RB: Oh no, I was writing fiction. I had written a novel before I got here, which I still have—it's in a file in the darkness. I think I have a fantasy that it will somehow be magically transformed into a really good novel if I leave it in the dark long enough and then open a drawer and re-read it some day. I did re-read it about fifteen or so years ago and was horrified by it, but I still hold onto it as if it were going to somehow molt and then turn into another beast altogether—but it doesn't.

Anyhow, I had been writing fiction. In fact I was talking to some students this morning here and realizing, remembering—it's amazing both what I had forgotten and what I have remembered. One of the things that I had forgotten and have remembered here was the fact that I, like most of my peers at that time, was writing everything. I was writing poems, prose poems, short stories, long stories, novellas, novels, short poems, long poems, plays. We were all trying everything. We were engaged in a process that most young writers do engage in and probably should if they don't—a process of mapping out the contours or the limits and extensions of our own imagination, and finding out by doing it both what you were good at, if anything, and what you were truly interested in, if anything. You don't know unless you try, and that was one way of doing that. Writing from all different points of view, too, writing from all different aesthetic points of view: writing realistically, writing surrealistically, writing metafiction and writing straight realism, writing formal verse or writing open verse. I was trying it all, and with great energy, as were most of the people whom I learned from and admired at the time around me.

I think that what happens when you do that is that you really do discover, relatively quickly, the nature of your own obsessions and what literary genres and forms will allow you to access those obsessions, to act on those obsessions in some way. So it was a crucial freedom to indulge in, to work like that. I don't think I would have known to go into the directions that I ended up going in had I not tried other directions and found them inadequate, or found myself inadequate in going in that direction. The biggest difference that I notice between myself as a writer now and myself as a writer then is that I almost never now start something that I don't finish, because I know what I want to work in. I know the mode I want to work in and that works for me, as it were. I don't have to try a lot of things now that I did then.

CT: The difference between the writer you are now and the writer you were then is something that also came up in the fiction forum discussion: the issue of your generation, the sixties generation. Do you think that the political environment then at UNC has had a lasting impact in your sensibility as a writer, so that there's still a strong continuity with the writer you were then?

RB: I don't think of it quite as continuity, but rather as a very important formative element in my life. It was what I found when I came South to Chapel Hill for those four years, and what I took from Chapel Hill when I went back north and back into life outside the university. When I walked into Chapel Hill I walked into the middle of the civil rights movement and very shortly after that the anti-war movement, and got caught up in it. I know that it sprung me into a world and a set of ideals and ambitions that I would never have had otherwise. I think this is generally true of writers of my generation: it was very hard, especially if you were in the South, not to get caught up in the civil rights movement, and it was very hard anywhere in America, especially on university campuses, not to get caught up in the anti-war movement. You almost had to work at it. And so most writers of my generation have—I won't say profited or suffered—but have been affected by the activism of that period. I think the work is different from the generation that preceded us and the generation which follows us—insofar as we are, I think, more engaged on that edge where the private meets the public, or that zone where the personal meets the political, than the two generations on either side of us. I believe that's because in our earliest adult years, this was the social trauma, as it were, that we endured.

I think generally this is the case—for fiction writers, perhaps, more than for poets—but generally it's true that artists of any kind are influenced profoundly by the social experiences of their early adulthood. When you first leave the family and that small community that surrounds the family and enter the larger world, the conditions you find when you enter there have an enormous impact on the rest of your life and therefore on your work. If you leave and go to war, that's going to have an enormous impact. If you leave and—as, say, happened to many writers in the depression era—you find extreme poverty and strife between classes and so forth, then chances are very good that you will be deeply influenced by that, as writers like Richard Wright and Nelson Algren and other writers of that generation were. You could identify the war generation that way, like Mailer and Styron and Jones and so on. Or the so-called "Lost Generation"—you know, they got "lost" at the age of eighteen, nineteen, twenty. I think the sixties generation, as I tend to call my own and as we tend to get called, we weren't much older than that. I mean most of us were in our late teens and early twenties too, and what we met when we came out of the family, out of the towns we were raised in, was social activism and the idealism of that era, and the bitter disappointment that followed, and the attempt to somehow hold the two together in our hearts and in our minds: both that idealism, the belief in activism, and the sad knowledge that followed in the seventies. Like many people in my generation, I lost a lot of friends to drugs, lost a lot of friends and family members to the Vietnam War; there was a dark side of all that activity as well.

CT: The struggle to reconcile idealism with action, and seeing the limits to that—when I read *Cloudsplitter*, seeing Owen's experience, I could certainly see that it was deeply a part of Owen's voice. I almost couldn't imagine that book being written so well by someone who hadn't experienced that directly in the sixties.

Julius Raper: Do you think that saved you from what caught Kesey? Kesey's a step ahead of you in a way, and a great talent. I ran into him a few years back, and it seemed like a waste.

RB: Yes, he has an enormous talent and was a powerful voice, and you could just see it get diminished as he went along. It's hard to know. You know alcohol destroyed, say, Jack Kerouac, and drugs—or alcohol, alcohol's a drug—obviously could destroy any individual writer from any generation. So if that's the case with Kesey—and I suspect it is—I don't think it's because he was of a particular generation really. It was just a particular temperament . . .

Julius Raper: He went to Stanford and got into civil rights . . .

RB: Right, that's true . . . He got involved in drugs actually when he was still at Stanford, right. But I'm not sure about the nature of the question . . .

Julius Raper: I just wondered about that—what came along that sort of kept you out of going into the direction that he did.

RB: Oh, the activism . . . No I don't think so, because there were so many of us who had no problem with that! Handling both . . .

Julius Raper: Stone was out there too—

RB: He kept on working . . . I'll tell you what I think saved me finally, and it saved me from—from wretched excess, really, is basically what we're saying. And I think it saved me in a way from my own self-destructive impulses, which came out of my childhood, by and large: it was really the discipline and rigor of art, and learning early enough that that was the direction I wanted to go in and what I wanted to bend my life to. The requirements of art were such that I really couldn't get away with too much. That's what I wanted to do and it was very clear to me by the time I was here. I knew it was going to put stress on my marriage, it was going to put stress on my economic life, it was going to probably not let me drink as much or take as many drugs as I'd like, and it was even going to confront my desire to become politically active as well. And it did—all those areas of my life were affected deeply by the requirements of art.

It forced me to pay attention to the world in a way that almost forbids throwing yourself into it. I mean, this is obviously an old, almost clichéd observation now, but it does compel one to step back a little bit, to keep a certain distance from the chaos—to keep it from being chaotic, I suppose—that flows around you. And so you don't enter fully into that activity. Whether it's political activity, or domestic, or personal, you're somewhat distanced throughout, and that isn't necessarily fun, but it is necessary for the work.

Brian Carpenter: I have heard Robert Morgan say that you did throw the best parties around here then . . .

RB: [*Laughs*] Did Bob say that—?

Brian Carpenter: I was talking to him about the cultural climate here at Chapel Hill then, and I told him that you were coming, and he said, "Well Russ Banks threw the best parties."

RB: Well, I think that's OK! [*Laughs*]

CT: We need to get that on the record!

RB: That's good to know—

CT: The need for some kind of distance—whether from this or that self-destructive behavior, or the sort of urgency towards direct, violent political action out of sheer outrage—this reminds me of what you said about the letter that you received from one of the Weathermen about *Cloudsplitter*. I don't know if you would feel comfortable talking about it, but it struck me as such a meaningful experience.

RB: I'd just as soon not have her name in it, because I don't have her permission to discuss it outside. But it is true that a few months after the book appeared I got a long letter that has prompted a continuing correspondence with a woman who was a very prominent Weatherman. She's been imprisoned for twenty-four years now, serving a life sentence for a bombing and a robbery in which people were killed. This is now her life and her fate. She said that she had always felt that the only way her story could be told would be a novel, and she thought that Owen Brown was telling her story insofar as it braided together the strands of personal psychology and the social-political conditions of the time, and the idealism. So that the actions that he was led to, and the progression that he and his father followed—the progression that began with idealism and proceeded through activism and then violence against property and violence against other people and then violent terrorism and even martyrdom—was a march that she understood all too well.

And that was intentional on my part. It's kind of interesting I guess that my ideal reader is a white woman terrorist serving a life sentence in prison in New York State. But I do think of her as my ideal reader.

CT: She struck me that way—I can't think of anyone who could have really gotten into that book the way she must have.

RB: And that's turned out to be the case. She is extremely intelligent, and she has read it very closely and she understands. It validates much that I hoped would happen with the book because I was also writing out of a desire to understand some of the mysteries that characterized my own life experience. One of the reasons, for instance, why the narrator Owen Brown speaks his story at the turn of the century when in fact the historical Owen Brown died in 1889—so that I had to, by authorial fiat, give him another eleven years—was so that the light from his experience, as he plumbed it and probed it, could be cast to our own time more recently. If he had told his story from 1889, the year he died, then it would seem more antique and somehow blocked off from our own time. I didn't want to do that; I think historical fiction is really only of any use if we can take it personally now, in the time of the reader, which is true I suppose of any fiction.

CT: I still wonder if you regarded it as a struggle to depict Owen's racial psychology while drawing on your own confrontation with this question, or your own psychology. That is, I wonder if it was a concern of yours to think, "OK, I need to keep a distance between my psychology with regards to race and his psychology, because he is from a different century"—even though part of the point is that he does still speak to our anxieties now. Were you concerned about that distinction, or did you feel free or even welcome the opportunity to allow yourself to get implicated by that?

RB: Very much the latter. I never felt the need to keep myself clear or distant or objective with regard to Owen, or with regard to any of my literary characters. They become as real to me in the process of writing as my siblings or children or spouse in a way; their landscape becomes my landscape, their moral life becomes my moral life, their quandaries and mysteries and puzzlements become mine. So I never prohibited that or wanted to. Quite the opposite. In fact, I think that any fiction writer or novelist or story-writer is going to end up looking at the world from the point of view of his or her characters. As it happened, Owen's preoccupations and observations, even his memories, correspond in many ways to my own. The danger might be that I would end up speaking for him—and that happens any time you're writing about a character who resembles you in various ways, even historically long-dead characters. That's the danger . . .

CT: Speaking for him instead of through him . . . ?

RB: No, not even that . . . speaking for him, using the character as a ventriloquist uses a dummy. Long ago, I began to see I wrote best when I could imagine myself as a listener rather than a speaker, and that my characters were able to speak more clearly and see the world and say the world more clearly and authentically if I got out of the way and imagined myself as a listener. So that, for instance, in writing *Rule of the Bone*, I really imagined myself as another kid in the next bed in the dark, both of us looking at the ceiling, and him talking to me because I knew that that was when I told the truth when I was an adolescent. Practically the only time I told the truth was when I was in the dark lying next to a good friend whom I trusted, and we would tell our stories to each other and tell the truth about what we were afraid of, what we dreamed of, what our fantasies were and so on. Or in the case of *The Sweet Hereafter*, I imagined myself as a lawyer deposing those characters; they were speaking to me as a result of that. It's always been easier for me to let a character speak if I could first imagine myself as a listener. In the case here with *Cloudsplitter*, of course, I had to imagine myself as Catherine Mayo, the person to whom Owen Brown is trying to communicate, and then in a way he could speak directly and as truthfully as possible.

Julius Raper: Is Owen's nineteenth-century voice based on any particular literary sources?

RB: He's a type of American speaker/writer that you hear—that we heard, all of us, who saw the Ken Burns Civil War documentary—in those letters and diaries back from the front or kept at home during the war. It was the American middle-class writers, the non-literary writers of English of that period. I think it was a moment, a period of great genius—like New England architecture of the eighteenth century, or music from New Orleans in the early twentieth century, or Haitian painting of the twentieth century. There's a period, I believe, when occasionally a people can have genius. Where everybody seems to be really good at it. And at that period in America, everybody with about four years of formal education—North and South—was really good at writing. I think Grant's memoirs are a literary masterpiece, and they're written in that plain, direct American vernacular English of the mid-nineteenth century. And so I was aiming for that, and I used an 1853 edition of Webster's as a lexical guide: I didn't want to use any term that wasn't there and I didn't want to use it in a way that wasn't permitted by that dictionary.

I also wanted an inflection and tone that I associate with late- or middle-nineteenth-century working men who are formal, and who are speaking on a somewhat formal occasion. I have a friend, an elderly man in upstate New York, who is a very intelligent man without a great deal of formal education, who went to work in the woods in the early part of the century—1910 to 1912—in rural America, and was working alongside and learned to speak with men who were probably born in the 1850s or so. I love the way he speaks, and his voice was in my ear much of the time. It was sort of the template I was using, the oral template that I was trying to use to hear Owen's voice. I was trying to get this man's particular voice, so that was there.

And then there were, in fact, transcriptions made by the historical Catherine Mayo of the surviving children of John Brown—around 1905–06—that I uncovered. I didn't discover them, they were lying moldering in the rare book room of Columbia University: the research materials used by Oswald Garrison Villard, the historian and biographer of Brown. I pulled this material out and found these transcriptions, and she had just written their answers to her questions with the voice that they used. The Brown family voice was exactly that voice. They were elderly people at that time, very elderly people in their eighties, but they were too young or weren't present at all the events that I wanted to have as part of my story. No one had ever interviewed Owen Brown, and he had left no memoirs; he disappeared in silence, really, after Harper's Ferry. He was present at all the important moments of Brown's career and he was his father's—not his favorite son, but his right hand, certainly. He was at his side throughout, and he escaped from Harper's Ferry and disappeared into the West and lived as a hermit-shepherd on a mountaintop near present-day Pasadena, California, where there is now a little marker on his grave.

CT: So his grave is marked . . .

RB: A marked grave, yeah. But that's where that voice came from—those several different sources. And once again, once he started speaking it wasn't a problem to tune it in. You know, it's like listening to one of those big old Hallicrafter's radios: you get long-distance broadcasts, and every once in a while there would be static or it would fuzz over with other voices and I'd have to fiddle with the dial to tune it back in again. But it was pretty much there throughout.

CT: That's something that has really struck me about a number of the more recent novels—that you've moved more insistently into using a first-person voice in the novels. After reading *Cloudsplitter*, and thinking of its concern with racial boundaries, I couldn't help but wonder what you would think at least theoretically about adopting the voice or perspective of an African-American—the way that Faulkner tried to do in his own way in *Go Down Moses*, or as Styron tried to, more controversially, in *The Confessions of Nat Turner*. Do you think the inherent problems of this would be perhaps insurmountable, or do you think it would still be a risk worth taking as an author?

RB: Oh, sure—I wouldn't hesitate any more than I would hesitate to write with a female narrator, and I've done that, or a teenaged homeless mall-rat, I've done that. So I wouldn't hesitate. But you have to remember that in all those cases, and it would be true in this case too, it depends on who the person is talking to: what they say is shaped enormously by who is being spoken to, who the listener is. So I don't think I could write from the point of view of a black narrator unless I imagined that person as speaking to a white person. I don't know—any more than I know what women say when there are no men present—what black people say when there's no white person present. I suspect that they don't say the same thing as when there is one, just as I suspect that women don't say the same things when there aren't any men present—

CT: So there is a structural limitation that you would need to be aware of . . .

Joseph Flora: And men also speak differently when women are present . . .

RB: You bet. Yes, exactly, I know that much is true! I just returned from a month of mountain climbing in the Andes with six men—you spend a month with six men with no women present whatsoever, and you get pretty funky, I'll tell you! [*Laughs.*] Linguistically funky—every once in a while we'd recognize it and say, "Jesus, we sound like a bunch of fourteen-year-olds on a campout or something!" Really uncivilized behavior!

So yes, I wouldn't have a problem with that at all. As long as I understand that there is a formal construction here that is restricting, conditioning what is said—just as there always is, you see, in any statement. Any narrative is contained and constrained by the context in which he or she speaks.

Julius Raper: Is Styron in that book of "novelists responding to historians" that you mentioned in the forum?

RB: Gee, I don't know, that's a good question. He is still very much wounded by the attacks he received, not from historians but from black intellectuals, and some whites but mostly black intellectuals, back when the book was published—in '68 I think it was published. I think he was unfairly attacked for having chosen the subject matter. I mean the territorial imperative; no one "owns" any subject, I don't think, in that sense. But on re-reading that novel, which I did do not too long ago—I didn't read all of it, I just went back and looked at it and tried to check out again the premises of it—I was really struck by how implausible it was. As a novel, it had problems. In literary terms, I found it an absurd novel because it contradicted the premises that it had set out: that it was in fact a confession of an illiterate thirty-four-year-old African-American slave in Virginia in the 1830s, when instead it sounds very much like a late Victorian white American Virginian with a very elegant education. So that he bypassed, I think, all the questions of plausibility, and that's what in some ways probably made people react to the novel so intensely. But it wasn't a problem of the subject matter; it's a problem of plausibility.

CT: I wonder, once an author like yourself reaches a certain level of acclaim, whether you still have the same time to read other authors. Or do you feel that now you've got the sort of momentum that you currently have, it's much more difficult to make the time to read the way that you used to? Is it something that you miss, or is there not that much of a change?

RB: I don't think there's much of a change. It's no more difficult for me to find time to read than I'm sure it is for an attorney or a dentist or a janitor—everybody's got pressures on their time. What has never really been possible for me, and is still not possible, is to read as if I weren't a writer, and that's what they can all do. So everything I read has usually some relation to my work. The reason I went back and re-read *Nat Turner*, for instance, was because I was interested in seeing how he dealt with many of the same technical problems that I was dealing with: a first person narrator from that era. I couldn't remember how it was set up and so I re-read it strictly for those purposes. Or *Moby Dick*: I went back and re-read that because I was trying to find out the music of the ending and what I vaguely remembered as the tone. When I got to the end or near the end of *Cloudsplitter*, I knew there were lots of similarities in terms of structure and the format—the narrative by what appears to be a secondary character about a figure not unlike Ahab, a long quest that ends in a cataclysm. And so I was looking for the music of the ending, and re-read it with that concern. That sort of reading has always been the case, and it's pretty much the same as it always was too: I'm reading it and trying to bring it back into relation to my own ongoing work. A lot of it is non-fiction as a result—

CT: The research involved—

RB: Yes—I think when I was younger it was in some ways more difficult, because I was trying to work on several tracks at once. I was trying at first to extend and deepen my education, my knowledge of and experience of the classic American and classic European literature, in particular fiction. And also I had—as I was saying earlier—a great need and desire to read everything being written by the generation just older than I to find my own way. So it was hard then to just read in a way that would feed my own work. Now I feel much less the obligation to read that way, and I find myself re-reading with great pleasure and to considerable good use, I think, in my work.

Tennessee Williams said, when asked a similar question—I think it was more to the point of "What do you think about all the young playwrights today?"—he said, "Honey, when you reach my age, you don't have to cover the waterfront." [*Laughs.*] And I sort of feel the same way: the younger writers that I read generally tend to be ex-students and I'm reading out of a sense of responsibility to them, or it's a request for a blurb, or a letter of recommendation for a Guggenheim or something like that, but otherwise I tend not to read the writers younger than I am very often. I tend to still work with my own generation and the older writers, the classics.

Brian Carpenter: What was it like to go back and re-read your early stories?

RB: It was a very useful and enlightening experience for me in many ways. I went back and re-read over a hundred published stories that had been previously collected in books, covering a period of about thirty-five years of writing in that short story form. I wasn't surprised to find as many of them that were bad, and that I didn't think were worth preserving or collecting in a volume of this type, which is kind of a retrospective volume. I expected that that would be the case. In fact, I was somewhat surprised that there were twenty-two of them that I felt were worthy of including and keeping—I was grateful for that. But there were interesting differences between the author who wrote those early stories and the author who wrote the later stories. In the reading last night, I was trying to suggest some of that difference a little bit, too. The earlier author was in a way much more self-consciously literary than the later author, the older author. And I think the work reflected that.

Brian Carpenter: "The Caul"—

RB: Yes, "The Caul." I wrote that I think when I was about twenty-eight years old or so. I think I wrote that here because that was when I was spending time travelling back and forth to Richmond, and obviously it's informed by the time I spent in the South and came out of that period. So, yes, that author was a little more self-serious than I try to be now [*laughs*]. But also, I think, less forgiving, maybe less compassionate and a little more judgmental towards his characters than I feel I am now. And less trusting of humor, and sentiment, than I am now—a little bit on guard against those two qualities of mine, I think.

I didn't see a vast difference in terms of competence, though. I think that I had reached a level of competence in my late twenties that is what you hope that you can have: sufficient craft to make a life's work. It seemed to be there then. And from there on out what seems to happen with most writers is that you either do or you don't deepen as a human being and broaden as a human being—that that's what makes the later work more interesting if it is going to be more interesting than the early work. Not because the writer got better as a writer, but the writer got more interesting as a person and the work conveys that. That's what you hope is happening. Although I'm probably the least qualified person in the world to judge them, that's what I believe happened as I look back over the early stories compared to the later stories. That, and also the earlier stories tended to be more varied formally because, as I was saying earlier, I was trying everything—trying all the shoes in the store to see which one fits.

Brian Carpenter: There is an early story in *Lillabullero* called "The Adjutant Bird," that begins with the narrator saying, "I'm a New Englander here in the South with my wife who also happens to be Southern, and she's asleep now but I'm sitting here with *Walden* on my lap. And I'm thinking to myself how she doesn't know how different we are. I'm a New Englander here in the South and I see the future differently than she does or anyone does who's from another part of the country . . ." Then the story trails off into digressions on Walden Pond and ice, of all things, and Rudyard Kipling. I thought it was interesting because, again, you're experimenting with form, but then there's also the idea that you're self-consciously a New England writer in the South. Did you ever struggle with that? Did you ever play with these identities or have you always been just "Russell Banks"?

RB: Oh, no, I think that's very shrewd of you to pick that up, and that probably, while there's much about my youth that I'm having a great time remembering here, there are also aspects of it I'd just as soon forget [*laughs*]. And one of them—not necessarily that I'm ashamed of that particular aspect of my youth—is that insecurity about my social identity, and how that affected me. That certainly was there then, and it manifested itself in several ways. One was with regard to region and my desire to have a firm identity—as any young person has the desire—and my attempts to satisfy and meet that desire through a regional identification and that was sort of exacerbated, perhaps, by living in the South at that time. But it forced me also to confront that as well, and eventually to reject that identification of myself in regional terms, or in strictly—and parochially—narrow cultural terms. On the other hand, it was also a door that I could walk through that would let me engage with and take very personally the writers of New England, the New England Renaissance writers: the Transcendentalists, and so forth, Hawthorne and Melville—as I understood him to be a New Englander, although he was from New York. I just roped him in and brought him over to Massachusetts!

So it's interesting to see that, and the insecurity that that reveals in some ways in that story. I haven't read that story—I did see it the other day, someone showed me—who was it? Oh, it was Jim Seay. He had an early issue of *Lillabullero* and showed it to me and I said, "Oh, boy, that's one I never even collected in a book later—I just let that one go . . ."

Julius Raper: You were publishing all over the place by the time *Lillabullero* got into its fourth or fifth edition—had you been doing that before you got to Carolina, or was that something that publishing a campus journal led to?

RB: No, I started publishing in small magazines before I got down here. And I had a growing collection of publications—poems and stories in small magazines. And, as I said, I had also written this novel that I was trying to—

Julius Raper: The Hemingway novel that you were referring to?

RB: Yes.

Julius Raper: You've got a Hemingway in your trunk too . . .

RB: [*Laughs.*] Yes, I know, and this has been a bad year for dead writers because their estates are pulling all this stuff out of the trunk and patching them up and putting band-aids on them and sending them out into the world. I mean the Hemingway novel, and then Ralph Ellison's *Juneteenth*, and then the "newly discovered" Raymond Carver stories coming out—

Joseph Flora: That earlier novel you talked about is going to come out—

Julius Raper: You'd better get your money while you're alive!

RB: [*Laughs.*] Either that or burn it, if I don't want to see it in print—that's for sure.

CT: My early impulse when I was thinking about the stories was "OK, well they're like a testing ground or a transitional form that allowed him to go to the novel," but I guess in that sense this would certainly be wrong. The short story to you is still just as alive as a form and has just as much potential, if not more, than ever?

RB: Oh, yes. I hadn't written any stories for a long time after—oh, let's see, from about 1987 or so. That was when I published *Success Stories*. Then I got really sidetracked into writing novels one after another for awhile: there was *Affliction*, and then *The Sweet Hereafter* and then *Rule of the Bone* and then *Cloudsplitter* over the next twelve years or so. And at the end of that—after *Cloudsplitter*—I was kind of burnt out; I felt exhausted. So I thought, "Well, I used to love to write short stories," and I turned back to writing short stories and wrote about nine that are in the new collection. I realized anew how much I loved the form, how different it was from the novel, and how different the experience of writing a story is from writing a novel. You know, you don't learn how to write novels by writing short stories. You learn to write prose by writing short stories, but you don't learn to write novels. You learn to write short stories, maybe, by writing short stories.

CT: So it's a misleading assumption to see it that way—

RB: I think so: it's a wholly different beast. Short stories in fact are much closer to poetry to me. That's why I noticed how a number of the early stories particularly—the one I read last night, for instance, "The Caul"—are structured very much the way poems are structured, where basically they're governed by a controlling image that's unpacked over the course of the narrative. If there is any drama to it, the drama usually arises from the imagery, from the metaphors themselves, rather from plot or any kind of accumulation of incident. That's true for me, I don't know if that's necessarily true for other writers. But it seems natural that there's a bridge that's between poetry—lyric poetry, in particular—and the short story.

CT: I felt that way about "The Moor," too—there were the shifting moods, the humor and the sadness, and it had a certain lyricism that reminded me of the sort of response that I typically have to poetry as opposed to fiction.

RB: Well, it's very hard to generate a sustained drama over a long period of time with atmosphere and imagery and metaphor. But you can, certainly with a short story, obtain drama through the interplay of atmosphere, character, and imagery and metaphor, if you're compelling enough—if your metaphors are compelling enough, and complex enough, that you can unfold them or reveal them slowly over time. Like the metaphor of the ductwork in the hospital story ["Plains of Abraham"]—it's eventually complex enough that the unfolding of it provides drama, you hope. The two chambers of the hospital, the one that's sort of empty and arid and the other one that is full and alive and vital, and so forth, where the heat works—it's rich enough, I think, so that just by revealing it you end up creating drama. But you couldn't do that over a whole hundred pages. Then you're stuck with it—you gotta make up a plot and tell a story.

CT: I liked that metaphor. But at least at one point, I remember that you also used it as a nice transitional device: you were with the husband and started going through the ductwork as you described it, so the image becomes a structural transition to the other scene—I loved that too.

Could you talk a bit about your current and upcoming work? The Liberia novel, for instance?

RB: It's interesting in a couple of senses to talk about in this context, because I got to it by the work I did on the novel which precedes it—*Cloudsplitter*. And I think that generally this is true for most writers, as least writers who don't end up repeating themselves—and one hopes that's not going to happen: that each book teaches you or gives you information in the process that allows you to write the next book. You couldn't have written the next book, you hope, without writing the one that preceded it. And that's been true for me generally: I couldn't have written *Affliction* without having written *Continental Drift*, and I couldn't have written *The Sweet Hereafter* without having written *Affliction*, and—to move on down—I couldn't have written *Rule of the Bone* without having written *The Sweet Hereafter*. And I think it's even true—although it may not be obvious or easily apparent—that I couldn't have written *Cloudsplitter* without having written *Rule of the Bone*.

Well, in the course of the research for *Cloudsplitter* and the writing of it I became terribly involved with the abolitionist movement of the era that precedes the Civil War, and as a part of that I came upon the formation of Liberia in West Africa. The civil war erupted in Liberia in the early nineties, and that bloody, terrible tribal war between the descendants of the Americo-Liberians, as they call them—the descendants of the African-Americans who were placed there and colonized the area—and the descendants of the tribes who were displaced by the Americo-Liberians. And I thought how this was such a sad, ironic, tragic end to the whole African diaspora—the diaspora that starts in the seventeenth century with the picking up of the slaves, and the forced migrations to the Caribbean and North America and ultimately the curve back to Africa. Here we are in the late twentieth century, and these tribes are hacking each other's arms off, and the kids are running up and down the streets of Monrovia with Kolyshnikovs in their arms—this is a horrifying thing. Yet it's not something that's happening out there in the world that has nothing to do with us. It's very much a part of our whole story, too. Whether you're a white or black American, it's part of American history: the fate of these people on the streets of Monrovia in Liberia in the 1990s. So I came to that material really through the work that I was doing that preceded it.

And that's where I'll be, I suppose, for the next few years. I'm writing a screenplay adaptation of *On the Road* for Francis Coppola, and I've got plans to write another screenplay—an original story idea with Atom Egoyan, who did *The Sweet Hereafter*, next year . . .

CT: You're going to work with him again?

RB: Yeah, I love Atom, I just adore him. He's like my smarter younger brother: a brilliant, brilliant man and great man. I love him.

CT: I noticed that you played the doctor in *The Sweet Hereafter*.

RB: I had my fifteen seconds on the silver screen, that's right!

Julius Raper: And your daughter too, is that right?

RB: My daughter—well, she's a real actor, I'm not. She plays Zoe, the daughter of Mitchell Stevens—she's the one who's always calling him on the phone. She was so sweet, too. She was scared—it's hard for her to be in a film that was so directly connected to me, and for me to be there on the set as I was, hanging around—it put a lot of weight on her. On the one hand, it was great fun—it got her a nice movie role, it got her an enormous amount of attention, and she got to go to the Cannes film festival and got to go to the Oscars and everything else. That was great fun. And she's a real actress and so it was a nice little accomplishment for her to build on. But on the other hand, I'm sure it wasn't that much fun being in daddy's movie. [*Laughs.*]

Julius Raper: Do you have your own home-grown take on American violence or do you kind of draw upon some of the theories floating around?

RB: Well, it sort of depends on what form of violence you're talking about. For instance, children are violent in ways today that they never seemed to have been violent in the past—with a greater intensity, a greater destructiveness, than ever. Some of the destructiveness, of course, is aided and abetted by the technology of weaponry that's available to them, and some of it is aided and abetted by drugs and alcohol and so forth that's available to them. Some of it just takes the form of body mutilation, and tattooing and so on.

And so I have thoughts about that form of violence—the violence of our children, which we used to feel was more or less confined to the inner city and children of the inner city. Because that's how it was then, we didn't regard it with quite the same horror that we regard violence once it steps outside into the suburbs and it's white kids shooting up the cafeteria and each other and themselves. Then we start to react with horror. And so now there is some awareness of widespread violence amongst children.

And I think that it is a direct expression of a number of things. I could talk about two of them and they are intimately linked. First, the gradual and now nearly complete abandonment of children over the last several generations—partly driven by economics and changes in our economic structure—and the destruction of the family as a result. This in turn is linked very directly to the gradual takeover of that family or community role by the consumer industry. So that children have been turned into a consumer group of enormous importance to the national economy—over 14 billion dollars, I think, was spent last year in advertising for children's goods alone. Yet that was a concept in my childhood that was basically foreign.

CT: The whole idea of the "youth market."

RB: The youth market, right, and it's very specified, very specific. We've objectified children by turning them into a consumer group, and we've done it with enormous sophistication and subtlety since the 1950s or so, step by step, so that no one younger than me can remember the time when it wasn't the case and knows anything different in a way.

But the impulse of our species has been for the adults in a family unit or a small group to protect the young from the amorality of the economy. That's the natural impulse, and all those old jokes in cartoons about slamming the door in the salesman's foot and so forth are really about that and the sanctity of the home. That's what it's really about; those myths and ideals are designed to reinforce that species-wide impulse to protect the children. It's like protecting them from the weather, anything that's mindless. And the economy—especially the consumer economy—is mindless and destructive to children who aren't sophisticated enough and skeptical enough to avoid it.

But in the fifties, we opened the door to the salesman, basically, and brought him in and sat him down in the living room by the television. Basically, that's what television is: the programming exists so that the ads can be played, not vice-versa. They would like us to think that the ads exist so that the programming can be done, but it's really the opposite.

Julius Raper: That's an image—inviting the salesman in . . .

CT: . . . and he's staying.

RB: Not only is he staying, but we've got him in the bedroom and in the kitchen, and he's babysitting. We're off now—we're over at the factory, or downtown, or we're running a keyboard somewhere—and kids are being taken care of by the salesmen for four to six hours a day, and they're being pummeled by consumer goods.

Julius Raper: Entitlement and rage . . .

RB: So what we've done then—they know, they sense that they have been depersonalized, commodified, and abandoned, but they haven't a vocabulary for it, an ideology for it. They haven't anyone telling them this is what's happened to them, so they can't defend themselves against it. And they're going to become parents themselves very soon; they know that too. And I think that the only way sometimes you can re-claim yourself is to express— is to destroy yourself. And I think that bulimia, anorexia, body-piercing, tattooing, disfiguration of the self in all those possible ways are really about that, are about re-claiming the self that has been commodified and depersonalized to such an extreme degree that it's not even acknowledged.

CT: So that maybe certain kinds of mutilation, fetishes, and violent behavior could be seen on one level as desperate attempts to re-engage with one's own humanity in a world where one forgets what it feels like to be human . . .

RB: I think that's a big part of it. And they're angry. When kids start shooting up the place, it's important to know that they are shooting two groups of people: they're shooting their parents, and they're shooting other kids. And then they shoot themselves. So their violence is against their parents— almost always, occasionally a grandparent, but usually parents—but more often than not it's directed at kids that are just like them. They may mouth some kind of dopey racist ideology like the "trenchcoat mafia" from Colorado, but the fantasy is really about shooting other kids—the kids that they identify with really, and the most closely.

And I think we're about to have some more, because no one's quite noticed that it usually happens right before graduation, as the school season's about to end. They're going to be on their own in June. Paducah, Columbine, the one in Pennsylvania—they all occurred right around this time of year, starting around now, April through to June. I think that's not accidental, either.

Brian Carpenter: It was interesting to see you deal with that question in the John Brown documentary—the question about how you depicted the massacre in Kansas—

RB: The Pottawatomie massacre.

Brian Carpenter: You talked about how you tried to contextualize what happened—it was obviously cold-blooded murder—and how you tried to get inside these characters' heads and understand what they were thinking—

RB: Yes, it's not usually seen that way because we already have decided that John Brown was mad. It's not usually seen as an act of terrorism. We don't necessarily sympathize with or we certainly don't admire but we understand, say, terrorism in Northern Ireland or in the Middle East. Even up to a certain point, we understand it in the United States when it has occurred—we understand the rationale for it, let's say. There is a reason to terrorize: it is to sow terror in the minds of people who weren't killed in order to bring political pressure to bear on whatever issue is at hand and is at stake.

Well, that's what was happening with Brown: it's just that he was the first American terrorist, and we take it away from him because we need to think of him as mad. That way, we don't have to think of the issue that he was dealing with, and we don't have to contextualize the issue and realize how slavery appeared to an anti-slavery activist or radical activist at that time. It looked as though the cause—the abolitionist cause—was essentially lost at that time; the Southern slaveholders had in fact taken over all three branches of the government and were in the process of expanding slavery westward. And so I think that—I wasn't trying, as you noted, to justify it, but I was trying to contextualize the act.

As with the woman who wrote to me from prison. She's a terrorist, and that's why she was imprisoned: she killed people in acts of terror. And people don't think she's mad—they contextualize it: "Well that was the late sixties, the early seventies, that was the Vietnam War, that was the level of frustration at the radical edge—it was so high that they thought they could not change the policy of the government without acts of terror." And we say "They went too far" and so on, and we send them to jail—but we don't think she was mad. So that was what I was trying to establish in that film, and in the book too.

Julius Raper: Is your Liberia novel set in the nineteenth century or is it set in the 1990s?

RB: In the 1990s—it will be very much set right in the middle of that civil war. I've got it pretty much worked out, I think. It's narrated by a white

American woman my age who, as so many did, went over there in the Peace Corps in the late sixties and early seventies, and married a Liberian and had children and moved into that world. And then she's the one—with her family, her husband and her sons—who gets caught up in that civil war. So it's really her story, because I think it's an American story that I'm trying to tell; I'm not trying to tell an African story. And I have to be conscious of that—that I'm trying to tell an American story.

Julius Raper: It sounds like she's very sympathetic to the causes—

RB: Yes. I think that's part of the problem in a way: she's not African, she's an American too, and a white American as well. And yet she's certainly going to be aware that what's happening here in Monrovia, here in Liberia, implicates her because she is an American. She's sort of like the moral center of the story: her quandary, her mystery, her contradictions and conflicts would be the ones that are at the center of the story.

CT: It seems similar to what you'd said about *Cloudsplitter* in the forum about taking history personally—although in this case, taking a form of history personally that we might otherwise separate from our own "American" history. This bridging of the gap seems somewhat similar to what happened in *Continental Drift*, but in this case much more connected with American colonial enterprises . . .

Brian Carpenter: *The Book of Jamaica*, too.

RB: Yes, that certainly raises some of the same issues. I think that so many American writers—especially the younger ones, when I do occasionally read younger writers after all—forget the degree to which we are connected to the larger world. And this may be again a product of my own experience in the sixties, and my generation's understanding that we were connected, that we were connected to what was going on in Southeast Asia and so forth. And yet now here we are thirty to forty years later: we're even more connected to what's going on in the rest of the world than ever before. But very few novelists are writing about it, very few are exploring it and looking at the world from outside the empire—only from inside. And the world looks very different when you step outside of the empire and look around.

A Conversation with Russell Banks: The Path to an Answered Prayer

Lewis Burke Frumkes/2001

From *The Writer* 114.2 (February 2001): 26–29. Reprinted by permission of Lewis Burke Frumkes. Frumkes is the author of seven books and host of the Lewis Burke Frumkes Show in New York (www.LewisFrumkes.com).

LBF: Why did you write *The Angel on the Roof* and how did you select the stories?

RB: Well, it's not a complicated story. After I wrote *Cloudsplitter* and finished the publicity tour, I realized that I had given up five, maybe six years of my life for that one book. Then I realized that for the whole decade, I had written four novels without taking a break. My brain felt as though some of the fuses had gone out! I wasn't quite burnt out, but that side of the brain—whatever side of the brain writes novels—was exhausted. So I turned to short stories.

What I used to do was write a novel and then take a year off to write short stories, which would turn into a collection the following year. On re-reading the earlier stories and writing the new stories, I saw that, in fact, I had a deep personal investment, a long-time investment, in the form. I had done work that I really wanted to save. I had done work in my twenties, thirties, and forties that I thought was good enough, mature enough, and interesting enough to stand alongside the stories I had written in my late fifties—this past year. I also thought it would be interesting to save the best stories, put them with the new stories, and make a different kind of book than I had ever made before.

LBF: Why did you call it *The Angel on the Roof*?

RB: The title is a metaphor. It appears in the introduction as an image, which I tried to find a way to talk about, of what storytelling itself is. What are we doing when we are telling stories? It seemed to me that we are uttering a kind of prayer, and we are uttering it to the angel on the roof.

The angel on the roof is a figure—the Muse, maybe, or a genie, or an angel that makes us better, smarter, more honest than we might be otherwise in the telling of a story. So it refers to the figure, which is a figure of the imagination. All stories seem, in some way, to be prayers to that angel on the roof. The prayer in the introduction is essentially this—very simple but very complex. It's at the heart of the storytelling impulse. The prayer is that I hope you, the stranger, will love me for no good reason. It's for that unconditional love.

A storyteller is always, in some way, asking that of a stranger.

LBF: What draws you to the short story format?

RB: When I started writing, I was just a kid in my early twenties who had fallen in love with poetry. I wanted to be a poet. I had the intelligence, but you probably don't have to be awfully intelligent to be a poet—you have to have the gift. And I didn't have the gift. I had a formal intelligence. I loved form, the excellency of form, the exigencies of form—what it makes you do and say that's unexpected: the way a sonnet can force you to say and see things in a fine language that you couldn't if you weren't working within the restrictions of a sonnet.

A short story has form like that. It is rigorous and binding in many ways. The ways in which it binds you is also the way in which it liberates you. It's a kind of back and forth between confinement or restriction and liberation. It's very exciting for a writer. All poets talk about it, and I think short story writers feel it too. You don't feel it with novels. They have that great big baggy form and there isn't the same kind of restriction. They're not quite as formal in the rigorous sense that a short story is. As a result, it engages language very differently. The need for concision, the sense of a phrase turning the entire meaning of a story on its head—you go in one direction or the other and however you go changes the meaning entirely. It's a very exciting and intense kind of writing.

LBF: Has your love of poetry and your early interest in visual arts influenced the way you write fiction?

RB: Devoting myself to writing and reading poetry for a number of years certainly influenced my sense of language as a tangible thing, something with solidity and life outside my thoughts and desires. I like to think it has made my prose more interesting. As for my early experience as a visual artist, yes, that's had an effect on my fiction, I'm sure. It's at the center of my belief that a writer (and reader) must see what's being written and not just hear it.

LBF: Several of your novels have been turned into films: *Affliction, The*

Sweet Hereafter, and soon, *Continental Drift*. How did you feel about each of those films?

RB: Well, I'm one of very few writers who really likes the movie adaptation of the novels—so far. Yes, they've won awards, but they have been really interesting movies in their own right. Even if they weren't adaptations of my novels, I would have gone to see Atom Egoyan's *The Sweet Hereafter* or Paul Schrader's *Affliction* and say, "Boy, that was a good movie." I was very lucky in that both Atom and Paul invited me into the process right from the conception, with our arms around each other's shoulders looking at everything step by step, line by line. It was a very intimate and collegial kind of process.

LBF: Have you considered writing a screenplay?

RB: I've written two based on my own novels, *Rule of the Bone* and *Continental Drift*, neither produced yet, and have just finished adapting Jack Kerouac's *On the Road* for Francis Ford Coppola. I love writing screenplays and I'm not bad at it. It's nothing like writing fiction, however. A screenplay is mainly a set of instructions, a plan or blueprint, not the thing itself.

LBF: In *Affliction,* your most autobiographical novel, the narrator tells the story of his brother's decline because "his story is my ghost life, and I want to exorcise it." You grew up in a broken home with an abusive father. Has writing helped free the demons of your difficult childhood?

RB: Not so much "free the demons" as free me from them, to let me live a life not controlled by my childhood experiences. But that's not something peculiar to writing. It's the discipline and rigor of the life I've had to live in order to write my stories and novels that have freed me from those demons you mention. If you devote yourself to an art, or to religious study, say, or to scholarship, to anything that requires your constant best attention, you're not likely to suffer the leftover bad memories of a difficult childhood. They just have no room in your life to play much of a role.

LBF: Tell us how your career as a writer has evolved.

RB: I came out of a blue-collar family in northern New England. We are a kind of rough and hearty breed of people. Hard-drinking, hard-fighting, hard-working. The idea of becoming a writer or artist was very difficult for me to imagine, to apply to myself. I came at it in an awkward, unconventional way. I worked at a variety of jobs; the one I was best at and stayed the longest at was that of a plumber. That's what my father was, that's what my grandfather was. I knew the different fittings because I had worked as a plumber's helper when I was a kid during the summers. So that was the direction I was going when I began to take myself seriously as a writer.

The inevitable conflict got resolved in some ways when I married at age twenty-four. My wife's mother offered to send me to college. I ended up going to the University of North Carolina at Chapel Hill and finding my peers. In a sense, I found my world. By the time I got out [in the late sixties], I was published fairly widely and I began to teach. I liked teaching, and I think I was fairly good at it. So I began to have a new career. Teaching ran sort of parallel to my career as a writer.

LBF: You retired from teaching after sixteen years in Princeton's Creative Writing Program. Do you miss working with students?

RB: Definitely. But not so much that I want to return to teaching. When I gave up teaching, it was for me an exchange of the pleasures of the classroom for more time to write. And it wasn't an even exchange, because while I value both, I value my remaining time to write more than I do the pleasures of the classroom.

LBF: You have become one of the more successful writers, and deservedly so. You also seem to have kept things in perspective. What has success meant to you?

RB: Mainly, it's freedom. That's the point. I get to control my time. As you get older, time is of the essence. You really hear the meter running, and you know time is what you need most of all. You need your health, memory, and mind, but to utilize those things you need time. That's what success has provided for me. But this all came to me in the last decade. If this happened when I was a kid, in my twenties or thirties, I think it could have been harmful in many ways. But by the time it arrived, my habits were set, my routines were set, my relation to my work was set, my friendships were set. What am I going to do? I might buy some nice copper-clad cookware or something, but that's about it. It doesn't change your life too much, except for the fact that there is a lot more time.

LBF: Are there certain books you'd like to be remembered for?

RB: Yes. The next one. The unwritten book, the one in which I'm trying to get it right, finally, and actually do get it right. You know, it's impossible for a writer to second-guess how his or her work will be seen in years to come. All one can do is hope that one is given enough time, energy and talent to write one book that will outlive the author. Sadly, the author will never know which—or if he or she has done that already.

It's like not being able to see who shows up at your funeral.

LBF: Do you have favorite words, or words that you use frequently in your writing?

RB: That's a tough question. So many words dazzle me. Looking over my work from earlier years, there are some words that do reappear. They aren't necessarily pretty to the ear; but they are, in my mind, interesting. These words are transformation, reconfiguration, words that suggest starting over, a re-evaluation or a fresh beginning. Those words and concepts show up over and over again in my stories. I think that's a lot of what the stories are about. They are about people who return to a breach in their lives or to betrayal, abandonment, or failure, and try to recognize and grasp it. People who try to reconfigure their lives, their futures, as a result of the re-engagement of the past.

LBF: That might actually be a theme to *The Angel on the Roof.* What advice would you give to young writers starting out?

RB: A number of people gave me advice when I was young. There are many things I would say. First of all, don't quit your day job. That's an important one. Also, trust your dreams more than your intelligence. It's very easy to be an intelligent young writer, very hard to be a dreamer who trusts his dreams. I don't mean the dreams that are your fantasies; I mean the dreams that bubble up from your unconscious. Trust the dreams that wake you up in the middle of the night, the ones that stir you and move you in mysterious ways. Which leads to my next bit of advice: Try to penetrate the mysteries.

Russell Banks: Views from the American Crossroads

Marc Weitzmann/2001

From *Autodafe* 1 (2001): 95–101. Reprinted by permission of Russell Banks.

MW: The twentieth century has been a golden age for American literature. But when one looks at the young generation one may think that the legendary social diversity that once made this golden age possible has started to disappear.

RB: It is true that the young writers who are published seem to be primarily white, primarily middle-class, and, I think, somewhat provincial in their point of view. This evolution is due to a number of things. First to the linkage that exists between the publishing industry and the creative programs in universities. Which, by and large, are in the control of, taught by, and filled with, white middle-class apprentice writers. Now this is not the fault of the creative programs. When the first generation of poor or minorities, let us say the children of immigrants, end up at universities, they rarely feel like studying the arts, they don't study literature, they want to become doctors or lawyers, and so forth. And so Blacks, Asians, or Latinos rarely end up in creative writings programs. That's just the way sociology works. But the problem begins in the linkage between those classes and the publishing industry, because the publishers themselves are not sufficiently engaged in claiming the Latino, Asian, or Black writers and developing an audience for them. It is a sign of inertia, laziness, institutional racism, and ignorance. They use the creative writing programs in the same way as the National Basketball Association uses the basketball players. This tends to manufacture mediocrity, conventionality, and predictability. Just as any academy does. But also, by the same token, it brings its own downfall in that. I can see a period coming where young writers will abandon or sabotage the conventions and find their own audience by different means, just as they did in the fifties and early sixties with the beatniks. There was a similar kind of ossification, of linkage between, publishing and academy, with the prizes and so forth, in fiction particularly. And this is in many ways what the beatniks were reacting against. So they created their own samizdats. All those magazines appeared at the time, small presses like City Lights in San Francisco, Evergreen in New York. This exploded in reaction to an academic freeze that had occurred in the previous years. And I think that's what's going to happen here in the electronic media, on the internet.

MW: Important public matters have been taking place in America those last years, from the Monica Lewinsky scandal to the death of Mamadou Diallo, who was shot forty-nine times by four policemen in front of his building for no apparent reason. All those events have been discussed on TV and in the press, but without the participation of writers or intellectuals.

RB: Well, those issues have been discussed endlessly between writers privately, in emails, letters. And in a few periodical magazines, people like Grace Paley, maybe, or Doctorow have made statements about it. But it is true that major wide circulation magazines or newspapers don't solicit the writers. That is an editorial decision based on their understanding of their readership. Their readership doesn't take writers or intellectuals seriously. Being afraid of literature and literary values is a long tradition in America, or in American imagination. You can see it happening right now in our primary elections, as Americans begin to discover that for instance Bill Bradley, Al Gore's rival in the Democratic party, might in fact be an intellectual. They thought he was a basketball player, so he was okay. But now that they've discovered he went to Princeton, they're running away from him. Since the beginning of our culture there is a love for the primitive man and a fear of the man of thought, and that still holds today on an unconscious level. Intellectuals are an object of derision here. Not that they don't deserve it sometime. But it's hard, very hard for an editor of mass magazines like *Time* or *Newsweek*, or newspapers like *The New York Times*, to sell the words and the opinion of an intellectual.

The New Yorker once asked a bunch of writers their opinions on the Monica Lewinsky scandal. Well, it turned out to be an interesting and provocative issue. Toni Morrison did a great piece. She, as she is inclined to do, was speaking metaphorically, but was taken literally, she said that Clinton was our first black president. She had hilarious and strong arguments, such as, Clinton plays saxophone, he's kind of sexy, likes to dance, he's kind of sloppy, he's lazy, he's coming from a dysfunctional family, et cetera. And I thought it was a very interesting way, first of all to talk about black people—not in terms of skin pigmentation. But you're certainly going against the tide here, when you're asking artists and intellectuals what their thoughts about public matters are.

MW: But at the same time, American literature has been one of the most powerful of the twentieth century.

RB: I think it's in spite of that. The American artistic tradition is a democratic one, with a commitment to witnessing. American writers since Whitman and Twain have understood that they have to witness the suffering and to testify. And it's as deep as American literature itself. But deep in the American imagination, there's always been a mistrust with that very witnessing and the conflict brought into it. We have a very powerful witnessing tradition in our literary life, and it really goes back to the beginning. We only have a very short history but our two first great writers are Walt Whitman and Mark Twain, and both were testifiers. And at the same time we produce a context that mistrusts them. It may be hard to understand from a European point of view. American writers both oppose that mistrust and use it to work in secrecy. We're not public figures and are not asked to be. We maintain a private status of primal opposition, we never identify with a party. The only and short period where American literary life was identified with a party was in the thirties when some writers were communists. And it was a very brief period, until they knew what was going on in the USSR. It didn't last.

MW: Contrary to the French intellectuals that apparently were never able to get the news.

RB: Right. So this is a good thing, too. If American writers had the public status of French writers or were treated the same way, I'm not so sure it would be a great thing. It would be nice if the American popular audience were more curious of what American writers had to say about Diallo or George W. Bush, or any other public matter, but it's not a necessity. It's not necessary for the works to exist. Writers have been writing about public matters in their books. Racism, political corruption, police violence: Twain had been writing about those very subjects. Whitman wrote about it.

MW: Could it be that the absence of the writers in public debate goes with a larger freedom in the work? For instance [Truman Capote's] *Cold Blood* couldn't have been written in France the way it was in the United States. Using a true story, writing a nonfiction novel would have exposed the author to justice immediately. Or Robert Coover's *Public Verdict*, written in the mid-seventies and where the narrator is Richard Nixon, at the time president of the country.

RB: It's worth something to have that freedom, and I'm not complaining really, about not being taken seriously as a writer. I don't particularly care about being invited or not by the president at the White House. Or by Rupert Murdoch or Ted Turner.

MW: Norman Mailer must have been one of the only representatives in American life of what the Europeans call *écrivain engagé*.

RB: Yes. During a brief period, from the late sixties to the early seventies, and he was remarkable then, he wrote some extraordinary books. But it was certainly not a typical relationship for an American writer—not even for Norman himself. But it was that brief period where we all thought that almost anything was possible.

MW: Nelson Algren has been your mentor since you started writing. What was his position on that issue of public debate?

RB: Well, he was quite engaged, both in his private and public life, he didn't see any discontinuity between the two. But he was never taken seriously by the larger public as a social critic. In a literary context, yes, he was. He's been on my mind lately, partly because of the publication of *The Man with the Golden Arm*. They reissued it and there was a big celebration around the book. His work brings an aggressive positioning of the writer—and of the reader as a result—against power, and a kind of deep compassion for the victim of that power. This is as much as anyone can ask of a writer. And this is very much in the tradition that flowered in Chicago between the late thirties and the forties, with people like Richard Wright and many others that had not necessarily the same status. He briefly was a member of the Communist party, for two weeks or so. But he couldn't take orders, so that took care of that. There has been a certain neglect of that tradition in American letters, partly because of the academics. At a university, you study books that can be deconstructed, not books that can change your life. Algren's books can change your life, and this kind of book you always have to discover on your own. Somebody passes them to you, you know, under the table as if it was an illegal gun or something: "Read this! Nobody else likes it but you will." I just love it when someone comes to me and says in a tone of conspiracy, "I just read this Nelson Algren guy, it's incredible, what do you know about him?" His books were almost out of print, you know, until a few years ago. Seven Stories Press has started to get all his work back into print, with a few writers like myself and Kurt Vonnegut writing introductions. He needs to be known not only as the lover of Simone de Beauvoir—the disappointed lover.

MW: Here in the USA when you talk of Chicago, you don't mention Algren, you mention Saul Bellow.

RB: Well, it's an old opposition in American literature, there's always been Henry James here, and Mark Twain there.

MW: Would you suggest that Saul Bellow is the contemporary equivalent of James?

RB: No. What I mean is geographical. There is a geographical line, an opposition between "east-west" writers on the one side, and "north-south" writers on the other side. For instance Mark Twain is writing about Mississippi. Whitman and Algren are writing about black-white relationships and working-class people. They are all north-south writers, and today you can count people like Toni Morrison and myself in the field. Whereas on the other hand the tradition of east-west writers goes back to Henry James and Edgar Allan Poe.

MW: Where would you put Faulkner and Hemingway?

RB: Faulkner is north-south oriented of course. As for Hemingway, well, with all his Caribbean, Latin interest, he was not writing European literature. He went back to Twain, said that himself. Sure, he is there, too. But not Henry James. Not Saul Bellow. Not Philip Roth, and not Cynthia Ozick. It's a kind of literature I admire in many ways, but not the kind I identify with.

MW: What about Don DeLillo?

RB: Oh, he's definitely one of the great American contemporary writers. He loves American language and everything about our culture. He's very much a writer of the American vernacular, and that, to me, makes him a north-south writer. There is this speech pattern he uses, the language he's attracted to. No one I believe has a better ear for the American vernacular, he just loves the way Americans talk, especially the urban working class. He also assembles his work in a way that is certainly not a European linear narrative by any means. It's a collage more than anything else. The pattern of the whole is not a complex narrative plot with a series of causes and effects controlling the events. It's like jazz, I would say. Not at all European.

MW: So the north-south line defines a kind of "*américanité*"?

RB: It's like jazz. I tend to believe that jazz can be a model for American literature, and jazz is probably the only true, the unique American art. It brings together African-American and Euro-American traditions of music. Instrumentations, and songs and melodies are complex and it's vernacular and democratic. And the best of American writing subscribes to those principles and uses pretty much the same methodologies.

MW: Do you think that American literature should cut its roots to the European tradition?

RB: No, I don't think we need to, because it's not a threat to us. Only if it were a threat should we have to do that. That's something that Hawthorne was worrying about. He was afraid of being influenced by what he called the "John Bull English," the English mentality. But it's not a threat to us anymore. Not since Henry James.

MW: Why does this line you show between north-south writers on one side and east-west on the other, seem to have political consequences, the second being apparently more conservative?

RB: Well, it's hard to say, unless you admit that commitment to language is a political act. If you commit yourself to the vernacular, you commit yourself to the people who speak it, to the demos. And if on the other hand you commit yourself to a more literary language, you commit yourself to those who speak it. This goes back to Chaucer, to Dante and Rabelais.

Engaging History in Collaborative Mythmaking: A Conversation with Russell Banks

Kimberly Rae Connor/2004

From *La Revue LISA / LISA e-journal* 2.4 (2004): 5–16. Reprinted by permission of Kimberly Rae Connor.

The following interview was drawn from a two-hour conversation between Kimberly Rae Connor (KRC), a professor at the University of San Francisco, and novelist Russell Banks (RB). Kimberly Rae Connor earned a PhD in religion and literature at the University of Virginia. She is on the faculty of the University of San Francisco. She is author of two books—*Conversions and Visions in the Writings of African American Women* (Tennessee 1994) and *Imagining Grace: Liberating Theologies in the Slave Narrative Tradition* (Illinois 2000) as well as many articles on African American religion and culture and multicultural pedagogy. This interview was conducted on March 19, 2004, at the Princeton Club in New York City. We began with an informal chat about Banks's collection of short stories, *Trailerpark*, which he is developing as a television series. That led us to a discussion of class and race, issues that deeply inform Banks's work and sensibility. In considering how one transgresses lines of class and race, the interviewer began with the following question.

KRC: Miguel de Unamuno, the Spanish philosopher and theologian said, "The secret of human life, the universal secret, the root secret from which all other secrets spring, is the longing for more life. The furious and insatiable desire to be everything else without ever ceasing to be ourselves." His insight reminded me of a previous interview in which you distinguished between *being* and *becoming* the other. Could you elaborate on that distinction?

RB: It is the difference between sympathy and empathy. Empathy tends to only recognize sameness and then appropriate difference as if it were the same. But sympathy is feeling *for* someone who is different.

KRC: That distinction prevents one from going into smug territory, which goes back to what we were talking about in terms of class issues and writing about who you are; then you don't stand in judgment. But I think that most people would tend to regard empathy as the superior trait.

RB: Well yes, but that is a kind of liberal prejudice, I think. Empathy sounds more substantial, but it is appropriational. As a white middle-class American man, I've had to be very careful of that. Because I am now at the top of the ladder and it is very easy to think you understand people who are just below you on the ladder.

KRC: Okay, but when you do acquire the wealth and the power, as you have now, what is your responsibility?

RB: It depends on what perspective you take, on your own identity. I have various roles in the world—as a writer, citizen, parent, spouse, teacher—and so I try to function in each of those roles as carefully as I can. Responsibly is a better way to put it. So I do a lot that my working class parents were never able to do. In terms of giving money away and taking care of other people, educating people—close to me and not so. Institutionally and personally. It is not problematic for me; it is a matter of me saying, "Okay, in this role, how do I deal with my resources and my powers in a responsible way?" You can react to all this neurotically because in some ways you are like a baseball player [offered a big contract] or a musician who suddenly had a hit record. It has nothing to do with you. Wealth is not a measure of your achievement in any way. It falls from the sky, in that sense, that kind of power and resources, and it isn't something one sets out to acquire.

KRC: It dials things up, raises the stakes. Although the recognition of the automatic entitlements is the first hurdle; but then whatever you accumulate just obliges you that much more. My problem with my white students is to get them to appreciate that they live in an entitled world, that things are happening to them because they are not happening to or for others.

RB: Yes, it is hard to make people with privilege see or realize that they have it. One of the privileges of privilege is to deny that you have privilege.

The interview then shifted to a discussion of issues pertinent to the theme of the journal and the relationship between history and fiction. I asked Banks if he had read Richard Powers's novel The Time of Our Singing—*he had not—to illustrate the ways Powers uses history and a particular historical moment as a backdrop and as a thematic focus, a more diffuse use of history than Banks employs in* Cloudsplitter. *I proceeded to ask him to describe his approach to the use of history in his fiction.*

KRC: What role does history play in the fiction writer's life? Is there a master narrative that isn't dominant, a middle ground between history and fiction that gets at truth?

RB: I think there is a master narrative that becomes dominant over time and controls the imagination of a people. But I think it is always historically a collective, or rather a collaborative narrative over time. Historians, filmmakers, novelists, poets all work with it, towards creating this dominant mythology that to such an enormous degree controls the imagination of a people for generations. I don't feel as though one type or perspective dominates but collaboratively they all contribute to the mythmaking. Take for example the Civil War and pick three different players, say the novel *Gone with the Wind*, the film *Cold Mountain*, and some serious historical work of that same period and they all three are kind of working together to create a (white) mythology that the next generation of Americans will hold in their minds and perceive the world through. So that is all I feel like I am doing. I am working with historical materials, trying to not compete with historians for some kind of ultimate truth. I have a different truth and a different use for the same materials.

KRC: But you are still interpreting history.

RB: I'm not. I am using the materials from history the same way I use materials from my personal life, my family life. I am using it knowing somewhere down the line some historian will come along—and they already have on John Brown—and use my work as a comment on how John Brown was perceived in the late-twentieth-century United States. Because John Brown is an iconic figure in our national mythology, our racial mythology especially. So someone will come along and say that this novel that was popular and widely taught gives evidence that the perspective on John Brown shifted in the late twentieth to early twenty-first centuries. There was a dialogue between the historically, conventionally African American perspective and the conventionally white perspective on John Brown going on. So that is sort of how you end up as a novelist engaging and being engaged by history. Which is somewhat different from seeing it as a dialectical relationship.

KRC: In other words, you are not intending to rewrite history. But there is an interpretative posture you take, a hermeneutic that asks us to look at history a different kind of way.

RB: Perhaps, there might be. But my main relation to historical materials is simply to appropriate them and use them in storytelling. My primary allegiance is to storytelling, the narrative that is necessitated by story, not history. That is a very different thing. But I think this perspective is true of most novelists who use historical materials. Not all, but most. Take Doctorow, for example. His use for it. Or Pynchon. Or DeLillo. You see a similar process there. I am using it to tell family stories. It always comes down to that for me.

KRC: You have alluded to myth in your discussion of history. What is curious to me, as a historian of religion, is that I accept the notion of myth as an energizing and compelling way of telling stories. It has essential and necessary elements for the individual but also for collective identities. And yet, somehow or another, as history and fiction merge, we get this notion of myth that carries an assumption of falsehood, as a story that is steering us away from what is meaningful and true.

RB: Well, I think of myth as empowering and defining. It basically operates for every population group to serve a basic, primitive function: defining what it is to be human and identifying the limits of our power. Myth is the narrative arc of our lives in terms that are connected to the perceivable realities of our lives. That is why the Greek myths don't work together for us anymore. We have to have nationalist myths. And religious myths are working less and less effectively. Although the film *The Passion of the Christ* seems to be flying in the face of what I just said.

A very hot topic in current social discourse, I could not resist asking Banks to elaborate his view of the film.

RB: That film is about its audience, as most slasher films are. It is a slasher movie for Christians. And there is a big component of homophobic, homoerotic S&M aspects. Mel Gibson justifies the film all the way to the bank, on religious terms. I won't go although my family, all born-again Christians, love it. But I won't go see the film. I am a practicing atheist.

To get the conversation back to novels, I asked Banks to speak specifically about Cloudsplitter *and inquired if it occupies its own narrative space in relation to history and testimony.*

RB: Well, maybe, but my own feeling about it is that it is a very basic story. It is an Abraham and Isaac story, from Isaac's point of view. That is its deepest stratum, I think. And the rest of it is built on top of that. My main concern was going to that part of the story and to use historical materials to tell that part of the story. It wasn't to rewrite history in order to clarify a particular historical period or issue or to retell or even correct the dominant or received version of that period and those issues. It was simply to tell, in a way that was for me interesting and insightful, the Abraham and Isaac story from Isaac's point of view. Because that was how I saw that story as a child. And that is the only way I can ever see it, even now—from the point of view of the child. I could never see it from Abraham's point of view. Even though Isaac loved his father.

KRC: But that posture is typical of your fiction. Rather than take the perpetrator's point of view, you take the victim's point of view. That is where you have the sympathetic (not empathetic) identification with the outsider, the marginalized. Which is really another version of history. I guess that is all I was trying to convey. That there are overlapping and competing narratives but some get heard and others do not.

RB: Yes, and we need all the narratives. In the end, it is interesting that historians have use for fiction that is primarily structural. They structure their work—historical narratives—after fiction, to give it a narrative dynamic. Otherwise it is just a shapeless accumulation of data. But the reverse is true for the novelist. The novelist has use for historians' work only in terms of the materials, the details, the characters, and the texture of it. The structure doesn't mean anything. Historical structure is all borrowed from fiction so why borrow it back? It is in the literary tradition to begin with. If I am interested in telling a story, really grappling with a powerful story, like Abraham and Isaac—a powerful father willing to sacrifice his son on principles—when I look around there is no better story than the story of John Brown and his sons, and in particular this one son, Owen Brown. So I could use the historical realities of John Brown's life and the issues there. There is no greater issue for me than to deal with that sacrifice, and race. John Brown is emblematic on these issues and these quandaries. So it was very easy to go and use those materials to tell this story. But there is a lot in it I made up, as you know. I tried to keep to the outline and the known conventions and historical realities, not in the interest of history but in the interest of plausibility. That is all that mattered to me. I couldn't violate what was conventionally known about the time or the biographies of the characters without blowing plausibility. But you do that in all fiction. I couldn't set a novel in New York City and have Broadway going from the Upper East Side to the Lower West Side. If I did that I would lose all plausibility, suspension of disbelief would break down.

KRC: So it is a question of how far you can carry your reader?

RB: Exactly. The same thing with history. I had to get the presidents right. I had to get the years in Kansas right. But I could also have John Brown listen to Ralph Waldo Emerson deliver his talk on heroism in a Charles Street meeting house, even though I know it never took place. I wanted those two characters there at the same time. You could see so much of John Brown's view of himself through his response to Emerson. But it was a fictional character's view of himself. So you can see what I am trying to get to here. This is a very different use of history that applies to a storyteller than is generally presumed. Historians and novelists are not colleagues, but we are collaborators in the larger sense, in the creation of mythology. Moviemakers, too, even most pop novels and movies participate in this process. It is a big, wide stream, this myth-making process.

KRC: Is that why you let your books be made into movies?

RB: Yes, that is part of it. I feel like I am involved with a big, wide cultural process. I have my little stream over here. But I don't mind swimming over to the left or right and trying it there, as long as I can have some measure of control and engagement with it.

KRC: It becomes an interesting metaphor for how your ideas can become part of a collaborative vision, in the way Gramsci describes creating a culture which is not just about one's own individual or original discoveries but how truth is diffused in a critical form, how ideas are socialized.

RB: Yes, that is good. And I am fairly conscious of that process and intentionally engaged in it, for better or worse. *Cloudsplitter* should be shooting next winter and spring. I didn't want to do it as a feature film. You cram it into two hours, have a big opening weekend and that is the end of it and it dribbles out over the years and you still have the same, racially divided audience that we are dealing with and that I am trying to overcome with this adaptation. I really wanted the film to overcome the divide, to reach a trans-racial audience. I didn't want it to be another story about race for white people or another story about race for black people that is shown during Black History Month. So I wanted to do it on TV (HBO) so it would get into people's homes. And you don't have to put them together in the same theatre. It will get in all homes—white, black, upper and working class. TV takes place in a more intimate space than the movies. Something really interesting to me, and I am not exactly sure what it implies, but people almost never dream about characters they have seen in a film, but they always dream about characters they know only through TV. Now that means to me that TV is a more intimate medium. As if a member of your household, a member of your family, were in your home. The characters on TV, we live with them. Going to the movies is really like going to a high church service.

KRC: So theatres provide the illusion of a communal experience without really providing it. Or, to extend the high church metaphor, it is sitting passively at mass rather than being taken over by the Holy Spirit!

RB: Yes, so I wanted to get this on TV for those reasons. And HBO let me put together a team of producers and writers, like Martin Scorsese, and Raoul Peck, who made the film on Lumumba. Peck is a close friend and partner. Getting him was great. A black director who is not American. He sees it from a whole different perspective. His parents fled Duvalier's Haiti and he was raised in Africa and educated in France. Now he lives in Brooklyn. He has enough historical and personal and intellectual distance on it to really see the whole story.

At this point the conversation partners discussed the situations in Haiti and Iraq, especially as they pertain to U.S. global responsibilities. Banks is an acutely informed and active citizen. I asked him to consider if the world today is ruled more by heat than light, a dichotomy I had drawn in my reading of John Brown as portrayed in Cloudsplitter, *where heat is passion and light is reflection and insight and Brown possesses more heat than light. Banks had previously described Brown as the first modern terrorist, a man of heat, so we continued to discuss the tension between heat and light as represented in world culture. When I asked if people were passionate today without the knowledge or the vision to know how to use it, Banks agreed.*

RB: Yes, that is right. We are in a post-ideological age and there isn't any governing or coherent ideology that we can all gather around. We have ended up with a dominant ideology that is made up of sound-bites like "free market democracy" that link capitalism and democracy together as if they were the same word or two sides of the same object. And that started back in the Reagan years and it was just repeated and repeated as a rationale and justification for every aspect of American governmentally driven and corporately driven policy.

KRC: It seems to me that when the conversation really got opened, with Johnson's vision of a Great Society, when we wanted to allow all these voices in and create a more complicated and rich and diverse image of America, was also when we started losing a shared voice or a unifying voice.

RB: Well, I am not so sure a unifying voice is such a great thing. We had one there from 9/11 until about three or four months ago.

KRC: Yes, but it was kind of tenuous don't you think? Perhaps a bit phony and insubstantial?

RB: Oh yes, thank goodness! But unifying voices always scare me anyhow. Crowd noise, I don't like all that chanting.

KRC: I agree, but doesn't there have to be something that motivates people to accomplish something together, especially in redressing issues of social injustice?

RB: Well, I think it goes back to our discussion of mythology—the shape of it and the meaning of it. You know I was in Cuba twice in the last year and a half. I had never been before although I had been all over the Caribbean and Africa, and when I got there one of the things that fascinated me was it was the first, the only, postcolonial slavery society I had ever been in where the dominant national mythology was not defined against colonialism and against slavery. Instead they were defining themselves in terms of the revolution. They had taken the revolution and turned it into a narrative with characters like Che and Fidel, with a sequence of events that begin when they are at the university and are arrested for protests against the Batista regime, to their going to Mexico, to their getting to the boat, the *Granma*, to landing in the Sierra Maestra and going into the mountains and coming down like Robin Hood, and so on. The whole history and narrative of the revolution and then of course the history as it falls out and these signal events like the Bay of Pigs and the Cuban missile crisis, and the immigration and the enemy outside, but it is all the revolution. This is not Marxist ideology. This is simple narrative mythology. It is totally empowering in a way. In a way that no postcolonial, post-slavery society has been empowered. And I said to myself, "Where the hell does this come from?" I went to the museum of the revolution there in Havana, this fantastic museum—they've got everything there, all the artifacts from the revolution. But then they have rooms and rooms of photographs, black and white, going back to the fifties, mostly guys. They are scruffy with beards, little neckties, but they are all posed with great historical self-consciousness, with their arms around each other, very intense and clear that they have taken this picture for the record even though they were only in their late teens and early twenties.

KRC: So they were conscious of building the narrative or myth all along?

RB: Yes, they were conscious of making history, of themselves in history. And I said, "What the hell do these pictures remind me of?" They totally reminded me of something. And then I realized what it was, because I had just spent a lot of time working on a film adaptation of Jack Kerouac's *On the Road*. They looked like the pictures of the Beats. I know that generation of American writers really well. I have been close enough to see the mythology of the Beats unfold, how and why it did. And it was a self-conscious creation of themselves as part of myth, right from the start.

KRC: Yes, and their sources of inspiration were mythological too.

RB: Absolutely. But so was this true in Cuba. The pictures of the Beats and the Cuban revolutionaries look alike. They are iconic. They meant them to be in a way. They have that self-consciousness, self-awareness I should say, that they were shaping literary history just as the revolutionaries were shaping Cuban history. They were really aware of making a record. It was striking. That creation of mythology is something I think most American writers have abandoned, that responsibility, that high ambition. The Beat generation of writers was the last generation of American writers who had that high ambition for themselves. It is the same ambition Poe, Hawthorne, Melville, Whitman, and Twain had. Now it is individualistic, not in a selfish and egoistic way, but there is no group identity or belief that you can change the world if you hang together. I don't think we have that sense of being able to change the world. I think we have to get there. The idea of creating myth or a national or a people's identity is a grander thing than what most writers are doing now. That sense of creating a national consciousness, what the nineteenth-century American writers were up to, even the best of the twentieth century. Those phrases wouldn't have sounded ridiculous in the past and they don't sound ridiculous in Joyce's mouth. You know, when Hawthorne says he wants to create an American literature that is truly American. When Melville says he wants to find a metaphor that defines everything. When Whitman sets out to create an American mythos. This is grandiose, but it is necessary.

KRC: I think now you are describing what I was trying to allude to before, about a shared language or narrative that complements and includes diversity without splitting people apart.

RB: Yes, I see that now. But the Beats and their predecessors, all of them, in some respects, were writing in reaction to the oppressiveness of their eras—sexual, racial, and all that. I recently saw an old "educational" documentary from the fifties about the South and I had forgotten all the stuff I had seen in high school that described the history of the southern plantation and its beauty. I was looking at it and saying, "you do that enough times and show that to enough kids—black and white—and people start to buy that shit wholesale." To break that down is so hard.

We discussed further issues related to southern mythology about the Civil War, including recent novelistic and film treatments, and our own experiences living and being educated in the South, and the lack of information made available to us about slavery. Banks concluded: "There is a conscious agenda across white America to rewrite the Civil War as political quarrel, to ignore the fact that African Americans and people like you and me still have to point out: that the war was really about slavery." After this our conversation digressed further into particulars about our shared obsession with John Brown and his iconography, and other pop culture figures, like Elvis, whom *we admire for their mythological traits. This discussion led us back to the Beats, their vision, and especially to Jack Kerouac. Banks concluded by sharing his own personal experience with his literary hero.*

RB: Late Kerouac was so tragic in a way. He was lost to alcohol and drugs. I had strong feelings of connection to that generation of writers and Kerouac is very touching to me. In the screenplay of *On the Road*, I treat the novel as a period piece. Most of us forget that it is set in 1948. It has a post-war innocence that is unavailable to us after 1968. There is a moment there where two white guys can roll up a pack of Luckys in their T-shirts and get in their cars and play music real loud and drive across the country and make love to a black woman and listen to jazz and really think they have gone to another planet. It is a kind of innocence that is really kind of wonderful and sweet and doomed. If you can show it as doomed, and not get nostalgic and sentimental about it, act as if it is something we can get back to, then it is something interesting dramatically and also relevant as well. As it happened I met Kerouac and spent a wild week with him in 1967, two years before he died. He showed up at my house in Chapel Hill with two Indians driving him. He didn't know how to drive. He was very sick, physically and mentally. At moments you could see why he was so attractive. He was Memory Babe [his nickname] because he could recall everything he had read or listened to or seen. And he was a wonderful, radical, barbarian man. Then in the next moment he was this idiot anti-Semite. He was in a room of worshipful acolytes who were all political activists in the civil rights movement, anti-war veterans, young artists and writers, at his feet. And it was incredibly jarring to see both sides of him, and to see his visible pain. So I framed the script of *On the Road* through this story, the story of a young guy, me, who meets him at this point in his life. It is set in two times and places—the time of *On the Road* and threaded through it scenes from 1968, the year of the loss of America's innocence, like Kerouac who is a lost soul at this point.

An Interview with Russell Banks

Valentin Locoge/2005

From *Cercles.com* (April 24, 2005). Reprinted by permission.

VL: African-American culture has been an essential part of your writing, but in your latest two novels, *Cloudsplitter* and *The Darling* you seem to focus more particularly on the theme of slavery; why is that?

RB: That's sort of the central drama in the history of race in the United States, and in the entire hemisphere really. It'd be unavoidable, you couldn't step around it, not dealing with it some way or another. What I'm really interested in, in the long haul, is trying to enter that history of race from different points of views, from different periods, and in a sense write different chapters in it. *The Book of Jamaica* deals with it in the Caribbean, *Continental Drift* in some ways deals with it as it collides in Florida and in the Southern part of the United States in contemporary time, and *Rule of the Bone* deals with it from the point of view of an American boy in the 1990s. I'm dealing with it in different ways, it's just unavoidable, you can't get away from the issue of, and the history of, and the effects of, slavery in the United States. It's the residue of racism we still struggle with.

VL: In those two novels, you offer a view of white guilt towards slavery, but at two different periods of time; how does the theme of slavery evolve between the two periods?

RB: With *Cloudsplitter*, what white anti-slavery Americans were dealing with was the profound frustration, even the desperation, that they experienced in the pre–Civil War era. They sensed that there was no way for them to eliminate slavery except through violence. It's something very difficult for us to grasp today, because Americans see the history of the pre–Civil War era looking back through the lens of the Civil War, so it's very difficult for us to imagine what it must have been like when you didn't know the Civil War was coming, anymore than today we think there's a civil war around the corner. We deal with our present realities as best as we can, and as we perceive them. That point of view, going to that era—the 1840s and 1850s—through the eyes of Owen Brown, John Brown, and others in the radical wing of the anti-slavery movement, was very important for me. I wanted to see what it looked like to them and why they behaved the way they behaved, and they seemed intimately linked. Whereas for *The Darling* of course we're looking at a post-colonial world, and a formal denial of responsibility here in the United States for any events that take place in West Africa particularly, and Liberia even more particularly. That's another kind of blindness we have sitting here today. I suppose both of them are historical fictions in that they are about events, in the case of *The Darling*, in the near past, and, in the case of *Cloudsplitter* in the distant past. In both cases there is a kind of denial first of all of the scarifying historical experience preceding the Civil War, and then in the second case the denial of any colonial relationship to Africa.

VL: How present is the theme of slavery in contemporary American culture? In fiction?

RB: It doesn't seem to engage the imagination of contemporary writers, or should I say of contemporary *white* writers. It does obviously engage the imagination of contemporary black writers. Witness Toni Morrison or any black writer you may want to list. It's a central theme of their work one way or the other, either slavery itself in the case of Toni Morrison's *Beloved*, or the repercussions, and the aftermath of slavery in the case of so many others down from Ishmael Reed, to John Edgar Wideman, to Gloria Naylor. It's central to their writing, and it's central to mine of course and a few other white writers perhaps. Generally the issue of slavery, and its history, and its aftermath does not engage the imagination of American artists and intellectuals, other than African-Americans, because there's a kind of denial operating in the society generally with regard to that history. We like to think that was then and this is now, it's over now, let's get beyond it, let's get on with our white lives. That's why I guess I'm engaged in it, I'm not engaged in it because, obviously, I'm not African-American, but I'm not engaged in it either because I bear some kind of obsessive fix on it. It's really because I think it is the central story in the United States. It's what distinguishes us from so many other countries in the world, and I'm engaged with it because of the degree to which we deny that. This is where a novelist tends to work; anyhow it's in that part of our experience that we're in denial of.

VL: Hannah Musgrave, your Darling, has emerged from the turbulent 1960s, where she was very much involved in radical groups, and she seems to need to make amends, as far as the slavery heritage is concerned. However, when she goes to Liberia, and marries an African politician, she eventually finds herself unable to embrace his culture and that of his ancestors. Is she just realizing that there are cultural differences we cannot overcome?

RB: I'm not so sure she realizes that at first, because she's experiencing it not on an ideological or intellectual level, but she's experiencing it in an entirely personal, subjective way, a very particularized way, which is how we generally experience these things anyhow if we're going to do it authentically. I don't think she is that conscious of it at the time, I was conscious of it in the process of writing it of course. There's that one episode where she goes into the bush with Woodrow, before she's married him, to meet his people as he calls them. She's locked out figuratively and almost literally, first she circles the compound, she can't get in until someone finally escorts her underneath the palisade and into the compound. Then she's repelled by their dietary habits, if you will, and flees. That's a kind of figurative representation of her being left out, and that's how she experiences it. Of course this is not unusual, and she could have turned into, as she says it, an "anthropologist of my own family." She doesn't do that partly I suppose because of its difficulty, and she senses the inauthenticity that that would impose upon her. It's an intriguing question really, because the character of Hannah is a complex and mixed figure. She's like any of us I suppose in that she's conflicted, and self-contradictory in many ways. It makes some readers a little anxious about the book and her character, because they can't easily like her or easily dislike her. Whenever that question comes up I always say, what about Madame Bovary? She's a little difficult at times too!

VL: Do you consider that there are barriers that prevent people from understanding that even somebody with her background *cannot break*?

RB: I'm not sure we can't break them, but we can't break them easily. We certainly can't break them by means of ideology or intellection. We can't think our way through those barriers. We have to live the life. It happens when someone wants to understand what it is to be French, and they live in France for a while, they may even marry a French person, and they still can't get there. We're talking Western Europeans here, versus North Americans. Same thing when a French person comes here. I have many friends like that, who've been living here for a while, and they still, on some level, don't get it. I suppose one can though. I lived in Jamaica for two years in the 1970s, and brought to that experience all kinds of liberal attitudes and ideologies and principles and ethics and so forth to the process. But I came away puzzled, frustrated, unable to penetrate what it was like really to be a Jamaican.

VL: You mention the Fuama incident, when Hannah visits Woodrow's people, but she is the one who refuses to endorse the culture of Woodrow's ancestors. She steps out of it when they seem to welcome her. Is this a trace of "internalized racism" on her part, of the kind of "internalized racism" that is really inherent to the 1960s ways, and that has to be dealt with somehow?

RB: I don't know if I would go so far as to say it's an internalized racism. The way I feel is—and this is a side of the novel actually—if you are raised in a culture that is itself racist or sexist, the only way you can override that cultural default is through an ongoing, constant critique, and attack, on your own consciousness, to the degree that that's formed by the culture. It has to be ongoing. It's not something that you can say, "Oh, I see," and that's the end of it, because the pressure of your culture is constant and ongoing. It's not something that just hits you when you're a child and when you're raised in a particular context in family or community. It's ongoing, and steady. I don't think that's peculiar to the 1960s, or any other time, and I'm of that generation of course. It seems to me that one of the virtues of that era—and there were many despite the revisionist view of the 1960s and 1970s that's prevalent today—is the willingness of that generation, the whites in that generation, to confront their own racism, however ineptly and inadequately, and to confront their own sexism too, however ineptly and inadequately. That is to me an admirable thing given the norms of our culture. It is something that did not take deep root. It's not something that present generations are willing to do, or able to do it seems. I don't want to over-criticize, just because that particular generation of radical Americans was in many ways self-deluded, and naïve, and self-absorbed. Despite all that, there were these virtues, and I was trying to get that mix in *The Darling*. Yes, there was some really wonderful idealism in that era, and it has driven the people of that era. It has controlled and organized their lives as they've gotten older too. It's not for nothing that Hannah is running an organic farm with only women in upstate New York. In fact that's how many of the radicals of that era ended up in their sixties. They're living in cities like Cleveland, organizing welfare-moms, or something like that, or might get an AIDS clinic set up here in Portland perhaps. You see them all across the country with a grizzled kind of gray ponytail and granny glasses. You've got to admire those people, what they have done, even though historical shifts and changes have made it impossible for them to change society in any radical way, they've kept those ideas and ideals alive. That's going to prove important down the line, to the young particularly. If we let those ideas die, those ideals die, as history shifts so fast—in this country particularly—and people forget so quickly, then there will be no way to resurrect those ideals and ideas and apply them further down the line. *The Darling* is a way of both acknowledging the historical and social reality on the one hand—and the change between the 1960s, 1970s, and today—but also of affirming a few of the central ideals of that era as well.

VL: When Hannah/Dawn tries to learn the native language in Liberia, she explains that whenever the natives did not want her to understand what they were saying they simply spoke faster or changed tones. At that point we realize that by its very humanness language is a quality she almost totally mistrusts. The only pure communications she has during the novel are with her chimpanzees, and her father when they have a wordless conversation with eye language on his deathbed. Why has language fallen so low in her mind?

RB: I'm not sure I have the answer to that. There's a sense that even though I wrote the book, I don't necessarily understand it any better than anybody else. It's funny you should ask because I'm looking here at this coffee cup, it has a quote from Roger Ebert. I had another one earlier this morning with a quote from Quincy Jones, the musician. I have a quote coming that's taken from *The Darling*. It's kind of funny that five million coffee cups will have a couple of sentences taken from *The Darling*, but it's very much about that, about silence. At some point Hannah says that silence is golden. She believes if we couldn't speak then we wouldn't be killing each other. She's thinking about the other species, but particularly chimpanzees. They seem so human to her, except for the inability to speak. There is, I suppose, underlying the very process of writing a book, writing that book or any book for that matter, a certain mistrust of language that any writer has. If you write long enough, you begin to realize how slippery language is, how manipulative it is. Even though you're a practitioner, you're one of those who is manipulating and utilizing language, and depending upon it for your life and for any kind of coherence. It nonetheless needs to be mistrusted. In Hannah's particular case, there's first the language of family. She does talk about how her mother talks and how her mother reverses the polarity. So when she wants to be seen as talking about someone else, she's in fact talking about herself in a narcissistic reversal of language. She uses that to reveal her mother's narcissism and failures of character. There's also her father who uses the language of an expert parent—he is a world expert on raising children—yet it is in some way always self-aggrandizing. Then there's the language of ideology, which she regularly talks about, how they used to talk about a revolution, talk about imperialism, and so forth. It's as if those terms and words are no longer functioning, yet they once believed in them. So, yes, she mistrusts language throughout. It is a theme, not a central theme, but it's certainly a theme in the novel: the ability of language to mislead and exploit us, and how language allows us to exploit others too.

VL: An interpretation of the opening sentence of the novel could be that her "human" dreams are not considered dreams anymore, and only when she dreams of the chimpanzees—her "dreamers" as she calls them—does she acknowledge it as a dream. What brings her so close to the chimpanzees?

RB: It's hard to know. Again, I have to keep falling back on saying that I don't really always understand why things end up the way they do in a novel. I can almost only revert to my own experience of chimpanzees from when I first started spending time with them, which was before I really began the book. Wanting to write the book reinforced my desire to spend time with chimpanzees, and spending time with chimpanzees reinforced my desire to write the book. When I first encountered them face to face in a chimp sanctuary just over the border in Quebec, I became friendly with the woman who runs it and visited fairly regularly. She has between fifteen and twenty chimpanzees that she has saved, mostly from medical experimentation and some from the entertainment industry. They are very powerful presences. It's very difficult to get around them, to ignore them and to objectify them. There's a profound connection that I think is unavoidable between chimpanzees and humans, if you allow yourself to be responsive to it. I had that connection very quickly and consistently. So when they appeared in the novel, it was not difficult for me to imagine—given her circumstances, and her background, and given her reasons for being, given all that, which is quite different from my own—that she would become fixated on them. They would replace her inability to connect to human beings, her sense of isolation, and her otherness. I guess that's why they're so central. I don't mean to have any large symbolic meaning, although there no doubt is. I don't have a scheme or some kind of emblematic grid that I was trying to lay down on the text; it's somewhat different from that—a looser and more intuitive process.

VL: Why have her dreams stopped belonging to the human sphere?

RB: Well I think the pain, and the shame. She says, "My story is a story of too late." It's too late to go back and redo her past. You can't redo your past. At another place she says, "My story is a story of abandonment and betrayal," which includes her sons, her husband, her husband's world, her parents, but also, as it turns out, the chimpanzees. She has a lot to be ashamed of from her point of view, not from mine because I don't judge her. With the opening of the novel I was hoping I would just open the door of the beginning of her confrontation with her past. The book is essentially one long confession.

You can't do it all at once. Every now and then she pauses and says, "I can't tell you that now, but I'll tell you later, maybe I'll get to it, maybe I won't," because it's gradual, a process, as it would be for any of us who had a complex and painful past, as she had.

VL: A consequence of the abandonment of speech is that she appears cold both as a woman and as a mother, something she keeps denying throughout the novel. Why does she have to keep denying it?

RB: I think it's because she isn't simply cold, or she wouldn't be able to tell this story. She's conflicted, she's afraid, and angry on certain psychological levels. She's removed from people like her because of her ethical and political views, and she's removed from people who are unlike her because of culture, race, and class. In a sense she is an isolated person, and I think that's why she appears cold, but she's not cold. She's unable to express that except in the course of the novel, otherwise you wouldn't have any feelings for her.

VL: Has her loss of confidence in language anything to do with it?

RB: Not necessarily. As a character, as a human being, she's a kind of borderline narcissist. There are very few characters in literature, at least in the West, who we could call a narcissist. Madame Bovary is one of them actually. There's a Chekhov short story called "The Darling." I don't know what it's called it in French, in fact I advised my translator to find the Chekhov story "The Darling," but he hasn't been able to find it in French. That woman in the Chekhov story and Madame Bovary are the only two figures I can think of in literature who are narcissists and who are also sympathetic at the same time. I was attempting to do that with Hannah. It's a kind of person that many of us find it easy to love at first and then difficult to embrace in an ongoing way; and yet it's a painful kind of narcissistic consciousness to experience. I think those two works of fiction grasp that, and I was attempting to do that as well. If you're a full-blown narcissist like Hannah's mother, it's almost impossible to feel sympathy for her except in a detached way; but Hannah's not that full-blown. She is struggling with it and under certain circumstances she could be like her mother.

VL: At the end of the book, she sadly witnesses the rewriting of American History after 9/11. She defines herself at some point as a "battered woman [. . .] victimized by ideology." If we relate those two events, can we say that here again language is turning against her because History is not a truth, but a matter of point of view, and it can be erased and modified, and more importantly *rewritten*, to suit ideologies?

RB: I don't know if I can follow quite that far with regard to the issue of mistrusting language. I think you are projecting something into the text that

I had no great ambition for. It's a theme I don't argue with you there—but it's not a central theme for me. These things do end up in a book regardless of the author's intentions, so I'm not going to argue too hard with you about it. For me the central theme, and it's one I've gone back to in other books in other ways, is the unintended consequences of good intentions. She is in many ways emblematic even of American foreign policy if you want. Today in other areas of the world, especially in a post-9/11 world, we are suddenly filled with good intentions and are killing people as a result and probably radically altering our society in the process in a very dangerous way. You can look at the history of Liberia for instance: the creation of Liberia. In its conception there were good intentions lying behind it. There was a nefarious and a dark side to those good intentions, as there almost inevitably are, because pure motives don't exist. The bloody civil war that started in 1980 is in fact the unintended consequence of good intentions, which started in the 1820s. Let's send them back to Africa, make the world safe and pretty, make it civilized and Christianized, and at the same time solve our race problem here in the United States with all those free blacks appearing in the streets of Philadelphia or New York. That to me is the central theme running through the book. I like to think of Hannah as emblematic of that; her life is that, the good intentions of the 1960s and 1970s, and the unintended consequences of it that she experiences very directly. Her engagement with the chimpanzees, her hope to save them, leads to their death. Instead of freeing them into the jungle she puts them on an island to save them, but they can't swim, so that imprisons them as well.

VL: Why did you choose to include this massive process of historical fictionalization in the novel, as in the end it's only Hannah Musgrave's truth; *The Darling* is still a work of fiction and should be read as such?

RB: It does have historical figures in it, like Charles Taylor, Samuel Doe, and John Kerry who was in the text before he ran. Kerry was an interesting figure to me. I knew him in the 1970s; he was an extremely promising young man, and a very brave one back then. He was just the kind of figure that seemed to be, like Hannah in some way, emblematic of that theme. He is someone who—over the period of twenty-five or thirty years in between his youth and now—had become in many ways a different person, so I thought he would be appropriate to be in this novel. Then of course he ran for president to prove my point by the kind of candidate he became. Having historical figures brings several things. I could have excluded all that, by setting the story in a fictional African country. Actually I even thought of it. I talked to a friend of mine who was raised in Congo, a man who understands and knows the history of Liberia very well. I told him I was thinking of putting this story in a fictional African country, which is generally what's done. Then I thought, "Why would I do that?" I could be afraid that someone would draw connections to this historical reality. Well I want those connections, it's part of the context. If I were writing a fiction that I would set in New York City in the 1960s or 1970s, I wouldn't exclude the historical realities or geography of that place. I wouldn't call it "Metropolis," or "Megalopolis," I would call it New York City. There's no reason not to do that. The more complicated decision comes with regard to using historical figures in a story, as I also did in *Cloudsplitter*. Historical figures show up all the time in that novel, like Frederick Douglass. Even Ralph Waldo Emerson shows up, he makes a brief appearance. Once again I could have excluded those historical figures, but why shouldn't I put them in? It is highly likely that they would have met each other. In fact they did; I know John Brown did meet Ralph Waldo Emerson, but I don't know that he heard Ralph Waldo Emerson read that particular lecture on heroism at Charles Street Meeting House. I know he met Frederick Douglass on several occasions, and Douglass was a big part of his plan. Same thing if you go to a small country like Liberia and you're a white American. If you marry a minor minister in the government, you're going to end up meeting everybody in the elite class at some point or other, including the president. What am I going to do? Make up a name for the president? Once you commit yourself to a certain level of realism in fiction, then your problems are primarily those of plausibility. It seems only plausible that her parents would know John Kerry and go on a whitewater rafting trip with him and William Sloane Coffin, the great reverend; why not? So there they are, present mainly out of a desire for plausibility, but also out of a desire to utilize the iconic quality that certain figures bring. If you evoke Che Guevara in a story of fiction, who has such an iconic quality, just the mere mention of his name invokes a visual image. It invokes rich associations. Same thing if you evoke Charles Taylor. You see a face, well if you've been reading the newspapers, there is a figure to that—same with John Kerry. A public person has this sort of iconic figure, and there was a desire to tap into that as well.

VL: What effect did you intend to produce when Hannah concludes that her story is irrelevant—a conclusion that also puts into question the very purpose of your novel? Why write the story at all?

RB: Of course that's her perspective, that she sees in the context of the unfolding events after September 11, 2001. She's telling the story, the story about her return to Africa, and her return to the United States from Africa takes place over that period. She's returning right on the same day in fact.

Her view of it is that it redefines American history, and she sees it as one of those hinges. Her history in the way it is connected to American history is really of the past, of the preceding era. Then there was a historical shift, and she's no longer connected to that post-9/11 world. My own personal view is somewhat different from that, which perhaps answers the question, "Why bother to write the book?" because it does subvert the intentionality of the book. I don't feel as though I'm merely and only and solely connected to the era that precedes 9/11. I'm obviously living in a post-9/11 world, and writing in a post-9/11 world. What has happened is that I view the years leading up to 9/11 differently as a result of that event. I do think the world has changed. You could not live as she lives in a post-9/11 world, you could not travel the way she travels, as you could not engage in the forms of opposition she did as a young woman. Today the kind of terrorist acts and the profoundly engaged opposition that she engaged in couldn't take place simply because of the security apparatus put in place since 9/11, and because of the technology that exists today. She notes that in the days before computers you could slip and slide right through the net—you couldn't track people, nor was there a particular desire to track people in so many numbers. Now in this post-9/11 world her principle of opposition to the government, to its policies, and the ways in which it was expressed could not occur. I really believe that we are in a different era in that way. We are in a much more closed-down society, a much more top-down controlled society, and a much more carefully secured and enforced society. I'm trying to watch the shift. It's a tectonic shift in our culture right now. As a novelist—as a citizen really—I feel one of my responsibilities is to track those shifts. I'm sixty-five years old, so I have a long memory compared to kids coming up. One of the things a novelist does is preserve memory because we forget so fast. I was thinking the other day that we're now nearly four years on after 9/11. Someone coming out of high school into college today was probably thirteen or fourteen when 9/11 occurred. His or her idea of society is shaped by those years; they have no memory of anything before. Therefore the security apparatus you go through at an airport, the tracking of people, the profiling of people, the idea that somewhere out there, there are a billion people who hate us for our freedom all seem normal. These are normal conceptions of the world because there's nothing to compare it to in their lives. In another four years, anyone entering adult life at ages eighteen, nineteen, or twenty would have been nine or ten years old when 9/11 occurred. Add another four years, and then they will not even have been born in 2001. That means there is no memory left for those kids. What I'm trying to do—and I think any novelist is trying to do that in some ways—is to preserve that memory. I have a very clear memory going back to the 1950s, and I don't want it lost because there was a difference. I'm not being nostalgic or sentimental about it. There is a structural difference.

VL: When did you start writing *The Darling*?

RB: It was right about 9/11, but I was bringing the materials forward before that. The framing of it around 9/11 was intentional from the very beginning. I was aware that this leads right into that era when she leaves for Africa, so I set it deliberately in late August 2001 when she wakes up that morning and begins this return. I didn't know for sure how it would play into the story, but I wanted it leading to that point. I didn't want to write about 9/11 as such. I wanted it to be the context, sort of the shadow that lurks in the background. You're not even aware of it as you read the book, but the information is there if you want to find it in the opening pages.

VL: The book opens with her dream of Africa, and when it closes she says her story has no relevance in a "larger world;" is that a call to keep looking at this larger world?

RB: Well, again, we must distinguish between her perspective and my own. She believes at the end of the book that her story has no meaning in a larger world today because it's a life that no one could live again. I don't believe that, or I wouldn't have written the novel. My own personal intention is obviously engaged by the larger world today. I think her story is relevant and does have meaning in a larger world. It certainly does for me personally. We have to make a distinction between the author's perspective on the world, which is represented by the book as a whole, and the narrator's perspective on the world, which is represented by her subjective experience of her own life.

Russell Banks, Toulouse 2006

David Roche/2006

Interview conducted June 17, 2006. Previously unpublished. Used with permission.

DR: Let's start with *Hamilton Stark*. How did the novel come about?

RB: Well you know it's really hard to go back that far and remember the origins of a book, when it wasn't a clear moment, where something came to me and I said: "Ah-ha," one of those moments. And I think that one evolved out of something more mysterious to me, and gradual, too, at the time. I think its origins lie in many ways where the origins for *Affliction* lie. It's definitely a precursor to *Affliction* in my mind. In obvious ways, certain themes are picked up and developed differently and I think more effectively later. And it was material that was, at that time—which probably would have been early seventies, when I was first getting into that book—I was not really ready to deal with. It was too emotionally close to me, too historically close to me, and was rooted in my relationship with my father, his relationship with his father, and certain events that had transpired that had kind of *clarified* those things for me in the previous decade, in my twenties. And so the material was difficult of access for me, and yet there was a kind of compulsive need to write about it, to put it into fiction, exactly. The kind of attraction-repulsion that I felt for a character *like* my father—that I myself felt for my father—and to find a way to do that was very difficult at that time for me, and yet I found it irresistible. So I think that partly explains the elaborate formality and artifice of the book because, in fact, that was the only kind of dance I could do to get close to the material. And I'm not sure I *did* get close to the material, either. I mean I haven't looked at that book in years and years. Literally, decades.

DR: Did you re-read it before writing *Affliction*?

RB: No I didn't, I didn't go back to it after that, no. I don't think I went back to it after it was published, or maybe for a few occasions where I read from it or something like that in public, but otherwise I didn't go back to it and re-read it. It was a learning experience for me, the book where I learned an awful lot about writing fiction, both what to do and what not to do, for my-self. And a lot about who I was as a writer, what I was eager to do and able to do, and what I was merely *challenged* to do, and for various reasons, some of them neurotic or based in insecurity, or defensiveness. So my relation to that book today, and has been for some time, is really an ambivalent one. I see it as an apprentice work that I probably had to write in order to write a later book—to get certain monkeys off my back. But I don't regard it in any way as a successful book, as artistically successful, or even for that matter in dealing with the theme I was trying to approach, which is basically betrayal, abandonment, violence, alcoholism, and so on. I don't think I was able to get close enough to make it really meaningful in any way, for myself, artistically. But it doesn't mean I don't *value* that book in my own sort of evolution as a writer. I think that I do very much. It wasn't a *wasted* effort for me. It was necessary effort, and that was valuable to me.

But so far as its origins go, it's very much—but so was *Affliction*—rooted in New Hampshire, in my childhood memories of New Hampshire, physi-cal memories, I mean, geographic and physical, and then also historical and geological, and some of that layering that's in that book appears in a more easeful way, in a more natural way in *Affliction* later on. They make an inter-esting contrast of study, I think, to put the two together to try to see them as a two-step progress, you know, and see what is left of *Hamilton Stark* that shows up in *Affliction* in a different garb, in a more naturalistic format, and contrast them. Some people really love it, you know, *Hamilton Stark*, really hover over it. I'm always sort of amazed when they do.

DR: Were you in New England or Jamaica when you wrote it?

RB: No, I was partly in Jamaica, partly in New England. I think I wrote it mostly in New England, in New Hampshire, before I went down to Jamaica in '74. I was teaching at the University of New Hampshire, living in North-wood, and I think I'm pretty sure that's where I did most of it. And I submit-ted it to Houghton Mifflin, to an editor there, a very nice woman named Daphne O'Neil. She was a junior editor, and she tried to convince them to publish it, and they didn't want to publish it. I was about to say to let it go. I mean it had been around to several other publishers, but she was the one who was the most eager to publish it, but she just couldn't convince her editorial board to take it on. This would have been around '74. I forgot what the copyright date was. I think it's—

DR: '78.

RB: Is it '78 before it finally turned up? So I made the round to several dif-ferent publishers, quite a few I imagine, and none of them wanted to take it on although there was a great deal of interest in it for various reasons. But it was not an inviting book. It wasn't funny; it was in a mode of writing which was fashionable enough at the time, but it had a serious darkness in it, and I think that that was perceived as inappropriate, almost, given the form, and I think they were right. I mean I think what they were sensing was the kind of conflicting demands that I was making on myself and on the book, trying to write it. I hadn't found the appropriate form for the material is what I'm saying, and I think that that was sensed. Until I was in Jamaica—now that would have been around '75, maybe '76—and Daphne wrote me again that she had a small list of suggested edits; she had been re-reading it. She said, "Would you be willing to rewrite it?" It wasn't a radical rewrite, but small changes, as I recall. "I think there's been a change here at the top and I think I might be able to get it through this time." So I was sort of by then reaching a point where I would as soon park it, and start again on something else and not worry about it anymore. Because I already had another novel in the drawer that I had done that with and I was glad I had done it: parked it. So I said, "Well, all right." It seemed like reasonable changes and useful ones. And so I went ahead and did the editing, the changes that she suggested, and then she took it back, and after months and months, I remember kind of finally just throwing up my hands and saying: "I don't want to talk to her anymore. She's got a fantasy that's never going to be realized and I don't want to catch it." But eventually she did talk them into publishing it and they did, and it was nicely done and nicely published; it got around. It was not a bad event in my life to publish it.

And as soon as it was over, it was over in terms of my relationship to the book. I'm glad now I didn't park it, though, really. I mean it's not something I'm embarrassed by in any way. And I'm glad that it's out there, and exists. It has its readership and so forth. But I don't use it; I use it as a marker in a way, a marker of maybe the end of my apprenticeship.

DR: Were you consciously parodying eighteenth-century novel-writing in that novel, or maybe Edgar Poe and Nabokov? It kind of reminds me of *Pale Fire*.

RB: Yeah, but you know I was never a great fan of *Pale Fire* or of Nabokov, but I certainly was a huge fan of eighteenth-century fiction, and I was certainly modeling a lot of it on that, consciously modeling it on eighteenth-century English fiction. With an overlay of American classical fiction as well, I mean that was where I was, that's what I had immersed myself in for a number of years by then. So that was certainly an influence. Poe, no. I mean there's a kind of florid quality to the prose that I think could suggest Poe or Nabokov, for that matter. But that was in a way in spite of myself. Or it was perhaps more likely to be influenced by Hawthorne, who at that time was an important writer to me. But Hawthorne seen through a modern or postmodernist gaze, really, although he didn't use that particular expression then. But I've never really had a great affection for Nabokov.

DR: What I had in mind was the relationship between the narrator and the character, and all the ambivalence and homosexual connotations.

RB: Yes, that was there, but I think that was more coincidence than actually modeling. I remember having long, not arguments so much, but discussions with friends, because *Pale Fire* was such a warmly embraced book by a certain kind of intellectual in the United States in that period in the seventies, mostly academic intellectuals, and I think I was resisting that pull, in a contrarian way, and backing away from it, not wanting to be drawn along. Even so I can, of course, appreciate the pyrotechnics and the intellectual gymnastics that were being used, but I wasn't that deeply attracted to it anyway.

DR: Nevertheless, re-reading *Hamilton Stark* in the light of the first interview in the book, the Constance Rooke interview, it seems that back then you fully endorsed postmodernist fiction. Was there a sort of tension at that time—and maybe that's why you feel that *Hamilton Stark* doesn't work—between your desire to endorse postmodernism and your content which is closer to realism? And maybe because realism wasn't really *à la mode* back then, you were trying to find a middle ground?

RB: I think that's definitely true, but it wasn't because realism wasn't in fashion, particularly. I think it's more complicated than that for me. I think when I became a writer, when I *wanted* to become a writer, first started imagining myself as a writer, I was doing it from a rather insecure and defensive position, coming out of my particular background and needing therefore to affirm to myself, not necessarily to anybody else, that I was smart enough, that I was literate enough, educated enough, and sufficiently intellectual and so on, to actually do this, to achieve this. And alongside that was, I think, a kind of nagging fear that, when it came right down to it, I didn't really have the material, that the stories that I could tap into, and the people that I grew up with and knew, and the lives that I knew intimately, weren't sufficiently meaningful material for fiction. So there was a kind of defensiveness and insecurity that motivated me as well, rather than a desire to be fashionable. Certainly I wasn't courting success in that regard. But even so, maybe it was fashionable amongst intellectuals, so-called postmodernist fiction, but it wasn't fashionable among general readers, you know: it was really a niche fiction, always, at its most popular. But it was a particularly intellectual and

highbrow niche, and I think I needed to convince myself that I was appropriate to be initiated into that niche myself before I could begin then to
say: "Okay, stop worrying about that. What do you really want to do here?
What's your natural gift? And what's your natural impulse? What's the real
shape of your imagination?" Because I started late in a sense, not really at
an *older age*, but I did not, growing up as an adolescent, think of myself as
an intellectual. It was only something I came at a little later through the
backdoor, and I was walking *backwards* when I came through the backdoor
so I could get out fast if I had to, you know. I didn't stride manfully into the
library [*laughs*]; I timidly peeked in. So I think that those were all factors.
But you're quite right: I mean there was this deep suspicion that maybe this
is not the right path for me to go, given my instinctive response to the world,
you know what really moves me and terrifies me.

DR: We'll come back to this later, but I think you actually found a way to
articulate both the realistic content *and* the postmodernist artifice—

RB: You do in that book?

DR: No, later on.

RB: Yes, later on; I agree with you. I think that I found that it was a very useful way to structure fiction, and that it was an *unavoidable* aspect of fiction,
not necessarily an *undesirable* aspect of fiction. Instead of using it as an
exo-skeleton, I managed to interiorize it, and realize that it was very useful
to me *personally* to know this, but it wasn't necessarily useful to the reader.
I began to realize that, actually, in a very conscious way with *The Book of
Jamaica* where you can begin to see this. I think there's a very big jump,
an evolutionary jump between *Hamilton Stark* and *The Book of Jamaica*,
and also with *Trailerpark* in that same period. Those two books came after
Hamilton Stark, and they came after the period where I was living in Jamaica, and I really think a lot changed in that period. And in some ways, the
truth of the matter is, publication of that book, *Hamilton Stark* at Houghton
Mifflin, it sounds like a small and maybe a vain thing, and a foolish thing,
but for someone like me at that age it was a very important thing. Publishing at Houghton Mifflin in Boston then, meeting with my editor, and by
then I had graduated to a senior editor, Robbie McColey. And you know it's
Hawthorne's publisher, it was the same damn building Hawthorne used to
go into to meet his editor. I was conscious of all this, and the book coming
out as it did, and it got generally good responses where it *was* reviewed, and
it was reviewed favorably by and large. And I think it got me a couple of
fellowships and things like that, it got me a job teaching. I think that it was
a *tremendous* boost to my confidence, and liberated me in a certain way to

go ahead and take a deeper plunge, to trust my instincts more afterwards. It was a form of endorsement, validation, really, that liberated me and allowed me to move on, with a certain amount of, not swagger, but a certain amount of confidence that I hadn't had up to that point.

DR: You pointed out the similarities between *Hamilton Stark* and *Affliction*, but structurally they're very different. It seems to me that the first kind of circles round the character [*laughs*], whereas *Affliction* starts right in the car with the main character.

RB: Yeah.

DR: So how do you see that evolution? Because *Affliction* is still very complexly structured, it's just that it's disguised.

RB: Oh yeah. And some of it's overt, too. There are several themes that are replaced slightly differently in each time. There's an unreliability of the narrator; it's a minor character telling a story about another character. Actually, those are similarities to *Hamilton Stark*. But the texture of the prose is different; the narrative is a much more straightforward linear narrative; the characters are not burlesques in any way, whereas they are in *Hamilton Stark* to some considerable degree. There isn't any self-parody going on; there's not any elaborate references to other texts, yet they're *there*. I mean there are a lot of allusions to other texts in *Affliction*, but they're only for me, they're not for anybody else necessarily. You can find them if you want, but they're the secret structure to the novel. What's the nature of the question, I'm not sure?

DR: Well, in *Hamilton Stark* the main character is the narrator. *Hamilton Stark* may be the title, but we never actually approach him, we just circle round, until the subject that is Hamilton Stark is actually split into the "100 Selected, Uninteresting Things Done and Said by Hamilton Stark." Whereas in *Affliction*, Wade Whitehouse does occupy the center as the main character.

RB: Yeah, he does, but it's through the gaze of a minor character, always, who is the unreliable narrator. And so, there's a scrib between the reader and Wade Whitehouse, and that scrib is Rolfe Whitehouse, the brother. I felt the necessity to have that for perhaps some of the same reasons that I felt the necessity for the much more *elaborate* distancing of *Hamilton Stark*, but I discovered it differently. In fact, I wrote 150 or more pages of *Affliction* without Rolfe as the narrator. It was a straightforward third-person narrator. There was no intervention, no speculation, no unreliability at all; it was dead-on realism. And I got there and, at 150 pages or so, you know this is really *deadening*. It's also condemning of the character; it is not redemptive of the character. I'm forced to see him in a way that turns him into a kind of Frankenstein, the monster.

DR: The monster.

RB: Yeah. Not the doctor, but the monster.

DR: Doesn't he still remain a monster if Rolfe is the narrator?

RB: No, because Rolfe loves him. And if you can talk about a monster from the point of view of someone who loves him, then he isn't monstrous anymore. It's the same thing in *Cloudsplitter* with John Brown: if you can see him from the point of view of his son who loves him, then he's not a monster. Still, you can see his behavior is kind of monstrous, but you end up compelled to see him through the eyes of someone who loves him and that changes how you see him, I think. And that was what I realized when I was about 150 pages into this thing, you know. It's really hard to care about this guy, unless I can find somebody who does, somebody whom I can get along with, in a sense, and whose point of view is more or less reasonable and sympathetic to start with. I did have the brother already there, the character who was becoming a historian, or a low-grade scholar, a high school teacher of history, I think. And so it occurred to me that if I told it through his point of view—he couldn't know everything, but he could *speculate* about a lot, he could *imagine* a lot, and if I just granted him that power, that authority to speculate, to remember, mix memory and imagination together in a kind of obsessive fix on his older brother, then I could get close enough to Wade Whitehouse, but not too close to get burnt by him, so that I could find distance, that mixture of distance and closeness that would allow me to feel affection for him. And I was doing it in a much more elaborate and contrived way than *Hamilton Stark*, which I grant is interesting in its own terms, too; in some ways the artifice of *Hamilton Stark is* kind of more interesting than the much simpler artifice of *Affliction*. But I still feel that emotionally it's not as mature as *Affliction*, given the material.

DR: One more question concerning *Hamilton Stark*. This is actually a general question on your work. It has to do with the evolution of irony. It seems to me that in *Hamilton Stark* the irony is very straightforward, linguistic irony on the part of the narrator, and paradoxically, re-reading it, it's not very funny.

RB: No.

DR: And it seems to me that over the years your use of irony has become more of a critical distance embedded in the structure of the work, instead of this sort of humorous irony on the part of the narrator.

RB: I think that's true.

DR: Is this something conscious on your part or is it something that's more generally linked to your use of artifice and narrative strategies?

RB: No, it's *conscious*, well I mean in the sense that I *desire* to have that certainly ironic distance on the material; I want to maintain that if I can. I don't have any great desire to be funny. I do as a person, in my relationship with other people—I like being funny if I can—but as a writer I have no great desire to be funny. I want to deal with material in fact that is not at all humorous, that's really dark, and I'm willing to risk that darkness in as direct a way as possible. Let me put it this way. There's a kind of tension between my reliance on ironic distancing structures, on the one hand, and my desire to deal with the material in as compassionate and sincere way as possible. And it helps me avoid melodrama, basically, and I think I consciously use it for that. And I could see *Affliction* as an example, that without having Rolfe as a kind of intervening figure in the narrative, I ran the risk either of portraying a *very* unsympathetic character on the one hand, or melodrama on the other—a kind of *Dreiserian* melodrama—and neither one of them were attractive to me; I wanted to avoid both of them. So I think you're right in that sense, in irony in that sense: there is a built-in distancing mechanism in almost everything I've done, and it's usually the formalism that lies behind the book. Even in something like *The Sweet Hereafter*, which no one would call an ironic book, yet there is a kind of artifice; certainly there's one with the four narrators and the spiraling structure, but also in the *slightly* formalized language that the narrators use. There's no attempt at flat-out realism there, in the way people speak—there is in the intervening dialogue—but in the narrative itself, each of the characters speaks in a slightly artificialized way, very small, but it's enough so that it makes you conscious a little bit of the page. I mean imagine that book without it: a school bus accident, a bunch of kids get killed. That would fall down into melodrama in a minute.

DR: And it also enabled you to speak about ethics without actually moralizing, even though some have gotten the impression that you *were*, confusing the author and the narrator.

RB: Yes, that's true. They don't say that anymore, though; they stopped saying that after awhile.

DR: Well that's because you use the first-person narrator all the time.

RB: Yes, that's true, I have for some time. Not now. The book I'm writing now is not; it's omniscient. But they don't say it typically though; I think they just sort of gave up and said: "To hell with it, he's going to do it anyhow [*laughs*]. We just better deal with it."

DR: Let's talk about *The Book of Jamaica*. Same thing. Brainstorm. Back in time.

RB: I have a much clearer memory of the evolution of *that* book, probably because I'm less ambivalent about it. I *like* the book still. I had the occasion a year ago, May—went to a festival in Jamaica called Calabash, which is all West Indians and a few others, and I was one of the others. I read to an audience of about two thousand Jamaicans and I read from *The Book of Jamaica*. I figured: "What the hell, why not? Do it!" It was great. It was under a big tent, right there on the water, over on a cliff overlooking the sea, outdoors, with the wind, and a fabulous Jamaican sound system—gigantic boxes, you know the speakers that they heap up—and two thousand Jamaicans swelter-ing out there under that tent, and I said: "What the hell?" So I read a long episode from it, and I really liked it; I said: "This is really not bad." And they loved it, the Jamaicans just adored it, because they recognize all the place names and everything, and all the details are familiar to them. It was enor-mously successful at the reading. But it was also, for me—For one thing I was revisiting the place; I hadn't been in Jamaica in years and returning to a lot of my remembered experiences there or *forgotten* experiences there, freshly remembering them, and I had this similar relationship to that text because I hadn't looked at it for years, and I was returning to that text and recalling then the context of writing it and so on, freshly. And it was actually quite satisfying. I realized it was not a bad book at all, in fact it's pretty good, and it does certain things that are kind of interesting to me still, formally and thematically, politically, linguistically; it's still very much alive to me, and I was pleased by that, and maybe relieved as well, in some ways.

But its origins obviously lie in my own personal experiences—from living in Jamaica, from travelling there. And I have said it before, it's true: it is the most directly autobiographical of my writings. Because my marriage was coming apart then, and I was very *aware* of it; it wasn't happening without my observing it and I'm aware of the causes of it, which were different from the causes that the marriage in the book comes apart. But nonetheless, I was undergoing a lot of the same kind of stresses and tensions and conflicts as the protagonist, Johnny, in *The Book of Jamaica*. And also the kind of gradual slow accumulation of understanding about race and racial differ-ence and class that the book dramatizes was something I was going through at that time as well, and wanted to be able to write about and dramatize in some way in fiction. So it cuts very close to my own personal experiences at the time.

Some of the characters are recognizable to anybody who knows them, modeled on Jamaicans that I knew, people that I *still* know in fact. Terron corresponds very closely to a single person who's still living there now. They're based on very specific people that I knew. The Maroons, particularly, are.

DR: You visited the Maroons?

RB: Oh yeah. I had a little cabin up there, too, stayed up there. It was one of the reasons my marriage was coming apart. Both a cause and a symptom [*laughs*]. That I was spending so much time up there. (You know, there is such a cave.) And all that is very close to the bone, as it were. In fact, when we started putting together the film a couple of years ago, and they wanted me to write the script, I just said: "You know, I don't think I can write this one, I'm really not just close to the book, but I'm close to what the book is *about*, and I'd have a hard time, I think, distancing myself from it enough to write a screenplay." So another person has written a screenplay, Jeremy Pikser, who wrote *Bullworth*, and is quite a good screenwriter. But the reason I didn't think I could write the screenplay comfortably was that, because it is so close to my own experiences, unlike anything else, more so than anything else, I felt the need to distance myself from it, that I couldn't do that. But one way I was able to distance myself in the writing of the book was through a kind of dynamic interest in narrative point of view, and by that shifting point of view, starting and moving slowly through the different narrative perspectives and gradually getting close to the material. There's a kind of reverse shift in it, where you start with an intimate point of view, but then you're distanced from the material, and then each time it moves, it moves closer to the material but the distance, the point of view, leads to a more detached perspective, and to a more objective perspective on it, till finally, in the end, I think it's third person fast. And I'm trying—striving for that kind of gradual shift in perspective that the narrator or the protagonist himself is going through from a totally subjective perspective to a distanced and objective perspective on these experiences. And I suppose implied in that is a kind of metaphysics or some implied moralizing with regard to the obtaining of knowledge.

DR: The distance occurs when he starts appropriating their culture.

RB: It leads him finally to the disillusionment at the very end, and the recognition of the impossibility of identification with the victim, with the oppressed, and acceptance of recognition of his own *power* defined by his own race, that he *cannot* penetrate that other culture or that other race, that there are experiences that cannot be penetrated, that—by virtue of one's class, or one's skin color, or one's gender, one is *excluded* from, and—one can observe it, but one can't necessarily experience it. And so there's an implied ethics to that, I think, a political ethics that's somewhere in there that has to do with, and arises from, the shifting point of view.

So even though it is very personal material that I was drawing on, I think that the structure of the book allowed me to work with it in a way that didn't make me feel as though I was writing autobiography or memoir, or anything of the sort.

DR: Did you write it back in New England?

RB: Yes, I did. I didn't start writing in Jamaica, no. What I wrote down there was *The Relation of My Imprisonment* and I finished *Hamilton Stark*, now that we're talking. I did the revisions on *Hamilton Stark* and rewrote that.

DR: *Imprisonment* is that old, then?

RB: Yeah, yeah. That has a long history before it was finally published. But I wrote that down there straight through, as a result of two things. The reading I was doing then. I was reading a lot of seventeenth-century history and, also religious tracts and odd things. I just got into it, at some point, starting with John Bunyan and others, and Jonathan Edwards, New England Divines, Puritan Divines, and then I was *hearing* Jamaican English in my ear all the time, which has a kind of seventeenth-century root to it. It is based on English of the seventeenth century, Jamaican *patois*, in some ways, the mixture obviously, but there are a lot of aspects to Jamaican English, even a lot of vocabulary as well as the syntax that I was hearing, and the mixture of those two gave rise to the language of *The Relation of My Imprisonment*, I think. But then when I returned home is when I wrote *The Book of Jamaica*.

DR: Did you start immediately after?

RB: Immediately after. I may have started it in Jamaica, I can't remember. No, I certainly was accumulating notes and material. I knew I was going to write *something* that grew out of that experience in a direct way because I was too *obsessed* with it not to have a need to make a fictional use of it.

DR: So can this novel be seen as your coming-out as a realist? You do use documentary techniques in it.

RB: That's right.

DR: I mean there's the "how-to-make-a-daub-and-wattle-house" passage which is pretty funny.

RB: Yeah . . . Well I guess so. I think it's very much a transitional book in that sense, more so than *Hamilton Stark* or *The Relation of My Imprisonment*.

I always have looked at it like that. And then *Trailerpark*, which I believe came next, has very much a format and a structure too; it's not just a collection of stories by any means. I think that's when it tilted, definitely.

DR: But the difference between *Trailerpark* and *The Book of Jamaica* is that *Trailerpark* is an allegory of American society, which is not credible and not very realistic—

RB: No, it's not.

DR: —whereas *The Book of Jamaica* really has the feel of firsthand experience.

RB: Yes, it's the distance between the presentation and the material which it derives from, which is to say, I guess, the *representation* of the material, of the experience that arises from—It pretty much was in the conventions of realism. The formal structure of the book is not.

DR: It's still a little postmodernist, isn't it?

RB: Yeah, yeah.

DR: It's got a complex time scheme as well.

RB: And the shifting point of view. I think that it's transitional. But it's not necessarily—I wouldn't even call it transitional—I think you were right the first time when you said it's a kind of a coming-out, both because it is no more, no less postmodern than what follows from it all the way through to *The Darling*, really, when you think about it. So, yes, I would say that's the breaking one; it's the one that makes clear what direction I'm going to go in for the rest of my career, as it turns out. I didn't know that at the time, of course, but [*laughs*] these many years later, now almost thirty years later . . .

DR: When did you finish it?

RB: It wasn't very long before that. I had a contract by then with Houghton Mifflin and they were happy to continue with me at that point. And it got slowed up and it had an odd thing happen to it—I don't know if I ever told you this story. [Russell Banks discusses libel-based difficulties with a portion of *The Book of Jamaica*.] So they recalled the *entire* edition. They had over ten thousand copies out at the time: sent it to the binder, stripped the covers off, pulled the offending page out, tipped in a page, because it was only a couple of lines in there which I didn't really give a shit about, it was not essential to the novel or anything—it was texture rather than anything else; it wasn't a plot point or something, and it wasn't an essential characteristic of an essential character. And so it cost them a fortune, and the reviews came out on the book, and they were wonderful reviews. It got a lovely review in the *New York Times* and elsewhere; but the book was not in the bookstores because they'd missed the deadline, the release date, because they had moved the whole edition back, so they hadn't shipped any of the books. The books weren't shipped until six or eight weeks after the reviews came out. By then nobody gave a shit about it. It *died*; it died withering. Actually, it died unborn in a way. So they are out there actually—I have about ten of them left—and there are the galleys with offending paragraphs in there, which are probably worth quite a lot of money now [*laughs*].

DR: There's a very good example of this sort of structural irony we were talking about in the first part of the novel, "Captain Blood," which starts out as a sort of mystery plot where the narrator already knows who the criminal is and tries to apply this postcolonial grid onto the rumors he hears. And actually it turns out that from the Jamaican point of view, from the Jamaicans he interviews, it's more just a story of everyday evil, everyday—

RB: Yeah, everyday violence, everyday evil. Everyday criminality.

DR: And it actually ends up with him in the shoes of the very criminal he was chasing—

RB: So it ends up with a classic sort of Errol Flynn sword fight, in a way.

DR: Yeah [*laughs*].

RB: So he becomes Captain Blood himself.

DR: So this is already a form of irony that's very different from what we talked about before and that you went on to use again later.

RB: Yes, reversals, I suppose. And mirroring, and inadvertent or, it seems, inadvertent mirroring. Undercutting, using that doubling to undercut. With no attempt to be funny [*laughs*], again.

DR: I think you already talked about the fact that the novel deconstructs the universalist vision. At the very beginning, the narrator says that at this time in his life, like most Americans, he believes more in the essential sameness among people than in their differences. The rest of the novel is basically a deconstruction of this.

RB: Right, that's very good.

DR: So this is going to be my last question, and it's a general question. How can one discuss ideology, politics, ethics, race, etc., without adopting a superior position? How do you find a way not to end up yourself in that position? Is it only the distancing or do you use other strategies to avoid this?

RB: Let me think about that. That's a troubling question.

DR: In one sense you are after all trying to *show* things to people. And at the same time you don't want to—

RB: Yeah, I'm offering a critique. There's no question about that. That I have more or less consistently for nearly *half* a century, now, it seems, certainly for the last thirty or so years, I've been offering a critique. And the question is: How do you do that without feeling superior to the material?

DR: Yeah. Without actually being in a position of someone who's teaching or preaching, who's in a superior position to the reader.

RB: Hmm . . . that's a *tough* one. I've asked myself and worried myself over because I don't want to fall into that trap, the trap of ideology on the one hand, or feelings of superiority on the other. I trust my own instincts as a storyteller and the hierarchy, really, that I feel with regard to storytelling and character and aesthetic concerns vis-à-vis a political critique, that is that, ultimately, everything has to turn on questions of story, for me, aesthetic questions, questions of character, and only incidentally political questions. I mean I happen to see the world in such a way that everything is political to me, and it's almost inescapable for me that I don't perceive story, character, aesthetics, questions of form through some kind of a political lens. I do anyhow; it's unavoidable; it's in my DNA. And I think if I can trust that it is in my DNA, then therefore I don't have to think about it. I don't have to raise a critique on the basis of ideology and I don't have to raise a critique on the basis of any political agenda—that the critique will emerge inevitably from my sympathies as simply a storyteller and a perceiver of character, as a sensitive responder to formal options that appear on the page. At some level I'm making political decisions, I know, and I don't have to think about them. And I *don't*. I don't think about what's right or wrong, politically, or what's good or bad, or what's desirable or undesirable, I really don't. I know race is very important to me in an intricate, mysterious—And, of course, it is at bottom, on some profound level political; it's also at a profound level psychological, it's also philosophical, anthropological, historical: I can't get away from all those aspects of race. But I simply trust that they're there in my perceptions.

And I've never really had an agenda, not certainly to the degree that I've been granted one by the media. I don't carry that. I'm usually positioned very much in the left in the American scheme of things, but that doesn't particularly concern me one way or the other. It's just happenstance. I'm not there because I set out to be or because it's part of an agenda, anyway, to be on the left. So in a sense it's not something I concern myself with too much as long as I trust that all those other decisions that I make in the production of a work are already political anyhow. And even my grammar, I trust that there's a political dimension to it. My interest, for instance, I know, in *sharing* the narration, as in *The Sweet Hereafter*, or in first-person narration, for that matter, or in narrative from the point of a minor character as in *Hamilton, Affliction,* and *Cloudsplitter*: there's a political dimension to those decisions. Some are more democratic than others [*laughs*]; some are more generous than others.

One of the reasons I've avoided (without thinking about it too deeply) the omniscient narrator is because I'm reluctant to take on that kind of political authority. I'm actually writing a novel now that is omniscient narrator and it's interesting to me to see how I'm sabotaging it as I'm doing it, making sure I give equal time to all characters, rather than favoring any particular one, spreading the entire narrative out over four different characters, and I think that's in response to a sense that there is something autocratic about an omniscient narrator that needs to be sabotaged. So everything has a political dimension. And if I just trust that and assume it and then know that I'm going to respond to it in a sensitive way, and presumably in a democratic way, in a just way, then I don't worry particularly about the possibility that I will take on a kind of superiority to my characters, or condescension to them in some way, or on the other hand a romanticizing of them, and a glamorizing of them. I don't worry about it too much. I think that I'm making my political decisions *prior* to that, and that the politics rest in those prior decisions already.

So I'm not over-concerned with it, as long as I know that I don't have an agenda, a political agenda, and that the characters don't exist in order to serve a political purpose. The political purpose may end up in order to serve the characters, or the sentences, or the formal apparatus, or the imagery, or whatever, but not the reverse; they don't exist to serve the politics. And I think that as long as I keep that clear in mind, then I'll be all right. But it is a trap that a lot of writers fall into, where they have some kind of political agenda and characters exist to serve that, rather than allowing the political agenda such as it is—the political perspective—to arise from the characters, or arise from all the other aspects of the work, whatever they are.

DR: It seems to me you do leave room for different political views. And even though when *Cloudsplitter* came out you were often defending John Brown in interviews, your novel nevertheless leaves a lot of room to show that you're not actually glorifying him.

RB: Oh yeah. And the same thing with *The Darling*. I mean, it seemed to entertain an awful lot of readers who wanted to put a political spin on that book that way. They were saying: "How am I supposed to take her? Is she a heroine, sort of romanticized, or is she someone I'm supposed to judge and dismiss?" Of course the only answer to that is *neither*: you're not supposed to judge her and you're not supposed to romanticize her. That's not my job.

DR: Does the polyphony, the different voices you talked about, help that?

RB: I think it does. Yeah. Also, in a novel, though, it's almost unavoidable to have different voices, or at least different meters, different levels of fiction, different registers, in the course of the novel, which amounts, often, to different voices. Over a period of five hundred pages or whatever, if it were all done in the same note, the same tone, the same register, etc., you would be deeply boring. It would have no range of emotions. Or no range of perspective. You've got to have them. It's inescapable; you can't avoid it. Polyphony in that sense. Not in a literal sense where you have multiple voices as in the case of *The Sweet Hereafter*. But I think polyphony in the other sense, as well as in the sense of *The Sweet Hereafter*—the obvious kind—does permit you to keep on freshly approaching the material that you're writing about from a multiplicity of perspectives, many of which will cancel each other out, or negate each other. Very difficult if not impossible except when a psychotic person is dealing with the material to maintain the same perspective on that material over a period of time, especially if it's mysterious and complicated material. You can't deal with it the same way every paragraph, every page; you have to keep shifting and moving and angling yourself at it.

DR: Do you plan that or do you *feel* it as it comes when you're writing?

RB: Yeah, I feel it in the sense that it's inevitable; it's inescapable. It's kind of a cubism, kind of a cubistic perspective. But I think that that goes with the territory. A writer who doesn't have that cubistic perspective is likely to turn out to be a genre writer writing genre fiction, locking in to a predetermined set of conventions and holding on to them regardless of what the material is. But if you aren't a genre writer and you don't have that preassembled set of conventions, you're going to be constantly revising your take on the material that you're working with. I think it's unavoidable. Erasing what you wrote before, in a sense, and coming at it again and again. And it feels that way, you know; it's not something one plans. I don't even think one necessarily makes a decision to do that on principle. I think it's just inevitable; it goes with the territory. I don't know how one could write about anything as complex as human nature in its natural habitat without the need to constantly take and retake your angle of vision on it. It's too elusive. Human nature is too mysterious to hold, to grab a hold and keep it from one point of view for five hundred pages or however long you have to be there. The older I get the more I've learned that I can trust the process, the actual process, more than I can trust myself, or certainly more than I can trust my own *conscious* mind.

DR: What have you been working on this year?

RB: I did the screenplay for *Cloudsplitter* for HBO.

DR: So that's done?

RB: It's done for now. They'll come back to me. I expect by the time I get home I'll have a long list of notes of suggested changes. It's in the hands of HBO right now, and I'm waiting for their take on it. And I'll have to do another draft, but I think I can do that fairly fast. It was *hard* writing, very hard writing. It's a long script; it's a three-hour film. And it was a lot of material to try to squeeze into that. And also it's historical material that's very difficult to get across quickly, to find the right key, the right images, that would convey the historical context without getting in the way of the narrative. I mean, it was a problem with the novel; however, there's a lot more room to do it in a novel. And in a screenplay you have very little room to provide historical background. So I did that. And then I went back to a novel that I started last year that I hope I'll finish by the fall. It's not going to be a real long novel; I think maybe three hundred pages. And it's set in 1936–37 in upstate New York where I live, up in the Adirondacks where you've been. And I'm really enjoying it; I'm just really glad to be getting back to writing. I like writing screenplays; it's kind of fun, but it's more of a *game* than anything else, and a puzzle, you know, and so on, it's not real writing. It's collaborative, which is also enjoyable in its own way, and there's a side of me that really likes collaboration and working with other people, but I was so relieved to get back to my desk in April, May, and June, and just be able to write sentences, start groping my way through paragraphs again, and scenes. The *plastic* quality of writing, of language that you can experience in writing fiction, to me, is *so* satisfying, and necessary. I'll never be a screenwriter. I'll write screenplays though, but I'll never think of myself as a screenwriter, certainly.
DR: Are the other films still at a standstill?
RB: Well, we're casting *Continental Drift* still. We've got Josh Hartnett for the lead, and Robert Downey Jr. for the second lead, and we're hoping to have a financee—
DR: For Eddie?
RB: Yeah, Eddie, the older brother, who in the screenplay is a larger character than—well, he's a pretty large character in the novel—but he's a second lead. In fact, I'm meeting with the director in Paris and with some representatives of a big financial company there. We got to get things *moving* because we want to shoot it this winter in Florida.
DR: You said that two years ago! [*laughs*]
RB: I know, I say it every year. This year, I guess we're at a little bit more than where we were last year. But it goes forward two steps, back one, and then, you know, like that.
DR: And *Rule of the Bone*?
RB: Actually, I got so sick of waiting for those guys, for Chris Noonan, the

director, and Marry Mandel, the producer, that when the option expired I didn't renew it; I held it back. So I'm sitting on the rights again, and I've got my screenplay that I wrote for Fox about seven years ago or something like that. And so now I'm looking for a director for that. No, I think the one that's definitely going ahead, now, is *Cloudsplitter*. That's most likely the one that will get made before the others.

DR: And *On the Road* is looking like the least done?

RB: Yes, but who knows what's going to happen to that. That's in Coppola's hands. And I've heard so many different rumors about that. He's hired Walter Salles to do it, who in a sense has already done it with *The Motorcycle Diaries*, with Francis executive producing it. They're probably going to write a whole new screenplay and start over again, as far as I know. And at that point I don't really care. I'd just like to get paid, but other than that I don't care. Then, of course, if they did use my script, I wouldn't mind sharing the credit.

[Pause. Russell Banks started talking about his new novel before the tape was rolling again.]

My father was born in 1917, my mother in 1914. And I realized a while back that events, historical events that occurred in the generation *before* I was born, in many ways have a bigger impact on me than events that occurred *after* I was born, because those historical events so distorted or shaped my parents' lives, that, inasmuch as my parents affected me, I'm affected by those historical events. And my parents' lives were completely fucked-up by the Depression: my father had to drop out of school at sixteen and go to work as a plumber, his father was a plumber, they lost a house, my mother's father lost his little shop. He was a watchmaker. They had to rent out part of *their* house. My mother had to go to work as this shop girl in a department store right away, and they had no money, and they had no ambition, practically no future, everything kind of shrunk around them, they started scrambling, not that they were rich beforehand.

DR: How many characters are there?

RB: There are four main characters. They're not emblematic to me, not particularly. And they're male and female, male and female, they're two couples. Classic back-and-forth, kind of wandering is at the bottom of it.

DR: Any adultery?

RB : Real hot stuff, yeah, real hot adultery, cross-class *[laughs]* adultery. Yeah, some real mix-ups. But I'm interested in this . . . There's a level at which you write fiction and it's tactile, and you get *really* interested. For instance, one of my characters, he's not a bush pilot but he flies biplanes, 1930 Wickle biplanes, and I got really interested in flying, and those little aircrafts, like riding a motorcycle or something, you know, very *basic* airplanes of that era, twenties and thirties. And I've just gotten fascinated by them, collecting pictures, and information. Actually I started learning to fly.

DR: You're learning to fly?

RB: Yeah, I'm getting my license. My wife's a little pissed-off. She says by research I mean recreation.

DR: That's why you say that the research part is the funnest part of writing.

RB: Yeah, I want an excuse to do things I have no excuse for doing otherwise [*laughs*]. Go to the places where I have no other reason to go.

DR: So that's the part that actually stimulates your imagination, in some ways, allows you to get into it? Before you might just have a vague idea.

RB: You have a vague idea, kind of an itch that needs to be scratched. But more and more I realize what a great physical pleasure writing is for me all the time. I experience it in a very physical way: sentences, writing sentences, paragraphs. It's less and less in my head and more and more in my sensory apparatus in some ways, visual and aural, A-U-R-A-L—O-R-A-L too—tactile. All the senses get more and more engaged, but they get engaged just on that level of writing sentences. Or exploring material, like airplanes, old Adirondack type of beautiful handmade back boats . . . I think it's closer to writing poetry, you know. You don't give a shit about ideas. They come inevitably; it's like the politics, you know. Everything has a metaphysics to it, you can't avoid it, you can't control it, you're better off not bothering yourself with it, it's going to be there anyhow. So, I feel that way about the ideas whenever I'm writing. It's taken me all these years, I think, to learn how to be an instinctual writer . . . What I always envied when I was younger about certain writers that I knew among my contemporaries was they just trusted the process, in a way that I didn't. I had to *learn* to trust.

DR: What do you mean by that? Do you mean that they just sat down and wrote, they didn't plan—?

RB: Well, they might plan out, outline whatever, a story. But they'd trust that whatever ideas—philosophical ideas, political ideas, historical or whatever thesis if you like—that would arise from the novel *would* arise from the material regardless. You couldn't control it, you couldn't keep it out, you have no ideas that would show, you have stupid ideas that would show, you couldn't fake it, you couldn't improve it; if you're politically idiotic that would show. And you cannot avoid it. So gradually, I've come to that point where now I just trust it.

The Not-So-Glamorous Life: Russell Banks

Maryrose Flanigan/2008

From *Expressnightout.com* (January 2008). Used by permission.

Russell Banks's *The Reserve* is a page-turner from the moment mad beauty Vanessa Cole insinuates herself aboard the biplane of Hemingway-esque antihero Jordan Groves.

In this Depression-era tale, Banks abandons his grungy working-class subjects of past books, such as *Continental Drift* and *Rule of the Bone,* for the oasis of a private wilderness reserve in the Adirondack Mountains. Vacationing in private "camps" and served by the scattered natives, the privileged few manage to preserve the glamorous life—and its Paris Hilton–style (or maybe Barbara Hutton–esque)—hijinks during hard times.

"The characters are glamorous and romantic and, in some ways, doomed," Banks says, "which has not been the case with my previous work—the doomed part probably, but not glamorous and romantic."

Despite the glitz, Banks remains true to his bedrock themes of the "dueling truths" that families and lovers live with, the troubles of the poor and the real, unromantic reasons behind temptation and sacrifice.

"The story really unfolds around the clash between those two classes through romantic and sexual encounters between people from both sides," Banks says. "It's kind of a classic story in that sense; kind of a D. H. Lawrence story."

With two charmed film adaptations already—the gritty *Affliction* and ethereal *The Sweet Hereafter*—*The Reserve* seems camera-ready as well. Interspersed with the Adirondack scenes are chapters about the Spanish Civil War, Nazis, experimental lobotomies, and the Hindenburg.

MF: After having *Affliction* and *The Sweet Hereafter* made into well-received movies, has the possibility of a screen adaptation affected your writing?

RB: I don't really find myself thinking about movies in the slightest. You know it doesn't have any effect on me my while I'm writing. I'm married to the sentence and the paragraph and the literary voice—the voice of the narrative. It's only after the book is published and people start talking about it and come to me. Then I start thinking about it afterwards, of course, and some seem more likely than others to adapt to film.

Over the years I have gotten involved in film and screenwriting and so forth . . . in the last decade I think it has had an effect on me as a fiction writer but it's been a positive effect. I also heard [*The Hours* author] Michael Cunningham say something very similar—and it's made me realize that I don't need to spend so much time setting things up . . . I think I can write more efficiently and get in and get out of scene more quickly than I used to think I could when I was younger. I think that's a positive thing; it's been a good influence on my writing. I don't think I would have written it this way twenty years ago.

MF: The reader is made to feel ambivalent about Jordan Groves. He's wealthy, self-absorbed, and selfish, yet he sacrifices for an ideal. Do you think Groves has an equivalent in the real world today—say, an artist or a politician?

RB: I think there are a lot of artists—painters, writers, intellectuals, and so forth—actors, even; people in the arts whose politics ally them with people who will never be familiar with, never know their work, whose social life and whose audience for their work is really the class against which they are opposed and so they have a kind of built-in conflict.

Think of a writer like E. L. Doctorow, who's known for his leftist leanings and his politics are identified with working people, yet he himself is certainly not a working person; he lives out in the Hamptons. Or myself for that matter: I'm known for my sympathies for the oppressed and the downtrodden on one hand, and on the other hand I certainly don't live like the person that I identify with in some ways.

So I think it's a common conflict among Americans—particularly artists and intellectuals going back, oh, all the way back to the nineteenth century—but we especially see it in a very clear form in the 1930s when artists and intellectuals took a very radical stance left and yet they were still hobnobbing with high society in Manhattan and Washington and Paris and London and so forth. You think of all those leftists—even like Hemingway hanging out in the Riviera [*laughs*]. So it's an old conflict but it's one that's not been written about much or acknowledged much.

MF: Did you fly to research the book, or did the idea of a pilot character emerge out of your learning to fly?

RB: I've always wanted to write about somebody looking at the world from above. I have friends up there who are pilots . . . so I started flying around with them just looking at my own region from above. It so entranced me that the two kind of came together simultaneously. Then I figured I'd better know more about what I'm doing . . . so then I did much more deliberate, conscious research. That's usually the way it goes anyhow: you have an intrigue with a skill or a with a place and then you go there and say, "Gee, I can make a novel out of this," and you start becoming deeply involved in it and before you know it you have to go out and learn a lot more.

MF: How have your research methods changed over the course of your career?

RB: Well, I think I've become more efficient. When I first began I didn't know that you could actually [*laughs*] hire someone to do some research. "Can you find out what movies were showing in the summer of 1936 in upstate New York?" Then there's the kind of research where you just follow up on your own intuitions and I want to know, for instance, about a painter, an artist of that period: What kind of material would he use? What would be the art historical context you would fit in? What gallery would he show his work in New York?

There's a kind of research you don't know you're going to need until you get there and . . . I have to trust that process—the process of writing. Say there's a scene in the book where there's some cars and they're picking people up at the clubhouse to take them to the railroad station, I could just write, "The cars were waiting for them when they arrive." But that's not very detailed, not very visible, so I have to go out and find out what big cars were being manufactured and sold to people like this in 1936 because I want the detail—but I didn't know I needed the detail until I go there when I got to that scene.

MF: Vanessa Cole is another character who is tough to love.

RB: I have great sympathy for her, and it's hard to have sympathy for her, for most people, because she's a little, well—some people would simply say she's crazy. But she's more than that to me. She's a person I think who has suffered a great deal and has been broken by it.

I feel strongly about all of [the characters] but in particular I feel strongly about her. One of those things an author can tell about his own emotional connection to a character is "Who do you feel protective of?" When the book comes out and it goes out into the world you feel like, "God, I don't want to hear any bad things about that character."

MF: Each character creates his or her universe, their own veracities, in *The Reserve*. What are you saying about the notion of truth in this novel?

RB: There are dueling truths throughout. Everybody has a slightly different understanding of what's going on even between lovers; what's really the case.

So much of getting at the truth depends on self-knowledge, and I think all four of the [main] characters are struggling to obtain self-knowledge. They don't have much until we get closer and closer to the end. It's only in that closing scene when everybody has a clear knowledge of what they've done and why they've done it. It is a dramatization of the dueling truths individuals have—even those who are intimate with one another and share experiences. And I think this is true of our lives. It's true in families; I've done it in my family. I'm sure everybody else has, too—when you sit down with siblings and you start comparing childhood notes and you have a rather different account than your brother or sister have, and the same thing with spouses and lovers. You sit down and years later you say, "No, it didn't go that way! That wasn't why I did it!" It is very, very difficult to obtain a shared truth.

Index